REFORMING MARKETS
IN HEALTH CARE:
AN ECONOMIC PERSPECTIVE

EDITED BY

Peter C. Smith

Open University Press
Buckingham · Philadelphia

Open University Press
Celtic Court
22 Ballmoor
Buckingham
MK18 1XW

email: enquiries@openup.co.uk
world wide web: http://www.openup.co.uk

and
325 Chestnut Street
Philadelphia, PA 19106, USA

First Published 2000

A catalogue record of this book is available from the British Library

ISBN   0 335 20462 7 (hbk)   0 335 20461 9 (pbk)

Library of Congress Cataloging-in-Publication Data
Reforming markets in health care: an economic perspective / edited by
    Peter C. Smith.
        p. cm. — (State of health series)
        Includes bibliographical references and index.
        ISBN 0-335-20462-7 (hbk)   ISBN 0-335-20461-9 (pbk)
        1. Medical economics—Great Britain.   I. Smith, Peter (Peter C.)
    II. Series.
    RA410.55.G7R446   2000
    338.4'33621'0941—dc21   99-28981
                                                                                CIP

Typeset by Type Study, Scarborough
Printed in Great Britain by The Cromwell Press, Trowbridge

CONTENTS

LIST OF CONTRIBUTORS

Karen Bloor is Research Fellow at the Department of Health Sciences and Clinical Evaluation, University of York.

Roy Carr-Hill is Senior Research Fellow at the Centre for Health Economics, University of York.

Tony Culyer is Professor of Economics and Head of Department at the Department of Economics and Related Studies, University of York.

Huw Davies is Reader in Health Care Management at the University of St Andrews.

Diane Dawson is Senior Research Fellow at the Centre for Health Economics, University of York.

Mike Drummond is Professor of Economics and Director of the Centre for Health Economics, University of York.

Martin Eccles is Professor of Clinical Effectiveness at the Centre for Health Services Research, University of Newcastle.

Brian Ferguson was until May 1999 Senior Research Fellow at the Centre for Health Economics, University of York. From June 1999 he is Professor of Health Economics at the Nuffield Institute for Health, University of Leeds.

Nick Freemantle is Senior Research Fellow in the Medicines Evaluation Group at the Centre for Health Economics, University of York.

Antonio Giuffrida is Research Fellow at the National Primary Care

Research and Development Centre at the Centre for Health Economics, University of York.

Maria Goddard is Senior Research Fellow at the Centre for Health Economics, University of York.

Hugh Gravelle is Professor of Economics and leader of the National Primary Care Research and Development Centre at the Centre for Health Economics, University of York.

Russell Mannion is Research Fellow at the Centre for Health Economics, University of York.

James Mason is Senior Research Fellow in the Medicines Evaluation Group at the Centre for Health Economics, University of York.

Alan Maynard is Professor of Health Economics and co-Director of the York Health Policy Group, University of York. He is also Chairman of the York NHS Trust.

Nigel Rice is Research Fellow at the Centre for Health Economics, University of York.

Martin Roland is Professor of General Practice at the University of Manchester, and Director of Research and Development at the National Primary Care Research and Development Centre.

Peter C. Smith is Professor of Economics at the University of York, where he is based in the Centre for Health Economics and the Department of Economics and Related Studies.

Andrew Street is Senior Research Fellow at the Centre for Health Economics, University of York.

SERIES EDITOR'S INTRODUCTION

Health services in many developed countries have come under critical scrutiny in recent years. In part this is because of increasing expenditure, much of it funded from public sources, and the pressure this has put on governments seeking to control public spending. Also important has been the perception that resources allocated to health services are not always deployed in an optimal fashion. Thus at a time when the scope for increasing expenditure is extremely limited, there is a need to search for ways of using existing budgets more efficiently. A further concern has been the desire to ensure access to health care of various groups on an equitable basis. In some countries this has been linked to a wish to enhance patient choice and to make service providers more responsive to patients as 'consumers'.

Underlying these specific concerns are a number of more fundamental developments which have a significant bearing on the performance of health services. Three are worth highlighting. First, there are demographic changes, including the ageing population and the decline in the proportion of the population of working age. These changes will both increase the demand for health care and at the same time limit the ability of health services to respond to this demand.

Second, advances in medical science will also give rise to new demands within the health services. These advances cover a range of possibilities, including innovations in surgery, drug therapy, screening and diagnosis. The pace of innovation quickened as the end of the century approached, with significant implications for the funding and provision of services.

Third, public expectations of health services are rising as those who use services demand higher standards of care. In part, this is stimulated by developments within the health service, including the availability of new technology. More fundamentally, it stems from the emergence of a more educated and informed population, in which people are accustomed to being treated as consumers rather than patients.

Against this background, policy makers in a number of countries are reviewing the future of health services. Those countries which have traditionally relied on a market in health care are making greater use of regulation and planning. Equally, those countries which have traditionally relied on regulation and planning are moving towards a more competitive approach. In no country is there complete satisfaction with existing methods of financing and delivery, and everywhere there is a search for new policy instruments.

The aim of this series is to contribute to debate about the future of health services through an analysis of major issues in health policy. These issues have been chosen because they are both of current interest and of enduring importance. The series is intended to be accessible to students and informed lay readers as well as to specialists working in this field. The aim is to go beyond a textbook approach to health policy analysis and to encourage authors to move debate about their issue forward. In this sense, each book presents a summary of current research and thinking, and an exploration of future policy directions.

Professor Chris Ham
Director of Health Services Management Centre,
University of Birmingham

EDITOR'S PREFACE

There has been an international move towards the creation of explicit markets in health care, in which the purchase of care is separated from provision. The creation of such markets has undeniably led to improvements in certain aspects of health care. However, the widespread implementation of market-based systems has also raised important issues that have yet to be resolved – for example, is an escalation of management costs an inevitable consequence of the introduction of a market in health care? What sort of information is needed to make the market function efficiently? And can a market-based system be compatible with society's objectives relating to equity and solidarity?

In 1991 the Conservative UK government set up an 'internal market' in the National Health Service (NHS), in which the purchase of secondary health care was made the responsibility of health authorities and general practitioner (GP) fundholders, while the provision of such care was placed in the hands of NHS 'trusts', which remained within the public sector but had separate boards of management. The 1991 reforms were heavily influenced by the ideas of neoclassical economics, which predict that, under certain conditions, markets can result in the provision of socially optimal levels of a good or service, delivered at maximum levels of efficiency. In practice, as even the architects of the internal market recognized, health care is an unusual service which in certain important respects does not conform to the textbook notion of an economic good.

In 1997 the incoming Labour government announced its intention to reform the internal market. The principle underlying these latest reforms is that 'what counts is what works'. That is, aspects of the previous structure which secured the desired objectives are to be retained, while those that failed will be discarded. The principal aspects of the new arrangements are:

- Retention of the separation of purchaser and provider roles and an associated internal market.
- The creation of primary care groups (PCGs), based on populations of about 100,000, charged with the key role of commissioning services and promoting health.
- The abolition of GP fundholding.
- An emphasis on long-term commissioning of health care services rather than the short-term purchasing that has hitherto characterized the operation of the internal market.
- A much-increased emphasis on the quality of clinical services.
- The creation of a National Institute for Clinical Excellence to identify and promote best practice.
- Establishment of local 'health improvement programmes'.
- The provision of a much-enhanced information base, in the form of a 'performance framework' to measure activity and output.
- The creation of a National Commission for Health Improvement to oversee local services and intervene where necessary.

In summary, these reforms retain the general principle of a market, but introduce a number of innovations designed to make the market more sensitive to the peculiar nature of health care as a service.

Economists were highly influential in inspiring and shaping the creation of the internal market and the latest reforms could be interpreted as a retreat from the prescriptions of the economics discipline. However, that would be a misrepresentation of both the nature of the latest reforms and of the contribution of economics. In fact, many economists have noted the need for a far more subtle and sensitive regulatory system than that implemented in 1991, and it is perhaps more appropriate to view the most recent reforms as an acknowledgement of the need to refine and update the UK market in health care.

This book examines the new arrangements from an economic perspective. It comprises a series of commentaries from leading health economists at the University of York and collaborators. Authors examine the contribution of economics to the debate on the reforms, while seeking to make the analysis accessible to a general audience. Although focusing on the arrangements in the NHS, contributors have sought to draw out the general lessons for health care policy and management which might be applicable within a wide range of health care systems.

The scene is set by Smith and Goddard in Chapter 1. They summarize the history of the NHS internal market, and the research evidence that has emerged as to its impact on UK health care. The chapter then describes the salient features of the Labour reforms, which largely came into force in April 1999.

There is one clear policy direction which has survived the change of government: the attempt to place local leadership of the NHS in the hands of primary care. This takes concrete form in the creation of PCGs, and in Chapter 2 Bloor, Maynard and Street examine the implications of giving such a central responsibility to primary care professionals. In Chapter 3, Carr-Hill, Rice and Smith examine the key issue of how appropriate finance can be devolved to a primary care level. They examine some of the practical difficulties that need to be tackled if the important objective of securing a fair system of budgets for PCGs is to be secured, and discuss some of the potentially dysfunctional consequences that may emerge if the budgeting system is not sensitive to local circumstances.

The substitution of long-term 'agreements' for short-term 'contracts' as a means of securing control of providers is discussed by Dawson and Goddard in Chapter 4. They examine prevailing contracting arrangements in six local areas, and find that hitherto contracts have been perceived to be predominantly financial instruments. The question therefore arises: will the new arrangements offer a more favourable environment for longer-term contracting which is capable of accommodating non-financial considerations?

Important new regulatory issues are emerging in the new NHS. Seeking to control the local system in the light of national frameworks is the health authority, with its new duty to develop a local Health Improvement Programme. Ferguson (Chapter 5) examines the important new local regulatory role given to the health authority. At a national level, research and development (R&D) accounts annually for about £500 million of NHS expenditure. In Chapter 6, Culyer presents the economic issues underlying the highly specialized market for R&D that has now been established within the NHS. Hitherto, R&D expenditure has been distributed on the basis of historical accident and piecemeal decision making. Culyer discusses whether the new market in R&D will lead to a more efficient distribution of resources.

Information (or the lack of it) concerned many commentators when the original internal market was established. Their anxiety turned out to be fully justified, and the new arrangements seek to correct some of the system's more important information shortcomings. These are discussed in Chapters 7–9. Goddard, Mannion and Smith (Chapter 7) discuss the performance framework, which offers a much broader coverage of information on activity and outcome than has been available hitherto. However, they claim that the available data will still be incomplete, imperfect and open to manipulation, and examine the difficulties that such inadequacies might give rise to. In Chapter 8, Giuffrida, Gravelle and Roland focus on indicators of primary care performance, and examine the statistical issues that arise when seeking to make sense of performance data – notably the need to take account of local socioeconomic conditions, and the need to construct confidence intervals around any measures of performance. Dawson and Street (Chapter 9) examine the many roles expected of the system of provider reference costs, and the extent to which the chosen method of presentation will be helpful to the intended users.

Chapters 10 and 11 are concerned with how the new arrangements might affect the quality of clinical services, given such a central emphasis in the latest reforms. At a strategic level, Mason and colleagues (Chapter 10) examine how economic evidence on cost-effectiveness might be integrated with clinical effectiveness information in the promulgation of advice by the National Institute for Clinical Excellence. More locally, Davies and Mannion (Chapter 11) discuss the incentives that arise for individual clinicians under the new arrangements. Finally, in Chapter 12, Gravelle and Smith seek to draw together the major themes that emerge in the course of the preceding chapters.

Numerous people assisted in the preparation of this book. My colleagues Sarah Byford, Antonio Giuffrida, Maria Goddard, Brenda Leese, Anne Mason, Stephen Palmer and David Torgerson acted as referees. Administrative and secretarial assistance was provided by Helen Parkinson, Frances Sharp and Vanessa Windass at the Centre for Health Economics. Jacinta Evans and Joan Malherbe at the Open University Press provided invaluable support, and the 'State of Health' series editor, Chris Ham, offered wise counsel. The contribution of these and others improved the contents of this book immeasurably and thanks are due to all.

Peter C. Smith

LIST OF ABBREVIATIONS

A&E	accident and emergency
ACSC	ambulatory care sensitive condition
AHCPR	Agency for Health Care Policy and Research
ASTRO-PU	age, sex, temporary resident originated prescribing unit
CHCs	community health councils
CHI	Commission for Health Improvement
CPAP	continuous positive airways pressure
CRD	Centre for Reviews and Dissemination
DEA	data envelopment analysis
DHA	district health authority
DRG	diagnosis related group
EBHC	evidence based health care
FHSA	family health services authority
FCE	finished consultant episode
GMS	general medical services
HCFA	US Health Care Financing Administration
HCHS	hospital and community health services
HES	Hospital Episodes Statistics
HImP	Health Improvement Programme
HMO	health maintenance organization
HRG	healthcare resource group
HTA	health technology assessment programme
LMC	Local Medical Committee
MSGP4	Fourth National Morbidity Survey in General Practice
NEAT	new and emerging applications of technology
NICE	National Institute for Clinical Excellence

NICs	net ingredient costs
NRCI	National Reference Cost Index
NRR	National Research Register
NSAIDs	non-steroidal anti-inflammatory drugs
NSRC	National Schedule of Reference Costs
OPCS	Office of Population Censuses and Surveys
PACT	prescribing analysis and cost data
PCG	primary care group
PCT	primary care trust
PPA	Pharmaceutical Pricing Authority
PPA	Prescription Pricing Authority
QALY	quality-adjusted life-year
R&D	research and development
RCT	randomized control trial
SDO	service delivery and organization
SIFTR	service increment for teaching and research
SMAC	Standing Medical Advisory Committee
SSRI	selective serotonin reuptake inhibitor
TPP	Total Purchasing Pilot
TUIP	transurethral incision of the prostate

1

REFORMING HEALTH CARE MARKETS
Peter C. Smith and Maria Goddard

INTRODUCTION

> Practical men, who believe themselves to be quite exempt
> from any intellectual influences, are usually the slaves of some
> defunct economist.
>
> (Keynes Ch. 24)

Perhaps the single most influential contribution of the economics
profession, in the sense suggested by Lord Keynes, is the notion of
a 'market' – a place in which buyers and sellers can come together
to effect economic exchange. Ever since Adam Smith developed
the concept of the 'invisible hand', many economists and their
practical slaves have been in thrall to the putative beauties and benefits of such markets.

Yet even the most elementary course in conventional economics
tells us that markets unambiguously confer benefits on society only
in the most special circumstances – where there are large numbers
of buyers and sellers, where information is freely available to all,
where there are no transaction costs, where property rights can be
enforced, and so on. Once we depart from such circumstances, the
virtues of the market become much less obvious, and society may
need to implement measures (such as market regulation) to correct
what have become known as market failures, in the extreme perhaps abandoning market exchange for some other method of allocating society's resources.

In no sector of the economy can the departure from the neoclassical economist's assumptions underlying a competitive market be
more pronounced than in the field of health care. To name but a few
of the violations:

- Consumers (patients) are relatively uninformed about the characteristics of the health care on offer.
- Providers (in particular physicians) play a key role in influencing the health care received by the patient.
- In many specialties and geographical locations there exists little realistic choice of provider.
- Patients rarely bear directly the full cost of health care received.
- Many aspects of health care, such as research and development (R&D) and education and training, have the characteristics of a public good, which traditional markets cannot on their own deliver.
- Society frequently has objectives relating to equity which may conflict with the efficiency criteria underlying the market.

The extent to which these violations compromise the desirability of relying on some sort of market mechanism for delivering health care has become the subject of a prolonged if somewhat sterile debate (see, for example, Evans 1997; Gaynor and Vogt 1997; Pauly 1997; Rice 1997). To some extent the arguments become confused with issues concerning the ownership structure of the health care industry (state or private sector). And much of the debate is influenced by the clearly dysfunctional nature of the US health care system, which is superficially market-based, comprising a uniquely chaotic plurality of purchasers and providers (Reinhardt 1996).

Notwithstanding the apparently profound (if not fatal) obstacles to securing an efficient market in health care, many developed nations have over the last decade sought to introduce market mechanisms into their systems of health care. Examples include various aspects of managed care in the USA and the introduction of 'internal markets' into state health service systems such as those found in Sweden, Italy, Portugal and the United Kingdom (UK). These initiatives reflect a wider movement within the public sector towards reliance on 'quasi-markets' to deliver public services such as education, social care and social housing (Bartlett *et al.* 1998).

THE NHS INTERNAL MARKET

Developments in UK health care have been especially dramatic and are of particular interest because of the dominance of a single National Health Service (NHS) in the delivery of health care. Since its inception in 1948, although under nominal central government control, the NHS relied on a very loose form of governance. It was in effect a relatively small bureaucracy, seeking to reconcile central government policy with the preoccupations of the dominant medical profession (Klein 1995). Locally, the NHS (in the form of geographically defined health authorities covering populations of about 300,000) was responsible for setting priorities, allocating resources and delivering health care.

These arrangements were changed fundamentally in 1991 when an 'internal market' in health care was set up (West 1997). Economists appear to have been highly influential in inspiring and shaping the 1991 reforms. In particular, the new arrangements introduced fundamental changes to the incentives offered to key agents within the NHS along the lines advocated by some economist commentators (Enthoven 1985). In the event, academic economists gave the new policy a cautious welcome, albeit with some concern expressed about the managerial and informational requirements of the internal market (Culyer *et al.* 1990).

Under the 1991 reforms, health authorities remained in place, but rapidly lost their role of delivering health care. Instead, they became the primary purchasers of health care. Health authorities received a fixed annual budget from central government, and were now responsible for negotiating contracts with health care providers in order to meet the health care needs of their population within the centrally determined budget constraint.

The principal providers of health care were to be NHS trusts, the health care providers formerly under the control of health authorities. These providers remained public sector organizations within the NHS, but now had separate boards of management, appointed by the secretary of state. The income of NHS trusts was to depend largely on the contracts they were able to negotiate with NHS purchasers. Thus the trusts were competing in an internal market which was clearly intended to mimic the functioning of a more traditional market. In particular, according to the policy document introducing the reforms, the internal market was expected to deliver some of the putative benefits associated with competitive markets, including reduced costs of services, increased quality of service, better use of NHS assets and streamlined management (Department of Health 1989). The two stated objectives were '[a] to give patients, wherever they live in the UK, better health care and greater choice of the services available; and [b] greater satisfaction and rewards for those working in the NHS who successfully respond to local needs and preferences' (Department of Health 1989: para. 1.8).

One aspect of the 1991 reforms which received only modest attention at the time, but which turned out to be of profound importance, was the role given to the general practitioners (GPs) in the new arrangements (Glennerster *et al.* 1994). Traditionally, GPs delivered primary care and were the gatekeepers to secondary care, in the sense that (except in emergencies) patients could gain access to secondary care only after a GP referral. Larger general practices could now elect to become GP fundholders. Fundholders became responsible for purchasing a number of routine procedures from local providers. In order to do this, they received an annual budget from the local health authority, which therefore delegated part of its budget and purchasing responsibility to those general practices that chose to become fundholders. Fundholders could retain any budget surplus for spending on services to patients. In reality, budget deficits were made good by health authorities, so that the fundholding budgeting system was not in practice unduly demanding for participating practices. In addition to negotiating with local health authorities, NHS trusts therefore found themselves also having to arrange a relatively large number of smaller contracts with local fundholders.

Fundholding became much more widespread than many commentators originally envisaged, and by 1997 over 50 per cent of the population was registered with a fundholding practice, and their expenditure accounted for 15 per cent of NHS expenditure on secondary care (Audit Commission 1996). Fundholding became the model for a much more ambitious experiment in delegation of powers to general practice, known as the Total Purchasing Pilots (Mays *et al.* 1997). Under total purchasing, virtually all secondary care purchasing powers and finance were delegated to voluntary associations of general practices covering populations of about 30,000.

The introduction of the internal market has never been subjected to rigorous evaluation. Indeed the government at the time consciously repudiated the need for coordinated evaluation, and claimed that calling on the advice of academics for such purposes was a sign of weakness (Robinson and Le Grand 1994). Some aspects of the market reforms have nevertheless been the subject of a certain amount of desultory research effort (a full review of the evidence is given by Le Grand *et al.* (1998b). We draw the following broad conclusions, some stated with more confidence than others.

- The market was heavily regulated, or 'managed'. For example, a Byzantine set of pricing rules was put in place which was easily circumvented and led to perverse incentives (Propper 1995; Propper *et al.* 1998). And few of the providers in the market were allowed to exit because of financial distress (Dawson 1994).
- There were large variations in the degree of competition found in the market in different parts of the country (Appleby *et al.* 1994).
- Some aspects of the market imposed a heavy bureaucratic burden on the NHS. In particular, devolved purchasing arrangements (GP fundholding) appeared to result in large increases in management costs, most especially in the writing, management and monitoring of contracts (Audit Commission 1996; Mays *et al.* 1997).
- A new set of management skills was required to make the internal market work satisfactorily. In practice constant changes in the managerial environment meant that such skills were often in short supply or had little time to be developed (West 1997; Thompson 1998).
- The information base required to make the market work satisfactorily was very large and was in practice not available (McGuire and Anand 1997).
- There was some evidence that the quality of care received from a single provider often varied depending on the purchaser. Although research findings are contradictory, the bulk of the evidence suggests that patients of GP fundholders may have been given favourable waiting times in comparison with patients of non-fundholders (Goodwin 1998).
- There were a large number of experiments with innovative approaches to purchasing and commissioning care (Mays and Dixon 1996).
- In many parts of the country, GP fundholders received generous budgets relative to GPs covered by health authority contracts, and fundholders experienced few serious sanctions for overspending (Dixon *et al.* 1994; Audit Commission 1996; Ellwood 1997).
- Compared with non-fundholding practices, GP fundholders appear to have secured a relatively slower growth in prescribing costs, at least in the early years of fundholding (Baines *et al.* 1997; Gosden and Torgerson 1997).
- On the supply side, the introduction of the market was associated with many apparent improvements in efficiency, including increased use of day surgery, reduced lengths of stay, reduced

waiting times for some procedures, and increased throughput (Le Grand *et al*. 1998b).
- Prices have shown remarkable variation, although it is not clear whether this reflects cost variations or accounting variations (Ellwood 1996). There is some evidence that prices bear a weak relationship to market conditions (Propper 1995).
- On the demand side, there appears to have been a substantial increase in volume, but relatively little response to apparent incentives to change patterns of referral. Geographical proximity, perceived quality and long-term relationships seem to have been the principal criteria for GP choice of provider, rather than prices charged (Mahon *et al*. 1994; Baines and Whynes 1996; Ellwood 1997; Toth *et al*. 1997; Propper *et al*. 1998).

As with most inferences based on observational rather than experimental data, there is of course a strong possibility that some of the effects attributed to the market reforms may in fact have had other causes. Many of the conclusions summarized above were hedged around with caveats and cautions, and a typical summary of the received wisdom is 'how little overall measurable change there seems to have been related to the core structures and mechanisms of the internal market' (Le Grand *et al*. 1998a: 129). In short, there is 'no convincing evidence that the reforms have produced a better NHS' (West 1997: 154).

THE LABOUR GOVERNMENT PROPOSALS

In May 1997 a Labour government was swept to power for the first time since 1979, with a new reform of the NHS a central plank in its programme (Smith 1996). Its policies were duly set out in a series of White Papers. The English White Paper, which will be the focus of this chapter, was entitled *The New NHS: Modern, Dependable*, and was published in December 1997 (Department of Health 1997). The principle underlying these latest reforms, which in large part took effect in April 1999, was that 'what counts is what works'. That is, aspects of the 1991 reforms that were seen to be successful would be retained, while those that were seen to have failed were discarded. In particular, the English White Paper suggested that there would be no 'continuation of the divisive internal market system of the 1990s' (Department of Health 1997: para. 2.1). The proposals reflect the more general government philosophy of pursuing a 'third way' between state control and free markets.

In the light of the evidence summarized above, it is instructive to review the critique of the internal market given in Chapter 2 of the White Paper. It affirms the success of separating the planning and provision of hospital care, the increasing importance afforded to primary care within the NHS, and the more general need to decentralize. However, the Labour government also claims that the market was associated with dysfunctional features. This view forms the fundamental rationale for the new reforms, and is summarized in the White Paper under six headings:

1 *Fragmentation*: the large number of purchasers and contracts gave rise to an uncoordinated health service, poorly placed to address issues such as the integration of health and social care.
2 *Unfairness*: competition within the market gave rise to variations in the access to care offered to patients, breaching one of the fundamental principles of the NHS.
3 *Inefficiency*: the prime measure of efficiency used in the internal market was the so-called 'purchaser efficiency index', which introduced a number of perverse incentives for providers, in particular to emphasize the maximization of patient throughput and ignore clinical outcomes.
4 *Bureaucracy*: the large number of purchasers and contracts gave rise to unsustainable levels of management costs.
5 *Instability*: the competition for contracts and the short-term nature of those contracts precluded proper long-term planning and coordination of health care.
6 *Secrecy*: the business model adopted by providers led to a level of secrecy which precluded citizens from gaining information about the plans and performance of their local health services.

As we shall show, notwithstanding the claims of the White Paper, a market of some sort remains clearly in place. Providers remain largely untouched by the 1999 reforms (albeit with the potential for more significant changes at a later date), purchasers continue their functions (albeit in a new organizational guise), and contracts between the two parties remain a central feature of the NHS (albeit under the title of longer-term agreements). However, the rhetoric of the White Paper suggests a replacement of the internal market with what is termed 'integrated care'. The intention is that the perceived fragmentation, unfairness, inefficiency, bureaucracy, instability and secrecy of the market is to be replaced by a spirit of cooperation, coordination, longer-term perspectives and sharing of best practice. Among the more important mechanisms for securing this change are:

- The establishment of primary care groups (PCGs), intended to be responsible for commissioning virtually all NHS health care for the population they cover (discussed in more detail in Chapter 2).
- The implementation of statutory Health Improvement Programmes within each health authority, designed to coordinate the local improvement of health and health care (see Chapter 5).
- The establishment of a National Institute for Clinical Excellence to promulgate guidelines on clinical and cost-effectiveness (see Chapter 10).
- A commitment to improvement in clinical quality, reflected in an emphasis on clinical governance (see Chapter 11).
- The establishment of a National Commission for Health Improvement, intended to oversee the quality of local services, and empowered to intervene when necessary.
- The establishment of a new performance framework, providing a much broader set of local performance measures than hitherto (see Chapter 7).

In addition there are promised measures designed to cut management costs, to increase the use of information technology within the NHS and to provide rewards for good performance and sanctions for poor performance.

We do not intend to offer here a comprehensive review of the proposals (see Baker 1998 for further details). Rather, we shall focus on the reforms as they relate to the quasi-market in health care. We consider the proposals under six headings: purchasers, providers, regulators, contracts, information and management costs.

Purchasers

The biggest changes envisaged in the reforms are in the purchasing – or, more properly, commissioning – function. GP fundholding is to be abolished. In its place is to be a set of about 500 PCGs. PCGs will cover geographically defined populations of about 100,000, and will be led by local GPs and community nurses. Membership is compulsory for all GPs practising within the geographically defined area, which will lie within a responsible health authority. PCGs will be responsible for virtually all the NHS health care for their population, and can choose to operate at one of four levels, reflecting progressively increasing levels of autonomy and responsibility:

1 Supporting in an advisory role the health authority's commissioning of health care.
2 Taking responsibility for managing the budget for local health care, although formally remaining part of the health authority.
3 Becoming a free-standing body accountable to the health authority for managing a budget and commissioning care.
4 As Level 3, but with the added responsibility for the provision of community health services for their population.

Thus at one extreme virtually all commissioning responsibility might be returned to the health authority. At the other end of the spectrum a PCG might commission virtually all health care, making detailed reference to the health authority only in respect of major service developments. In between these extremes, it is expected that PCGs will exhibit great variations in the powers they adopt and the elements of health care they choose to 'block back' to the health authority. In the early years of the new arrangements it is expected that most PCGs will operate at Level 1 or 2, but that there will be a gradual progression towards more autonomy. There are also provisions for a Level 3 or Level 4 PCG to become a primary care trust, which is empowered to deliver community health care.

Using its usual weighted capitation approach, the national NHS Executive will set budgets for virtually all health care within health authorities, encompassing hospital and community health services, prescribing, and primary care support staff and premises. Using a consistent methodology, the NHS Executive will also set 'indicative' expenditure targets for each of the constituent PCGs within a health authority. The health authority is however expected to retain a good deal of freedom as to how it sets PCG budgets in the light of these targets. These health authority and PCG budgets will be built up service by service, and will be known as 'unified budgets'. Although a health authority will be expected to adhere to its overall budget, there is no requirement to conform to the individual service elements of the budget (see Chapter 3 for further details).

The 'New NHS' White Paper (Department of Health 1997: para. 5.27) is not explicit about how the advisory or commissioning roles of PCGs will work, and in practice it is expected that a wide range of models will be adopted. The intention is that local circumstances should determine detailed arrangements, in the light of 'national service frameworks' set by the NHS Executive, guidelines issued by the National Institute for Clinical Excellence, and the health improvement programme developed by the health authority. There will also be requirements to cooperate with local social services, and to involve the public in commissioning decisions.

Providers

The structural changes envisaged in respect of NHS Trusts appear to be relatively modest. They will be expected to enter into constructive dialogues with commissioners, and to incorporate standards for quality and efficiency into local agreements. However a major innovation in the new arrangements is the emphasis on quality and 'clinical governance'. This signals a move away from the previous preoccupations with financial performance and process measures (waiting times) towards a concern with clinical outcomes, to the extent that NHS trusts will be given a statutory duty for assuring quality of care. Ultimately the buck will stop with the chief executive.

The ideas sketched out in the 'New NHS' White Paper (Department of Health 1997: para. 6.12) are further developed in a discussion document entitled *A First-Class Service* (NHS Executive 1998b). The principal features of clinical governance are defined as the establishment of clear lines of accountability for health care, a range of quality improvement activities and effective procedures to identify and remedy poor performance. The particular procedures envisaged include thorough and prompt investigation of adverse outcomes, widespread engagement with evidence-based practice, continual professional and managerial development among clinicians and collection of appropriate data.

Although predominantly concerned with hospital services, the 'New NHS' White Paper notes the need to extend the ideas of clinical governance into primary care, particularly where PCGs are seeking to become primary care trusts (Department of Health 1997: para. 5.34).

Regulators

Under the new arrangements, health authorities will be given a strategic leadership role (see Chapter 5). This will include: assessing the health needs of their population and developing health improvement programmes; planning the broad development of local services; determining local targets and standards in the light of national guidance; and supporting and holding to account local PCGs.

The intention appears to be that the focus of health authorities should shift towards health (rather than health care), a priority of the Labour government (Department of Health 1998). This will be manifest in the development of a local Health Improvement Programme, which will cover a three-year period, and will form the framework for the development of local services. Major developments of services planned by PCGs will have to be consistent with the local Health Improvement Programme. The health authority will therefore in effect become the local regulator of health services, responsible for overseeing both the commissioning and provision of services in the interests of the local population, but taking increasingly less direct part in the detailed operation of the reformed market.

Contracts

Contracts in the internal NHS market have never been legal instruments. Rather, they can be characterized as formal service agreements between different parts of the same public sector organization. This reality is recognized in the new arrangements, which talk throughout of agreements rather than contracts. There will clearly be less emphasis on contractual form (for example, block contract, cost per case) and more on quality and outcomes. The intention is that, in order to economize on managerial effort, the national NHS Executive will develop model agreements for local use.

Indeed, cost-per-case contracts will be abolished, suggesting little or no direct financial reward for providers when treating extra patients. The 'New NHS' White Paper (Department of Health 1997) appears to suggest that cost-per-case contracts, widely used by GP fundholders, are inefficient for two reasons: first, they give rise to inappropriate incentives, encouraging trusts to seek out more cases to treat regardless of clinical need; and second, they involve large flows of paperwork and managerial effort. In particular, there is an intention to reform the widely criticized system of 'extra contractual referrals', whereby GPs could refer to a trust with whom no contract was held only after explicit permission was granted from the health authority.

Paragraph 9.14 (Department of Health 1997) affirms that the

focus of agreements between commissioner and trust will be longer term than the previous one-year time horizon, covering at least three years (see Chapter 4). The intention is to enhance the stability of health care provision. Furthermore, agreements will be based on specific services rather than whole hospitals. They appear to represent a formal manifestation of what is intended to be a broader dialogue between GP commissioners and specialist providers. This reflects the spirit of partnership and cooperation intended to permeate the new NHS, in distinct contrast to the 'opposite sides of the table' model implicit in the market.

Information

A central element of the new arrangements is the establishment of a performance framework, designed to address some of the informational deficiencies within the NHS exposed by the internal market. A later discussion paper gives details of the plans sketched in the White Paper (NHS Executive 1998a). The framework will present information on local performance in six dimensions: health improvement, fairness of access, effective delivery, efficiency, the patient/carer experience, and health outcomes of NHS care. These encompass many of the stated priorities of the government, including an emphasis on health (rather than health care), and the pursuit of equity, effectiveness, efficiency and quality of care.

The discussion document suggests that much of the framework will be opportunistic, tapping into existing data sources. Large gaps in coverage will remain. However, an important innovation will be a national survey of patients exploring their experiences of care. Under the internal market, performance measurement concentrated on provider performance. The performance framework will also include measures of health authority and PCG performance, reflecting the increased emphasis to be placed on population health.

The White Paper also promises provision of an annual set of 'reference costs', which will document estimates of costs of every treatment in every trust, to be based on standard accounting and casemix data (NHS Executive 1998c). The intention is that these costs will be used for a number of purposes, including benchmarking cost improvements, measuring relative efficiency, identifying best practice, funding transfers, and costing health improvement programmes (see Chapter 9).

Management costs

The minimization of NHS management costs has been a consistent theme of successive governments – indeed the attack on management has become a ritual part of the UK political dialogue across the entire public sector, and the transaction and management costs associated with public sector quasi-markets has become an important element of academic research (Bartlett *et al.* 1998). The White Paper implies that the abolition of GP fundholding will lead to large savings in the form of fewer contracts and a reduced volume of information requirements. It promises that 'management costs will be capped' in health authorities and PCGs (para. 3.10), with explicit mention of £3 per head of population as being the benchmark for management costs in low-level PCGs (para. 5.22). At the provider level, it is claimed that the abolition of the internal market will lead to a significant reduction in transaction costs (para. 6.24).

In total, it is expected that £1 billion will be made available for direct patient care by such reductions and efficiency improvements over the lifetime of this Parliament, implying an annual saving of £200 million, which Baker (1998) claims has largely already been secured.

DISCUSSION

The purpose of this chapter has been to set the scene for the commentaries in the following chapters. It has presented the salient features of the proposed reforms, and leaves detailed commentary to the rest of the book. The discussion has noted that the discipline of economics appears to have been influential in forming the NHS internal market, but that many features of the original arrangements are perceived to have led to unsatisfactory outcomes. The latest plans reflect a desire to retain what works but to discard what is unsatisfactory. In this respect, they offer an interesting insight into how research and other evidence is filtered through the political process to inform policy.

Only time will tell how radical this latest attempt to reform the NHS turns out to be. On paper it represents a major change of philosophy in a number of respects. The establishment of PCGs, with control over budgets for virtually all health care expenditure, signals a real determination to devolve operational decisions down to a local level. But will primary care be able to rise to this challenge?

And is the expected reduction in management costs either achievable or desirable?

At the same time, there is a significant strengthening in the regulatory framework at a national level, with the National Institute for Clinical Excellence as the advisor, the performance framework as the auditor and the National Commission for Health Improvement as the enforcer. At the local level, health authorities will assume an important – though to date poorly defined – new regulatory role in monitoring the performance of PCGs. A key issue will be the extent to which these new instruments and agencies – the introduction of which is largely an act of faith – work as intended.

Most commentators would welcome the increased emphasis on clinical quality. Yet here too there is considerable potential for the reforms to go off the rails. Can clinicians be persuaded to seek continual improvement? Can clinical outcome be measured in any meaningful way? If so, will it be possible to attribute outcome to a particular clinical intervention? And how will clinicians respond to the increased attention paid to their reported performance? In short, will an imperfect model of clinical governance, which can in principle be readily subverted, yield the hoped-for benefits?

More generally, much greater emphasis will now be placed on measurement (rather than competition) as a means of steering the NHS. The history of seeking to secure control by means of information is haunted by the experience of the Soviet Union. Will the NHS grasp the opportunities offered by improvements in information and avoid the obvious dangers, or will emphasis on measurement distort behaviour in an unintended and costly fashion?

Thus, the new arrangements appear to introduce a range of new instruments and incentives which may yield enormous benefits, but which also contain the potential for disappointment or even severe damage for the NHS. In addressing the sort of questions outlined above, there are important lessons that can be learned from past experience, other countries and other sectors. There is therefore a clear agenda for research, both in informing implementation and in evaluating the outcome. The following chapters seek to contribute to that process by examining these latest reforms from an economic perspective.

REFERENCES

Appleby, J., Smith, P., Ranade, W., Little, V. and Robinson, R. (1994). Monitoring managed competition. In R. Robinson and J. Le Grand (eds), *Evaluating the NHS Reforms*. London: King's Fund Institute.

Audit Commission (1996). *What the Doctor Ordered: A Study of GP Fundholders in England and Wales*. London: HMSO.

Baines, D. and Whynes, D.K. (1996). Selection bias in GP fundholding. *Health Economics*, 5(2), 129–40.

Baines, D., Tolley, K.H. and Whynes, D.K. (1997). *Prescribing, Budgets and Fundholding in General Practice*. London: Office of Health Economics.

Baker, M. (1998). *Making sense of the NHS White Paper*. Oxford: Radcliffe Medical Press.

Bartlett, W., Roberts, J.A. and Le Grand, J. (eds) (1998). *A Revolution in Social Policy: Quasi-market Reforms in the 1990s*. Bristol: The Policy Press.

Culyer, A.J., Maynard, A.K. and Posnett, J.W. (1990). *Competition in Health Care: Reforming the NHS*. Basingstoke: Macmillan.

Dawson, D. (1994). Costs and prices in the internal market: markets versus the NHS Management Executive guidelines. *Discussion Paper 115*, Centre for Health Economics, University of York.

Department of Health (1989). *Working for Patients*. London: HMSO.

Department of Health (1997). *The New NHS: Modern, Dependable*. London: The Stationery Office.

Department of Health (1998). *Our Healthier Nation: A Contract for Health*. London: The Stationery Office.

Dixon, J., Dinwoodie, M., Hodson, D. *et al.* (1994). Distribution of funds between fundholding and non-fundholding practices. *British Medical Journal*, 309, 30–4.

Ellwood, S. (1996). Pricing of services in the UK NHS. *Financial Accountability and Management*, 12, 281–301.

Ellwood, S. (1997). *The Response of Fundholding Doctors to the Market*. London: CIMA.

Enthoven, A. (1985). *Reflections on the Management of the National Health Service*. London: Nuffield Provincial Hospitals Trust.

Evans, R. (1997). Going for gold: the redistributive agenda behind market-based health care reform. *Journal of Health Politics, Policy and Law*, 22(2), 427–65.

Gaynor, M. and Vogt, W.B. (1997). What does economics have to say about health policy anyway? A comment and correction on Evans and Rice. *Journal of Health Politics, Policy and Law*, 22(2), 475–96.

Glennerster, H., Matsaganis, M. and Owens, P. (1994). *Implementing GP fundholding: Wild Card or Winning Hand?* Buckingham: Open University Press.

Goodwin, N. (1998). GP fundholding. In J. Le Grand, N. Mays and J. Mulligan (eds), *Learning from the NHS Internal Market*. London: King's Fund Institute.

Gosden, T. and Torgerson, D. (1997). The effect of fundholding on prescribing and referral costs: a review of the evidence. *Health Policy*, 40, 103–14.

Keynes, J.M. (1936). *The General Theory of Employment, Interest and Money*. London: Macmillan.

Klein, R. (1995). *The New Politics of the National Health Service*, 3rd edn. London: Longman.

Le Grand, J., Mays, N. and Dixon, J. (eds) (1998a). The reforms: success, failure or neither? In J. Le Grand, N. Mays and J. Mulligan (eds), *Learning from the NHS Internal Market*. London: King's Fund Institute.

Le Grand, J., Mays, N. and Mulligan, J. (1998b). *Learning from the NHS Internal Market*. London: King's Fund Institute.

McGuire, A. and Anand, P. (1997). Introduction: evaluating health care reform. In P. Anand and A. McGuire (eds), *Changes in Health Care: Reflections on the NHS Internal Market*. Basingstoke: Macmillan.

Mahon, A., Wilkin, D. and Whitehouse, C. (1994). Choice of hospital for elective surgery referrals: GPs' and patients' views. In R. Robinson and J. Le Grand (eds), *Evaluating the NHS Reforms*. London: King's Fund Institute.

Mays, N. and Dixon, J. (1996). *Purchaser Plurality in UK Health Care: Is a Consensus Emerging and is it the Right One?* London: Kings Fund Institute.

Mays, N., Goodwin, N., Bevan, G. and Wyke, S. (1997). *Total Purchasing: A Profile of National Pilot Sites*. London: Kings Fund Institute.

NHS Executive (1998a). *The New NHS, Modern and Dependable: A National Framework for Assessing Performance*. London: The Stationery Office.

NHS Executive (1998b). *A First-Class Service: Quality in the New NHS*. London: The Stationery Office.

NHS Executive (1998c). *Reference Costs: A Consultation Document*. London: The Stationery Office.

Pauly, M.V. (1997). Who was that straw man anyway? A comment on Evans and Rice. *Journal of Health Politics, Policy and Law*, 22(2), 468–73.

Propper, C. (1995). Regulatory reform of the NHS internal market. *Health Economics*, 4(2), 77–83.

Propper, C., Wilson, D. and Soderlund, N. (1998). The effects of regulation and competition in the NHS internal market: the case of general practitioner fundholders. *Journal of Health Economics*, 17, 645–73.

Reinhardt, U.E. (1996). A social contract for 21st century American health care: three tier health care with bounty hunting. *Health Economics*, 5(6), 479–99.

Rice, T. (1997). Can markets give us the health system we want? *Journal of Health Politics, Policy and Law*, 22(2), 383–426.

Robinson, R. and Le Grand, J. (eds) (1994). *Evaluating the NHS Reforms.* London: King's Fund Institute.

Smith, C. (1996). A health service for a new century: Labour's proposals to replace the internal market in the NHS. Speech, 3 December.

Thompson, D. (1998). Developing managers for the late 1990s. In P. Spurgeon (ed.), *The New Face of the NHS.* London: Royal Society of Medicine Press.

Toth, B., Harvey, I.M. and Peters, T.J. (1997). Did the introduction of general practice fundholding change patterns of emergency admission to hospital? *Journal of Health Services Research and Policy*, 2, 71–4.

West, P. (1997). *Understanding the National Health Service: The Creation of Incentives?* Buckingham: Open University Press.

2

THE CORNERSTONE OF LABOUR'S 'NEW NHS': REFORMING PRIMARY CARE

Karen Bloor, Alan Maynard and Andrew Street

Two remarkable aspects of the Thatcher 'internal market' reforms of the National Health Service (NHS) were the focus on creating a market for hospital services and the way in which primary care was treated almost peripherally in the 1989 White Paper (Department of Health 1989a). The 1991 NHS reforms introduced general practitioner (GP) fundholding almost as an afterthought, and the revision of the GP contract imposed in 1990 (Department of Health 1989b) was conducted separately from the implementation of other health care reforms.

In contrast, the principal focus of Labour's 'new NHS' reform is primary care (Department of Health 1997). The intention of the government is both to improve the efficiency and equity of primary care provision and to develop primary care groups (PCGs) and primary care trusts (PCTs) which both provide care efficiently and act as agents who purchase secondary and tertiary care on behalf of patients. This is an ambitious agenda.

This chapter explores the policy context of PCGs, describes and appraises the government proposals and identifies major issues involved in the implementation of change.

HISTORICAL BACKGROUND

The supply of primary care

In 1948, GPs were given independent contractor status, and for the first ten years of the NHS their role was ill-defined. Around 40 per cent of GPs were single-handed, and many had lists of 3000 patients, working from their own homes with little or no additional support. By the end of the 1950s there was a declining trend in the number of young doctors electing to work in general practice, and recurrent themes of 'low morale' and 'crisis' in general practice were firmly established by the early 1960s. After protracted negotiation between the Ministry of Health and the profession, a 'Doctors' Charter' was introduced in 1965 (Cameron *et al.* 1965). This created a remuneration system combining capitation and practice allowances, with the additional item of service fees. It also increased funding for premises and practice staffing, encouraging the formation of partnerships and establishing a stronger academic base for the specialty of general medicine.

The Doctors' Charter maintained the independence of general practice and the passive role of funding agencies. The 'red book' (Department of Health and Social Security 1974), which set out the terms and conditions of a practitioner, declared that a GP should aim 'to render to their patients all necessary and appropriate personal medical services of a type usually provided by general medical practitioners'. This circular definition went unnoticed by government, which trusted the doctors to practise efficiently and be rigorous 'gatekeepers' to the expensive hospital system. It has since been described as the 'John Wayne contract' – 'a GP's got to do what a GP's got to do . . .!' (Dowson and Maynard 1985: 15).

The system appeared to operate frugally because of the conservative practices of the GPs and the modest demands of the population in the 1970s. In the 1980s, general medical services (GMS) expenditure, in real terms and per capita, began to inflate more rapidly (see Table 2.1). The growth rates 1975/6–1989/90 were significant. However, there has been an even greater increase in real expenditure in the 1990s, and sharp differences in funding of primary care have emerged between the constituent parts of the United Kingdom (UK). By 1996/7, annual spending per capita was £57 in England, £156 in Wales, £85 in Scotland and £40 in Northern Ireland. This marked growth trend is the product of price and volume effects, particularly for pharmaceuticals and personnel.

Table 2.1   Increases in general medical services expenditure per capita, UK, 1975–96 (index 1974/5 = 100)

Year	England	Wales	Scotland	Northern Ireland	UK
1975/6	102	104	106	105	103
1979/80	107	107	108	105	106
1985/6	147	151	148	149	147
1989/90	176	176	172	172	172
1995/6	233	542	288	170	248

Source: McGuigan (1997)

The rate of growth of expenditure on pharmaceuticals over the last 20 years has been considerable, with over 12.5 per cent of NHS expenditure now devoted to drugs. This is partly due to net ingredient costs (NICs), which have increased by a quarter between 1985 and 1995 (see Table 2.2), again with marked national variations. Volume has also increased by one third over the same period, again with national variations. The rate of inflation in volume has accelerated considerably since 1985.

The other main cause of cost inflation in primary care has been expenditure on staff. Between 1985 and 1995 the number of GPs in England grew by over 11 per cent. However, more noticeably, the number of practice nurses and other staff increased even more rapidly, by 350 per cent and 117 per cent respectively (see Table 2.3). Thus, the average list size has fallen and new staff are available to substitute for GPs in providing care for patients in primary care.

Table 2.2   Pharmaceutical volume (prescriptions per capita) and net ingredient cost

Year	England		Wales		Scotland		Northern Ireland		UK	
	N	NIC	N	NIC	N	NIC	N	NIC	N	NIC
1985	6.8	101	8.8	100	7.1	100	8.5	111	6.9	101
1990	7.5	112	9.8	110	8.3	110	9.7	125	7.8	112
1995	9.0	125	11.8	124	9.9	127	11.9	155	9.2	123
% growth rate	32	24	34	24	39	27	40	44	33	25

N: Annual average prescriptions per capita
NIC: Net ingredient cost per prescription

Source: McGuigan (1997)

Table 2.3 General medical services staffing

Staff (England)	1985/6	1995/6	Growth rate (%)
General medical practitioners	24035	36702	11.1
GP practice staff (whole time equivalent)	27394	59476	117.1
Practice nurses (whole time equivalent)	2211	9966	350.7
Average list size	2068	1887	–8.8

Source: McGuigan (1997)

The primary care sector has grown rapidly during the last 15 years, with expenditure of £10.5 billion in 1999. The Thatcher government constrained hospital expenditure vigorously in the 1980s but did not focus on efficiency and cost control in the rapidly expanding GMS budget (Bloor and Maynard 1993). The secretary of state for health at the time of the 1991 reforms, Kenneth Clarke, was concerned about the 'black box' of primary care. He sought to tackle pharmaceutical expenditure, encouraging generic prescriptions and introducing a negative list, and to monitor GP activity more systematically.

The principal obstacle to improved control was the combination of inadequate information and little management capacity. There was no systematic measurement of the volume, quality and cost of services provided. 'One-off' studies demonstrated major variations in medical practice (e.g. hospital referral rates varied over 20-fold in the late 1980s) and there was evidence of 'on the job leisure': a study in Salford identified average patient contact time by GPs of only 26 hours per week.

The Thatcher government's response to such data was not to measure better and evaluate, but to impose a new contract on GPs (Department of Health 1989b). This increased the average GP's compensation from capitation funding to around 60 per cent. The politicians believed, in the absence of adequate evidence, that practitioners would be made more sensitive to patients' needs – if they did not provide what a patient wanted, the patient might move to a different GP, although this rarely happened in practice. A new system of fees per item of service was also introduced. There were graduated fees, depending on coverage achieved, for immunization, vaccination and cervical cytology, which have been successful in achieving increased coverage. Some of the other fees – for example those for health promotion clinics and minor surgery – have been less successful. Minor surgery fees led to increased activity in primary care which did not appear to translate into savings in the hospital sector, and health promotion clinics were inadequately defined. In one case a GP had to be reimbursed for showing a Jane Fonda workout video in his practice! The divergence in success demonstrates that fee for service payments can be useful only if 'success' is easy to measure and manage.

For the rest of the Conservative term of government, political rhetoric was to favour a primary-care led NHS (NHS Executive 1995). This was ill-defined but could be interpreted as primary care being 'A Good Thing' although the evidence base for such rhetoric is absent. Primary care in the UK over the last 50 years has been characterized by dominance of the GP, and failure to manage resources efficiently and openly. During the 20 years preceding the current government, the efficiency of GPs and their staff as providers of primary care was little questioned. Expenditure was demand determined and grew rapidly. Resource allocation formulae did not address the significant inequities in the geographical distribution of funding, as these applied only to the hospital sector (Bloor and Maynard 1995). In retrospect it is remarkable that primary care not only survived but thrived financially during successive Conservative governments.

Primary care practitioners as purchasers

Despite the insulation of the supply of primary care from the 1991 reforms, GPs were developed as purchasers of secondary care. GP fundholding was an 'add-on' to the 1991 reforms, derived from academic discussions in the early 1980s (Marinker 1984; Maynard 1986; Maynard *et al.* 1986). The rationale for fundholding was to increase the awareness of opportunity costs in health care. It was thought that if budgetary responsibilities were combined with clinical responsibilities, GPs would contain costs and use resources more efficiently.

Initially the scheme allowed only general practices with patient lists exceeding 11,000. Practices could apply for their own budgets from which to purchase a limited list of hospital services, including outpatient services, diagnostic tests and some non-emergency inpatient and day-case treatment. The budgets also included all the primary care services provided by GPs. A minimum list size was specified to reduce the risk involved with practice fundholding and a stop-loss arrangement was also included: if the annual cost to the practice of hospital treatment for a patient exceeded £5000, the excess was funded by the host district health authority. Subsequently, the scheme was extended, and fundholders ranged from practices with only 3000 patients (community fundholders) to schemes involving multiple practices, such as Total Purchasing Pilots. Figure 2.1 outlines some of the more common examples of GP commissioning arrangements which developed over time.

GP fundholders acted both as providers of primary care and purchasers of services on behalf of their practice populations. Despite their secondary importance in the 1989 White Paper, they appear to have been major catalysts for change, shifting marginal business between trust hospitals (Glennerster 1994). The scheme was introduced cumulatively, and by 1996 GP fundholders served over 50 per cent of the population in England (Department of Health 1996). Fundholding was introduced with considerable additional funding, which both encouraged participation in the scheme, and opposition to it, on the grounds of inequity and a 'two-tier service' (Dixon 1994: 772).

The Conservative government claimed great success from the scheme, but the evidence to support these claims of success is equivocal. Fundholding was introduced in the absence of formal monitoring and evaluation procedures, and the majority of studies are observational and fail to isolate fundholding effects from other concurrent influences. The published evidence focuses on identifying changes in three broad areas: in primary care, in referrals to the secondary care sector, and in prescribing.

One of the main benefits that fundholding was supposed to realize was a shift from secondary to primary care. As fundholding embodied incentives to reduce referrals, increased primary care activity was expected as a substitution for secondary care activity. There was some evidence for this. A comparison of 18 fundholding practices and 81 non-fundholders in Lincolnshire found that fundholders achieved better cervical cytology uptake, child health and preschool surveillance and undertook higher amounts of paid minor surgery (Baines and Whynes 1996). Fundholders also began to diversify their practices by providing new services (e.g. physiotherapy) and developing specialist outreach clinics (Corney 1994).

GPs were better contractors than health authorities as they had better information and more motivation to improve service standards and because they could make marginal decisions without causing the confrontation that health authorities would face if they changed provider (Glennerster 1994). GP Fundholders also had financial incentives to limit referrals which were not strictly

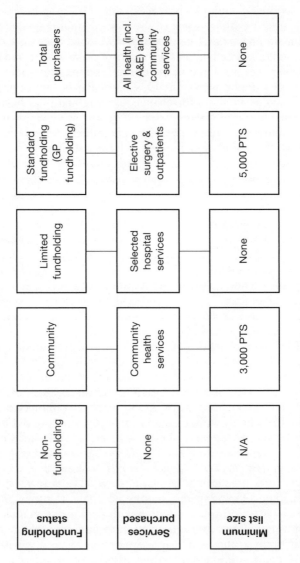

Fundholding status	Non-fundholding	Community	Limited fundholding	Standard fundholding (GP fundholding)	Total purchasers
Services purchased	None	Community health services	Selected hospital services	Elective surgery & outpatients	All health (incl. A&E) and community services
Minimum list size	N/A	3,000 PTS	None	5,000 PTS	None

Figure 2.1 Variants of GP purchasing arrangements

necessary so that the practice could save money, and to encourage patients with private insurance to accept private treatment, the cost of which did not fall on the practice budget. The extent to which these incentives influenced practice remains unclear (Dixon and Glennerster 1995). In a small study of ten first-wave fundholding practices and six non-fundholding practices in the Oxford region, which were matched according to various practice characteristics, Coulter and Bradlow (1993) found no evidence that hospital referrals were influenced by fundholding. In contrast, a study of fundholding practices in Scotland revealed a significant reduction in referral rates, matched by an increase in the use of direct access services (Howie *et al.*, 1995). In another study (Surender *et al.*, 1995) it was found that three years into the scheme NHS referral rates by GP fundholders had actually increased slightly, and that, contrary to expectations, referrals to private clinics had generally fallen. There was no evidence of a substitution away from specialist care.

Critics of the scheme have argued that fundholding offers incentives to have patients admitted through casualty rather than via referral, because fundholders do not have to pay for emergency care; however, evidence that this happened is weak. In an analysis of more than 50,000 episodes in the south-west region, no indication was found that fundholding had an impact on the proportion of emergency admissions to hospital (Toth *et al.* 1997). Baines and Whynes (1996) found referrals were contrary to the hypothesis: their comparison of 99 practices in Lincolnshire showed fundholders had a lower ratio of emergency to elective admissions. The authors suggest this may have been because GP fundholders were more successful in placing elective contracts than health authorities.

The impact of fundholding on prescribing has received more attention in the literature than any other single aspect of its activity. Early studies suggested that GP fundholders were more successful than non-fundholders at containing drug costs (Bradlow and Coulter 1993; Maxwell *et al.* 1993; Wilson *et al.* 1995), but longer-term analyses are less clear (Glennerster *et al.* 1994; Harris and Scrivener 1996). Over the period since the introduction of fundholding there has been a general and pronounced rise in overall prescribing costs, irrespective of the fundholding status of practices. Evidence about whether the rate of inflation has been lower for GP fundholders than other practices remains a subject of debate. In a study of prescribing habits among a small number of practices three years after the introduction of fundholding, Surender *et al.* (1995)

found that net prescribing costs had risen by a third or more, with highest costs among non-dispensing fundholders, while dispensing fundholders and non-fundholders had similar prescribing costs. A more extensive survey of 100 fundholders and 312 non-fundholders yielded a different conclusion: GP fundholders had contained costs more effectively than non-fundholders by reducing both volume and cost per item (Wilson *et al.* 1995).

Whynes *et al.* (1996) found that prescribing costs were lower for fundholding than non-fundholding practices in Lincolnshire. However, in a separate study of the same practices the authors argue that this observation may stem from selection bias of practices participating in the scheme, rather than the nature of fundholding itself (Baines and Whynes 1996). They conclude that 'control over prescribing costs is an inherited characteristic [rather] than one acquired as a result of fundholding' and that 'fundholders' prescribing performance as a whole will, in the future, regress towards that of the non-fundholders' (p. 138).

This prediction seems to have been borne out by the most comprehensive study of prescribing costs, featuring all general practices in England for the six years from April 1990 to March 1996 (Harris and Scrivener 1996). This analysis demonstrated that prescribing costs had increased by up to 59 per cent in fundholding practices and by 66 per cent for non-fundholders over the period. For each fundholding wave, a small relative reduction in prescribing costs was observed in the year prior to fundholding. Maximum reductions occurred in the first year but tailed off to the extent that increases in costs were similar to that for non-fundholders beyond the third year of fundholding status. Fundholding was associated with cost escalation of 6 per cent less than that of non-fundholding over the five-year period of its existence. This is not a particularly substantial return on the significantly more generous investment received by fundholding practices. This was the conclusion reached in an Audit Commission report: fundholders made relatively modest changes to patient benefits and management capacity, and may not have provided sufficient improvements to justify their higher cost (Audit Commission 1996).

Limited though these benefits were, questions have been raised about whether they could be attributed to fundholding at all. Fundholding was a voluntary scheme and it may be that those practices which participated would have been successful anyway. In an examination of the possibility of selection bias, Baines and Whynes (1996: 137) concluded that 'practices obtaining fundholding status in the early waves were those most capable of achieving success as officially assessed'. Consequently, caution should be exercised in attributing changes in activity to the fundholding status of the practices. Moreover, innovations were not exclusive to fundholding practices: practices were reviewing prescribing protocols and investing in new facilities long before fundholding was introduced (Corney 1994).

Fundholding also generated vociferous opposition, most particularly because it was perceived to be inequitable. This inequity took two forms (Bevan 1998). First, patients registered with fundholders appeared to enjoy preferential access to secondary care compared to those registered with non-fundholders in the same health authority (Audit Commission 1996; Beecham 1997; Dowling 1997). Second, per capita funding available for fundholder patients was more generous than that for patients funded directly from health authority budgets (Dixon 1994; Dixon *et al.* 1994; National Audit Office 1995).

In summary, it seems that fundholding was inequitable and had failed to generate benefits of significant enough magnitude to justify the expense of the scheme. The experiment was poorly evaluated and had not run its course. Various alternatives were being adopted towards the end of the Conservative government's final term in office. The most innovative of these was total purchasing.

Total purchasing

The NHS Executive introduced the Total Purchasing Pilot (TPP) initiative in 1994, following local developments in GP fundholding (NHS Executive 1995). Standard fundholders took responsibility for purchasing a much wider range of services, such as maternity services and inpatient mental health (Mays and Mulligan 1998). Unlike standard fundholding and other aspects of the 1991 reforms, the TPPs were constructed as experiments, and evaluated in a three-year 'before and after' study. TPPs were implemented with minimal central guidance, leading to considerable variation among them (TP-NET 1997). Mays and Mulligan (1998) refer to the TPPs as 'selective purchasers' because most were not, in fact, 'total' purchasers: many gave responsibility back to their health authority for the purchase of some services, such as accident and emergency and forensic psychiatry.

There were 53 first wave TPPs, which went 'live' in April 1996.

A year later, they were joined by 35 second wave TPPs. 37 per cent of TPPs comprised single practices, the median population covered was 23,000 patients and approximately 5 per cent of patients in England and Wales were covered by the TPP scheme (Mays *et al.* 1998).

Direct management costs of running TPPs varied from £10,000 to £99,000 for single practice projects and from £1000 to £339,000 for multi-practice projects, reflecting diversity in scale, scope, ambition and managerial infrastructure (Posnett *et al.* 1998). These figures relate only to the additional cost of managing the total purchasing budget over and above the management allowance for fundholding. Overall, it is expected that rolling out total purchasing more generally would have led to a net increase in the management costs of primary care commissioning (Killoran *et al.* 1998). The highest performing TPPs, in terms of their reported achievements, had considerably higher management costs than the lowest performing projects. They also appeared to have more GP involvement, contributing to these direct management costs (Place *et al.* 1999).

Evidence relating to total purchasing has been summarized by Mays and Mulligan (1998):

- TPPs varied greatly in size, management arrangements, budget arrangements and reported achievements.
- Total purchasing is more ambitious and more costly to run than standard fundholding. It added to NHS costs, but with highly variable direct management costs and higher reported achievements from those with higher management costs.
- There was limited evidence on whether TPPs have achieved service efficiency objectives, but projects have altered the use of acute services in terms of admissions and bed days, reporting achievement of around half their self-defined objectives.
- Total purchasing probably had greater scope for promoting equity than standard fundholding, depending on budget negotiations with the health authority.
- Little was known about the quality of services delivered under total purchasing, and most TPPs did not formally assess their patients' needs or systematically use research evidence to inform their service provision.
- There was limited accountability other than ensuring financial accountability, and TPPs did not give high priority to informing or involving patients in purchasing decisions.

PRIMARY CARE IN THE 'NEW NHS'

While acknowledging that it was not without benefit, New Labour's White Paper formally announced the demise of fundholding:

> Despite its limitations, many innovative GPs and their fund managers have used the fundholding scheme to sharpen the responsiveness of some hospital services and to extend the range of services available in their own surgeries. But the fundholding scheme has also proved bureaucratic and costly. It has allowed development to take place in a fragmented way, outside a coherent strategic plan. It has artificially separated responsibility for emergency and planned care, and given advantage to some patients at the expense of others.
>
> (Department of Health 1997: s.5.5)

The rhetoric of New Labour is that GP fundholding has failed. This voluntary and partial system was replaced in April 1999 with a comprehensive and compulsory system of PCGs, many of which, in time, are expected to evolve into PCTs, which will be freestanding organizations.

Primary care groups

PCGs for England were introduced in the White Paper *The New NHS: Modern, Dependable* (Department of Health 1997), with similar concepts presented in consultation documents for Scotland (Scottish Office 1998), Wales (Welsh Office 1998) and Northern Ireland (Northern Ireland Office 1998). The policy was described as 'going with the grain', aiming to 'keep what has worked about fundholding, but discard what has not'. PCGs will 'bring together GPs and community nurses in each area to work together to improve the health of local people' (Department of Health 1997: 27). The functions of PCGs are described in the White Paper (Department of Health 1997), and developed in later guidance (NHS Executive 1998b–f).

The government intends that PCGs will:

- Commission health services for their populations from NHS trusts, within the framework of the health authority's Health Improvement Programme (HImP), ensuring quality and efficiency.
- Monitor performance against the service agreements they (or, initially, the health authority) have with NHS trusts.

- Develop primary care, by joint working across practices, sharing skills, providing a forum for professional development, audit and peer review, assuring quality and developing the new approach to clinical governance, and influencing deployment of resources for general practice locally. Local Medical Committees (LMCs) will have a key role in supporting this process.
- Better integrate primary and community health services and work more closely with social services on both planning and delivery.
- Contribute to the HImP, helping to ensure that it reflects the perspective of the local community and experience of patients.
- Promote the health of the local population, working in partnership with other agencies.

Performance criteria for these functions have not been articulated. The form of PCGs is intended to be flexible and to reflect local circumstances, building on existing arrangements such as total purchasing, locality commissioning groups and multifunds. There will be four optional and progressive forms of involvement, and PCGs are expected to progress so that in time all assume fuller responsibilities:

1 Supporting the health authority in commissioning care for its population, acting in an advisory capacity.
2 Taking devolved responsibility for managing the budget for health care in their area, formally as part of the health authority.
3 Become established as freestanding bodies accountable to the health authority for commissioning care.
4 Become established as free-standing bodies accountable to the health authority for commissioning care and with added responsibility for the commissioning of community health services for their population.

The government has legislated to introduce freestanding Level 3 and 4 PCTs. PCTs may include community health services previously provided by existing NHS trusts, and community NHS trusts may merge with PCTs to integrate service and management support. Ultimately, PCTs will be able to run community hospitals and other services but will not take responsibility for mental health or learning disability services, although links with these services will be developed.

A core set of requirements applies to all levels of PCG/Ts. They will be accountable to the health authority and be required to:

- Be representative of all GP practices in the group.
- Have a governing body which includes community nursing and social services as well as GPs drawn from the area.
- Take account of social services as well as health authority boundaries, to help promote integration in service planning and provision.
- Abide by the local HImP.
- Have clear arrangements for public involvement including lay representation on the governing body and open meetings.
- Have efficient and effective arrangements for management and financial accountability.

Each PCG will have a governing body, consisting of between four and seven GPs, one or two nurses, a local social services authority representative, a health authority representative and a lay member and the PCG chief executive. This will be quorate only when there are a majority of GPs present and GPs will have first refusal on the chair (Milburn 1998). This policy permits continued medical dominance of primary care, which sits uneasily with the move towards multidisciplinary primary health care teams.

PCGs were intended to develop around natural communities and existing local groups, taking account of the boundaries with social services and typically serving around 100,000 patients, with the largest serving more than twice this number. It is unclear how this recommended figure was determined as it exceeds the optimum size to minimize management costs or to spread risk (Bachmann and Bevan 1996; Place *et al.* 1999). It may be that by covering large 'natural' communities, perceptions of a 'two-tier' service and rationing by postcode will be less in evidence.

Beyond Level 1, PCGs will be funded with a unified cash limited budget and will have the opportunity to 'deploy resources and savings to strengthen local services and ensure that patterns of care best reflect their patients' needs' (Department of Health 1997: 28). This budget covers hospital and community health services, prescribing and GMS infrastructure. For the first time this effectively cash limits the overall prescribing budgets, as overspends on prescribing will mean reduced expenditure on other services to stay within the overall budget. Up to now, prescribing budgets have been 'demand-determined', without an overall limit. Indicative budgets will be used for individual practices, but the PCG will have to develop mechanisms for ensuring that these budgets are not overspent. Practice level incentive arrangements are encouraged to promote best use of resources. Such incentives will require careful specification and monitoring. The inclusion of the practice infra-structure component of GMS in the budget has been of particular concern to GPs, but subsequent policy indicates that expenditure on staff, premises and computers will be subject to a minimum guaranteed floor (Milburn 1998).

Management costs for PCGs will be combined with those of the health authority, with a limit of £3 per head estimated for manage-ment costs initially, increasing as PCGs take on more responsi-bilities or merge with community trusts. Analysis of the transaction costs of TPPs suggests that PCGs may have difficulties living within this envelope, particularly if contributing parties (GPs, nurses and other professionals) are to be adequately reimbursed for their (management) time devoted to the PCG (Killoran *et al.* 1998; Place *et al.* 1999). Over time as PCGs move to higher levels, the balance of management costs between the PCG and the health authority may change, although this will require a scaling down of health authority duties, perhaps facilitated by further health authority mergers. It is also possible that PCGs will start to share functions without full merger (Smith *et al.* 1999).

HImPs of health authorities determine much of the work of a PCG. PCGs should influence the development of HImPs and will be accountable for their implementation. Preparation of docu-ments such as primary care investment plans and organizational development plans will also be required from PCGs. PCGs will specify and maintain service agreements with NHS trusts about the quality and level of care provided in hospitals.

Accountability is maintained through an accounting officer to the health authority. Health authorities will monitor and advise PCGs, offering additional direction if an individual PCG falls behind its peers, and have the power, *in extremis*, to withdraw or reduce responsibilities, or change leadership and management. As well as financial accountability through an accounting officer, a senior pro-fessional within the PCG will be nominated to be responsible for clinical governance and quality of clinical care. Individual practices will also be encouraged to identify a leader for clinical governance. To achieve trust status, PCGs must demonstrate that they have a systematic approach to monitoring and developing clinical stan-dards in practice. The primary care investment plan and annual accountability agreements, containing key targets, objectives and standards, will be required by the health authority.

These plans are ambitious and novel. The surviving dominance of GPs, much of it ceded by ministers in negotiation in 1998, makes them liable for the successes and failures of PCGs. The novelty of these reforms lies in seeking to manage (control) primary care, to reduce practice variation and enhance quality, openly and efficiently. Previously, GP practices, particularly when acting as providers rather than purchasers, have been independent 'islands' in the uncharted waters of primary care. This era of no accountability is clearly at an end: price taking is being translated into price making.

The current situation

In April 1999, 481 primary care groups were introduced in England. These are all constituted as committees of their local health authority with the chairs (usually GPs) accountable to the chief executive of the health authority. From 1 April 2000, 50–60 PCGs in England will be selected to move to trust status. The requirements for this move are not yet known and will be determined by future guidance.

The heterogeneity of PCGs is considerable. Some are based on existing arrangements, such as GP multifunds or total purchasers, and may find 'promotion' to trust status straightforward. Others are fragmented in terms of their previous status and the development of internal management and external collaboration. Such organizations have limited management capacity and lack the information systems required for the efficient development of practices within PCGs and appropriate collaboration across groups.

It is unlikely that the existing stock of PCGs will survive many years. As trust status spreads, amalgamation seems likely, and chief executives and other staff currently being recruited may be reorganized and even made redundant in such mergers.

FUTURE CHALLENGES

An underlying motivation for the introduction of PCGs is the belief that patients will benefit by further extending the role of primary care so that more (and, supposedly, better) decisions are made by those who are the first port of call for most users of the NHS. Moreover, by obliging all GPs to adopt one or other option, the two-tier system associated with fundholding will be less in evidence. Also, because PCGs have responsibility for more than simply a practice

list they may be able to plan more strategically for their local population than fundholding allowed, particularly as they will be
expected to commission in accordance with their local HImP. But,
in making primary care the cornerstone of their health care
reforms, the current Labour government faces challenges. Four
particular challenges relate to organizational size and structure,
quality and clinical governance, financial accountability, and
rationing.

Organizational size and structure

PCGs are to be larger organizations than most preceding models of
primary care commissioning in the NHS. It may be that this will
make them better able to manage risk but, apparently, larger
groupings are not required for this. A simulation exercise exploring
the budgetary implications of rare costly referrals suggested that a
risk pool of 30,000 may be adequate (Bachmann and Bevan 1996).
Moreover, risks may be more manageable over the longer time-
frames that Health Service Agreements allow.

PCGs may be able to realize economies of scale from amal-
gamating practices. As GPs commission for a wider range of services for a larger population the fixed costs associated with needs
assessment, writing the purchasing plan and contracting can be
spread among more patients. This suggests that costs will fall as
PCGs grow in size. However, at some point such economies will be
exhausted. Evidence from analysis of health maintenance organizations (HMOs) in the USA, which have been likened in certain
respects to PCGs (Ham 1998), does not provide a clear answer.
Given (1996) suggests that returns are exhausted at 115,000
enrollees, while Wholey *et al.* (1996) argue that economies are realized at only 50,000 enrollees. The continuing amalgamation of managed care companies on the basis of asserted economies of scale
casts some doubt on these figures.

One crucial difference between HMOs and PCGs (at least in the
short term) is the contractual status of their medical staff. The staff
of HMOs are typically salaried employees while GPs are likely to
remain as independent contractors. While it is relatively straightforward to achieve harmony among GPs and to get them to accept
budgetary responsibility when managing a single practice's fundholding budget, the administrative burden associated with coordinating GPs from the practices comprising the PCG may compromise
any economies derived from creating larger commissioning groups.

Analysis of the transactions costs associated with total purchasing suggests a substantial amount of management time is spent on co-ordinating GPs and communicating organizational objectives. Furthermore this cost increases the more GPs are involved (Place *et al.* 1999). To mitigate these coordination problems, PCGs may adopt a range of organizational structures which allow them to balance strategic against day-to-day management (Street and Place 1998; Smith *et al.* 1999).

Quality and clinical governance

The recent NHS reforms promise profound changes in the government of general practice. With acceptance by the General Medical Council and the Royal College of General Practitioners of the need for re-accreditation of all practitioners every five years, quality and guidelines will be central to the professional development of medical and other staff. The reforms also place a statutory duty of maintaining quality of clinical care on the chief executives of acute, community and primary care trusts. At present they have only a financial responsibility under the law (to break even and make a 6 per cent return on historic capital investment). The creation of this new duty of 'quality' introduces a new agenda in risk management, clinical audit and quality assurance for all managers.

The initial definition of clinical governance was vague (Department of Health 1998: 33) 'a framework through which NHS organisations are accountable for continuously improving the quality of their services and safeguarding high standards of care by creating an environment in which excellence in clinical care will flourish'. However, since then it has become clear that quality relates not just to clinical effectiveness but to cost-effectiveness. The discussion document about the role of the National Institute for Clinical Excellence (NICE) (Department of Health 1999) makes it clear that companies wishing to have their products accepted for reimbursement by the NHS must demonstrate cost effectiveness if they are to be incorporated into NICE guidelines.

GPs will receive these NICE guidelines, which will have varying levels of application depending on the robustness of the data. One of the earliest guidelines is likely to be for the use of beta interferon in the treatment of multiple sclerosis. This is an area where medical practice variation is considerable and 'postcode' rationing is much criticized.

A guideline like this will be issued with a degree of obligation to

GPs: they will be expected to adhere to the guideline or face management interference. An interesting issue, given the independent contractor status of GPs, is to consider how implementation of NICE guidelines will be monitored, and what are the implications if a GP refuses to adhere to the guidelines. Such behaviour will incur the displeasure of a PCG or PCT chief executive, who has a duty of quality related to NICE guidelines. Also it will attract the attention of the Commission for Health Improvement (CHI). This organization will audit trusts thoroughly every three to four years and will respond to high profile incidents where quality is in question. The pressures for GPs to conform will be considerable.

However, with the focus of NICE being predominantly on pharmaceuticals, at least initially, the need for improved management information will be acute. An obvious source of pharmaceutical prescribing information is the Pharmaceutical Pricing Authority (PPA). At present all dispensing chemists send their prescription forms to the PPA, who reimburse pharmacists and collate information. This information role could be developed by augmenting prescriptions with a diagnostic code and a patient identifier. NICE practice guidelines will target interventions at particular patient groups and an augmented PPA information system could be used to measure speed and the extent of adherence to guidelines by practitioners. There will be economies from a national system and such data will be an invaluable source for research and management.

The costs of this reform have not been estimated. At present, plans are vague and evolving, but the resource consequences of professional, trust, NICE, CHI and PPA investments will be considerable. There is a risk that parsimony and poor management may lead to the fragmentation and failure of some elements of this long-overdue process of regulating the quality of primary care.

Financial accountability

In general, attempts to increase GP involvement in commissioning have been rationalized either as a means to improve patient access and service delivery through the inclusion of a primary care perspective in the commissioning process or to make GPs directly accountable for the resource consequences of clinical decisions. The former aim may be achieved by introducing PCGs as advisory bodies only, but clearly the government envisages a more substantial role.

Experience suggests that in order to make GPs financially

accountable they must be actively engaged in the management of a budget. In many of the multi-practice sites forming TPPs, GPs were content to delegate financial responsibility to the lead GP and the TPP management team, and this reduced the extent to which GPs faced direct incentives to alter their own practice. Unless peer pressure is strong, the aim of engaging all GPs within a local group will probably require notional budgets set at practice level (even if budgets are aggregated for management purposes) and significant investment in coordinating the views and actions of GPs.

In order to make GPs financially responsible they must be sufficiently motivated to work with their colleagues in the PCG towards developing and realizing common organizational objectives. All GPs are obliged to participate in a PCG of one form or another. However, the incentive for these independent (and generally individualistic) contractors to cooperate with one another and accept interference in their decision making is not obvious (Butler and Roland 1998).

For those who were not opposed to fundholding on ideological grounds, there were clear incentives to taking on fundholding status, as it promised GPs greater leverage and autonomy in terms of where, when and how their patients were treated, and the prospect of generating savings to plough back into the practice. As much larger conglomerations it will be interesting to see how individual GPs, particularly fundholders and non-fundholders, grouped in the same PCG reconcile their differences and come to a shared vision about the overall objectives of the PCG. Compared to practice-based fundholding, it is likely to prove more difficult to reach consensus and to ensure that all GPs consider the wider interests of the PCG when making clinical decisions which have financial implications. We should not be surprised if some GPs resist any attempt to make them participate in a scheme which has the prospect of reducing their own autonomy.

Nevertheless, if PCGs are to be financially accountable and manage within their budgets, they will have to develop mechanisms for monitoring and perhaps limiting GP referral and prescribing behaviour. This is a major challenge and requires a balance of rewards and penalties. Health authorities have found it difficult to manage activity within their global budgets, in part because they are a step removed from the GPs who make many of the decisions which determine the pattern of service provision. It is hoped that PCGs will be in a better position to operate within a global budget by virtue of involving GPs in the management structure.

However, with a comprehensive budget set at PCG level, GPs will face restrictions on their referral and prescribing behaviour in order to meet the constraints of this global budget. This is in direct contradiction to government assurances:

> *Patients will continue to be guaranteed the drugs, investigations and the treatments they need.* If a primary care group over-spends, the overspend will be managed within the funds made available to health authorities generally and to the NHS more widely, much as health authority overspends are handled now. There is no question of anyone being denied the drugs they need because a GP runs out of cash. GPs' participation within a PCG, or membership of a PCG board will not affect their ability to fulfil their terms of service obligation always to pre-scribe and refer in the best interests of their patients. *I can guarantee that the freedom to refer and prescribe remains unchanged.*
>
> (Milburn 1998: 2, original emphasis)

One of the central concerns of the White Paper and subsequent documents is the variability in access to and use of services through-out the country (Department of Health 1997; NHS Executive 1998a). This is being addressed at all levels of the NHS, with the National Institute for Clinical Excellence providing overall guidance about effective and cost-effective practices, health authorities being monitored according to their performance in reducing variations, and trusts and PCGs introducing clinical governance mechanisms.

Clearly, referral and prescribing variations will have to be man-aged by PCGs to ensure greater efficiency and to remain in budget. Alignment of clinical and financial accountability and the desire to reduce treatment variations is incompatible with political assur-ances that the freedom to refer and prescribe remains unchanged. The get-out clause from the Department's perspective is that the Milburn letter states that 'patients will continue to be guaranteed the drugs, investigations and the treatments they *need*' (emphasis added). Responses to patient needs must be cost-effective: the free-dom to refer and prescribe remains so long as it is justifiable.

GPs appear to be under no illusion that limits are to be placed on their clinical freedom and that the 'best interests of patients' should be defined as the overall interests of the broader popu-lation for which the PCG is responsible, rather than merely the patient in the consulting room. Among the challenges facing those working in PCGs is their ability to manage a global budget and, in particular, what mechanisms they should employ to prevent over-spending.

The Department of Health, after 50 years of pressure from the Treasury, is attempting to cash-limit the GMS budget. However, it is realizing only partial success. The non-GP part of the budget is to be cash-limited and allocated using a weighted capitation formula similar to that used in the hospital sector. The reluctance to tackle the issue of the gross inequities in the distribution of GPs (e.g. many more per capita, even with need weighting, in the south-west than the north-east) is related to the power of the medical profession to resist change and influence policy makers.

Rationing

A paradox of the NHS debate is that the government denies the existence of rationing but, like its predecessor, it reforms the structures of the NHS to improve the efficiency of resource allocation (rationing). The allocative goal of the NHS is to use resources efficiently so that potential population health gains are maximized from its limited budget. The pursuit of this goal requires the practice of economics-based medicine. However, while governments reform vigorously and espouse the cause of 'value for money', they are reluctant to confront the rationing issue explicitly and fully. The logical consequence of Milburn's statement and the constitution of NICE is that resource allocation will be informed, if not determined, by cost-effectiveness criteria.

The Labour government also expresses concerns about equity. The Acheson Report on inequalities in health (Acheson 1999) described familiar findings about the growth of inequality, but failed to cost and prioritize its recommendations. This leaves a lack of clarity about the equity goals of the government, their ranking in relation to other goals, and the preferred nature of trade-offs.

What principles of rationing might be implied from the behaviour of politicians and the electorate? Williams (1996) suggests the following three criteria, which may form a basis for debate and consensus formation:

1 Equals should be treated equally and with due dignity, especially when near to death.
2 People's needs for health care should be met as efficiently as possible (imposing the least sacrifice on others).

3 Inequalities in the lifetime health of the population should be minimized.

At present, government policy, through the creation of clinical governance, NICE and CHI is focusing its rationing efforts on efficiency (2, above). This is incomplete. Health care professionals may at times practise inefficiently because of social objectives, such as the high valuation of new-born children, which may require resources not to be used cost-effectively. This implies a strong equity objective (3, above). The policy question is therefore how much efficiency (health gain) is society prepared to sacrifice to pursue equity goals? Ignoring such issues makes medical practice difficult and undermines the acceptability of evidence-based practice guidelines to be produced by NICE.

CONCLUSION

The failure to manage primary care provision in an efficient and open manner has been condoned by politicians, who nevertheless continued to advocate a 'primary-care-led NHS' and developed the capacity of primary care to purchase secondary care services. The paradoxes implicit in these policies are as significant as the variations in primary care practice and the relative absence of management systems.

Reform is likely to bring with it the gradual alteration of the GP contract of employment. In 1997 the Conservative government, with Labour support, passed legislation to facilitate pilots of salary-paid GPs. In late 1998 the then minister of health, Alan Milburn, indicated that it was the government's intention to reform doctors' contracts. Such reform has always been expensive (Klein and Maynard 1998) and this time is unlikely to be different. The creation of a new salaried system of GPs would require shift working, skill substitution and careful management of the new contract with performance criteria to ensure activity and quality.

The government's reform of primary care is of great importance to the sector itself and to the NHS as a whole. In the last decade there has been a failure to ensure openness and accountability in primary care performance, as reform energy has previously been directed at the hospital system. This failure means that the task of primary care reform is more difficult. For example, GPs are now having to respond to activities such as audit which were imposed in the hospital sector about a decade ago. The government have an ambitious agenda which is yet to be determined fully and which will be costly. As ever, this will raise hopes and antagonism. Aneurin Bevan's view was that 'the only way to get a message across to a doctor is to write it on a cheque'. Primary care reforms in the next decade may well require increased expenditure, but will also require clearly articulated objectives, shrewd management and careful performance assessment.

REFERENCES

Acheson, D. (1999). *Independent Inquiry into Inequalities in Health.* Report chaired by Sir Donald Acheson. London: The Stationery Office.

Audit Commission (1996). *What the Doctor Ordered.* London: HMSO.

Bachmann, M. and Bevan, G. (1996). Determining the size of a total purchasing site to manage the financial risks of rare costly referrals: computer simulation model. *British Medical Journal*, 313, 1054–7.

Baines, D.L. and Whynes, D.K. (1996). Selection bias in GP fundholding. *Health Economics*, 5, 129-40.

Beecham, L. (1997). GP fundholders can no longer jump the queue. *British Medical Journal*, 315, 209.

Bloor, K. and Maynard, A. (1993). *Expenditure in the NHS During and After the Thatcher Years.* (*Discussion Paper 113*). York: Centre for Health Economics, University of York.

Bloor, K. and Maynard, A. (1995). *Equity in Primary Care* (*Discussion Paper 141*). York: Centre for Health Economics, University of York.

Bradlow, J. and Coulter, A. (1993). Effect of fundholding and indicative prescribing schemes on general practitioners' prescribing costs. *British Medical Journal*, 307, 1186–9.

Butler, T. and Roland, M. (1998). How will primary care groups work? *British Medical Journal*, 316, 214.

Cameron, J.C., Jones, I.M., Kuenssberg, E.V. *et al.* (1965). A charter for the family doctor service, *British Medical Journal* (Supplement), 89–91.

Corney, R. (1994). Experiences of first wave general practice fundholders in South East Thames Regional Health Authority. *British Journal of General Practice*, 44, 34–7.

Coulter, A. and Bradlow, J. (1993). Effect of NHS reforms on general practitioners' referral patterns. *British Medical Journal*, 306, 433–7.

Department of Health (1989a). *Working for Patients.* London: HMSO.

Department of Health (1989b). *Terms of Service for Doctors in General Practice.* London: HMSO.

Department of Health (1996). *More than 50 per cent of patients are now served by GP fundholders* (press release 96/107). London: Department of Health.

Department of Health (1997). *The New NHS: Modern, Dependable.* London: The Stationery Office.

Department of Health (1999). *Faster Access to Modern Treatment: How NICE Appraisal will Work.* London: NHS Executive.

Department of Health and Social Security (1974). *The National Health Service (General Medical and Pharmaceutical Services) Regulations 1974.* London: HMSO.

Dixon, J. (1994). Can there be fair funding for fundholding practices? *British Medical Journal,* 308, 772–5.

Dixon, J. and Glennerster, H. (1995). What do we know about fundholding in general practice? *British Medical Journal,* 311, 727–30.

Dixon, J., Dinwoodie, M., Hodson, D., *et al.* (1994). Distribution of NHS funds between fundholding and non-fundholding practices. *British Medical Journal,* 309, 30–4.

Dowling, B. (1997). Effect of fundholding on waiting times: database study. *British Medical Journal,* 315, 290–2.

Dowson, S. and Maynard, A. (1985). General practices. In A.J. Harrison and J. Gretton (eds) *Health Care UK 1985: An Economic, Social and Policy Audit.* London: CIPFA.

Given, R.S. (1996). Economies of scale and scope as an explanation of merger and output diversification activities in the health maintenance organization industry. *Journal of Health Economics,* 15, 685–713.

Glennerster, H. (1994). GP fundholding – wild card or winning hand? In R. Robinson and J. LeGrand (eds), *Evaluating the NHS Reforms.* London: King's Fund Institute.

Glennerster, H., Matsaganis, M. and Owens, P. (1994). *Implementing GP Fundholding: Wild Card or Winning Hand?* Buckingham: Open University Press.

Ham, C. (1998). The new NHS: commentaries on the White Paper: from command economy to demand management. *British Medical Journal,* 316, 212–16.

Harris, C.M. and Scrivener, G. (1996). Fundholders' prescribing costs: the first five years. *British Medical Journal,* 313, 1531–4.

Howie, J.G.R., Heaney, D.J. and Maxwell, M. (1995). *General Practice Fundholding: Shadow Project – an Evaluation.* Edinburgh: University of Edinburgh.

Killoran, A., Griffiths, J., Posnett, J. and Mays, N. (1998). *What Can We Learn From the Total Purchasing Pilots About the Management Costs of Primary Care Groups?* London: King's Fund Institute.

Klein, R. and Maynard, A. (1998). *On the way to Calvary. British Medical Journal,* 5, 7150.

McGuigan, S. (1997). *Office of Health Economics Compendium of Health Statistics.* London: Office of Health Economics.

Marinker, M. (1984). Developments in primary health care. In G. Teeling Smith (ed.), *A New NHS Act for 1996?* London: Office of Health Economics.

Maxwell, M., Heaney, D., Howie, J. and Noble, S. (1993). General practice fundholding: observations on prescribing patterns and costs using the defined daily dose method. *British Medical Journal*, 307, 1190–4.

Maynard, A. (1986). Performance incentives in general practice. In G. Teeling Smith (ed.), *Health Education and General Practice*. London: Office of Health Economics.

Maynard, A., Marinker, M. and Pereira Gray, D. (1986). The doctor, the patient and their contract III – alternative contracts: are they viable? *British Medical Journal*, 292, 1438–40.

Mays, N. and Mulligan, J. (1998). Total purchasing. In J. Le Grand, N. Mays and J. Mulligan (eds), *Learning from the NHS Internal Market*. London: Kings Fund Institute.

Mays, N., Goodwin, N., Killoran, A. and Malbon, G. (1998). *Total Purchasing: A Step Towards Primary Care Groups*. London: King's Fund Institute.

Milburn, A. (1998). *The new NHS: Letter to British Medical Association* (17 June). London: Department of Health.

National Audit Office (1995). *General Practitioner Fundholding in England*. (HC51). London: HMSO.

NHS Executive (1995). *Developing NHS Purchasing and GP Fundholding: Towards a Primary Care-Led NHS*. London: NHSE.

NHS Executive (1998a). *A First-Class Service: Quality in the New NHS*. London: The Stationery Office.

NHS Executive (1998b). *Better Health and Better Care: Implementing 'The New NHS' and 'Our Healthier Nation'*, Health Service Circular 021. Leeds: NHSE.

NHS Executive (1998c). *Establishing Primary Care Groups*, Health Service Circular 065. Leeds: NHSE.

NHS Executive (1998d). *Setting Unified Health Authority and PCG Baselines*, Health Service Circular 120. Leeds: NHSE.

NHS Executive (1998e). *Developing Primary Care Groups*, Health Service Circular 139. Leeds: NHSE.

NHS Executive (1998f). *Governing Arrangements for Primary Care Groups*, Health Service Circular 230. Leeds: NHSE.

Northern Ireland Office (1998). *Fit for the Future*. London: HMSO.

Place, M., Posnett, J. and Street, A. (1999) *An Analysis of the Transactions Costs of Total Purchasing*. London: King's Fund Institute.

Posnett, J., Goodwin, N., Griffiths, J., *et al.* (1998). *The Transactions Costs of Total Purchasing*. London: King's Fund Institute.

Scottish Office (1998). *Designed to Care: Renewing the NHS in Scotland*. London: The Stationery Office.

Smith, J., Knight, T. and Wilson, F. (1999). Primary care groups: supra troupers. *Health Services Journal*, 14 (January), 26–8.

Stewart-Brown, S., Surender, R., Bradlow, J., Coulter, A. and Doll, H. (1995). General practice fundholding effects on prescribing habits three years on. *British Medical Journal*, 311, 1543–7.

Street, A. and Place, M. (1998). *The Management Challenges for Primary Care Groups*. London: King's Fund Institute.

Surender, R., Bradlow, J., Coulter, A., Doll, H. and Stewart-Brown, S. (1995). Prospective study of trends in referral patterns in fundholding and non-fundholding practices in the Oxford region, 1990–4. *British Medical Journal*, 311, 1205–8.

Toth, B., Harvey, I. and Peters, T. (1997). Did the introduction of general practice fundholding change patterns of emergency admission to hospital? *Journal of Health Service Research Policy*, 2(2), 71–4.

TP-NET Total Purchasing National Evaluation Team (1997). *Total Purchasing: A Profile of National Pilot Projects*. London: Kings Fund Institute.

Welsh Office (1998). *NHS Wales: Putting Patients First*. London: The Stationery Office.

Wholey, D., Feldman, R., Christianson, J.B. and Engberg, J. (1996). Scale and scope economies among health maintenance organisations. *Journal of Health Economics*, 15, 657–84.

Whynes, D.K., Baines, D.L. and Tolley, K.H. (1996). Explaining variations in general practice prescribing costs per ASTRO-PU. *British Medical Journal*, 316: 488–9.

Williams, A. (1996). *Priorities in Health Care: A View from Over the Garden Fence* (mimeograph). York: University of York.

Wilson, R.P.H., Buchan, I. and Walley, T. (1995). Alternations in prescribing by general practitioner fundholders: an observational study. *British Medical Journal*, 311: 1347–50.

3

TOWARDS LOCALLY-BASED RESOURCE ALLOCATION

Roy Carr-Hill, Nigel Rice and Peter C. Smith

INTRODUCTION

For some years there has been a move in the United Kingdom (UK) towards a 'primary care led' National Health Service (NHS). At the same time, a founding principle of the NHS is that equal access to health care should be available to those in equal need, regardless of individual circumstances. This chapter argues that a shift of the focus of care towards the primary care level will require increasingly careful definition of 'need'. The chapter therefore examines the implications of trying to measure need at the level of general practice, or groups of general practices.

The recently-elected government has continued the shift in focus towards primary care in the NHS, and the White Paper *The New NHS: Modern, Dependable* (Department of Health 1997), signals an increased emphasis on devolution of health care budgets. In this respect, the White Paper builds on existing experience with general practitioner (GP) fundholding, in which health care budgets for a subset of elective procedures and for prescribing have been devolved to individual general practices which choose to participate. However, the new policy differs in three respects from the fundholding experience: first, the budgetary devolution will be to groups of general practices, in the form of primary care groups (PCGs), rather than to individual practices; second, the emphasis will be on commissioning and planning services, rather than purchasing; and third, the budget will encompass a much larger proportion of total expenditure than the standard fundholding budget. In this respect, the new arrangements have much in common with the recently-evaluated Total Purchasing Pilots (TPPs) although they are even more ambitious in seeking to include primary care expenditure as well as hospital, community and prescribing services.

In this chapter we argue that, in order to secure an efficient and equitable distribution of limited health care funds, it is indeed important for devolved budgets to embrace all health care expenditure and not just a subset such as prescribing or fundholding procedures. However, we identify a number of serious practical difficulties that must be overcome if successful devolution along these lines is to take place.

The chapter is organized as follows. The next section outlines the importance and role of budgetary management in a health care system where resources are scarce. We then describe the essentials of the present 'needs'-based formula used to allocate budgets to health authorities. This is followed by a discussion of how health authorities currently secure budgetary control in primary care. In the next section we consider the move towards devolved budgeting and the implications this will have for resource allocation. Although we endorse the move towards a fully integrated system whereby PCGs will hold a 'global budget' from which they will be free to spend on all aspects of health care as they see fit, we acknowledge that – at least in the short term – the problems associated with this will be considerable. We therefore highlight some of the major obstacles that require careful thought and research. In a final section we call for the need for a comprehensive survey of individual NHS utilization designed specifically to address the issues expanded on in this chapter and to secure a move towards 'needs'-based primary-care-led budgetary management.

BUDGETS IN THE NHS

Budgets are perhaps the most important formal mechanism for securing managerial control. Emmanuel *et al.* (1990) set out five roles that budgets usually play:

1 authorization of actions;
2 a means of forecasting and planning;
3 a channel of communication and coordination;
4 a means of motivating organizational members;
5 a vehicle for performance evaluation and control.

While these roles may conflict, elements of all five can be discerned in most budgetary systems. In the NHS the principal role of the budget has probably been to signal command over resources, and thereby to secure adherence to public expenditure limits – a mixture of roles one to three.

Expenditure in the NHS can be considered under three broad headings:

1 hospital and community health services (HCHS) purchased (a) by health authorities and (b) by general practitioners;
2 prescribing;
3 general medical services (GMS), including expenditure on general practices.

This section outlines the systems of budgetary control currently in place in these categories. (see NHS Executive 1997 for further details).

Hospital and community health services

HCHS expenditure accounted for £20.9 billion in 1996/7, or 76 per cent of all local NHS expenditure in England. These national funds are in the first instance devolved to health authorities with populations of about 500,000. Setting cash-limited annual HCHS budgets for individual health authorities has been central to the objective of restraining government expenditure on the NHS. Of course such budgets could be set on the basis of crude criteria, such as a fixed *per capita* sum, or last year's expenditure plus x per cent. However, major efforts have been made to make health authority budgets as equitable as possible in terms of responding to variations in need (see below). It is almost certainly the case that the attention to equity has helped to make acceptable the imposition of frequently severe cash limits.

The methodology for setting HCHS budgets for health authorities has been developed and refined over a 20-year period. The general principle is known as 'weighted capitation' because a capitation allocation for each citizen is weighted for a number of relevant factors. Under weighted capitation, a target health authority budget can be expressed as follows:

$$Budget = PerCap * Pop * (1 + a) * (1 + n) * (1 + c)$$

The starting point for the budget is *PerCap*, the national *per capita* sum allocated for HCHS in the public expenditure system negotiations. This is first multiplied by the local population size, *Pop*. The crude budget this yields is then successively adjusted for the age structure of the population (using the relative age factor *a*), the health care needs of the population over and above age (using the relative needs factor *n*), and the relative costs of local health care (using the relative cost factor *c*). The national averages of *a*, *n* and *c* are zero.

The age adjustment *a* is relatively uncontentious, and reflects the clear propensity of the very young and elderly people to require more health care expenditure than the rest of the population. The needs adjustment *n* has been the subject of intense scrutiny. Current methods involve the use of a set of relative needs indices for different parts of HCHS. These include variables reflecting both health status and more general socio-economic status. For example, the index for acute care, used to distribute 64 per cent of HCHS expenditure, uses the following variables:

- standardized limiting long-standing illness ratio (under 75);
- standardized mortality ratio (under 75);
- proportion of economically active who are unemployed;
- proportion of pensionable age living alone;
- proportion of dependants in single-carer households.

The cost adjustment seeks to adjust for unavoidable differences in costs of capital and labour in different parts of the country, most importantly London and the south-east. A separate cost adjustment is calculated for each health authority.

Health authorities are responsible for living within their annual HCHS budgets. In this respect, they face a problem in the sense that HCHS expenditure is heavily influenced by the referral practices of a large number of individual GPs, over whom health authorities have little direct control. Until the advent of fundholding, the major restraining influences were supply-side restraints, in the form of waiting lists for elective procedures and (in extreme cases) a refusal to undertake certain procedures. Nevertheless, even before the 1991 internal market reforms, health authorities were generally successful in keeping within budget limits. This success could not have been achieved without the widespread acceptance by GPs of the need to restrain health care expenditure.

Primary care: purchase of HCHS

The introduction of fundholding allowed health authorities to devolve an average of 15 per cent of their HCHS budget to GPs, mainly in the form of standard fundholding budgets. This devolution encompassed a range of common elective procedures and prescribing (see below). However it did not necessarily absolve the health authority of all responsibility for that element of their budget, as the majority of any overspend was likely to have to be met by the health authority. Nevertheless, it was clearly hoped that the devolution would offer GPs a concrete incentive to restrain expenditure for the relevant services, as they were allowed to retain any underspend on their fundholding budget for expenditure on other patient services.

In contrast to the mature budget setting process for health authorities, setting budgets for GPs remained in its infancy. An early attempt to develop a needs index for standard fundholding procedures failed (Sheldon *et al.* 1994). Subsequent guidance from the NHS Executive (1996a) urged health authorities to use some sort of formula to set fundholder budgets, and to ensure that fundholders and non-fundholders were treated equitably. The Executive recommended use of a dampened form of the acute sector index mentioned above (NHS Executive 1996b), and in practice many health authorities have tended to use similar methods to the NHS Executive weighted capitation approach in setting fundholding budgets. This entailed weighting each patient on a practice's list by the patient's age, and the health and socio-economic characteristics of the small area in which the patient lives.

The standard fundholding scheme was augmented by the introduction of 'total purchasing', encompassing virtually all HCHS services, including emergencies, and usually involving coalitions of several practices. In contrast to standard fundholding, the total purchasing scheme is the subject of a thorough evaluation (Mays *et al.* 1997). Participating general practices continued to be the formal holders of their own individual budgets, although the architects of the total purchasing scheme envisaged that eventually an entire site would receive a fully integrated budget. Budgeting emerged as a crucial issue in the development of the total purchasing experiment which was never satisfactorily resolved.

Primary care: prescribing

In 1996/7 total prescribing costs accounted for £3.8 billion; 14 per cent of all local NHS expenditure. The NHS reforms and the creation of fundholding were intended, in part, to place greater emphasis on cost-effective prescribing in an attempt to control the rise in total prescribing costs. Fundholding budgets included an element for prescribing costs, and fundholding practices were required to meet prescribing costs out of the fundholding budgets which were allocated to them by their health authority. In contrast, non-fundholders were allocated an indicative prescribing budget. This was a notional budget or target, and penalties for overspending played a much weaker role than for fundholders.

Until relatively recently budgets for prescribing at the health authority level were largely based on historical costs adjusted for inflation. More recently, allocations to health authorities have moved towards a weighted capitation basis. In 1996/7, for the first time, a very small proportion of the prescribing budgets was based on a needs weighting. After appropriate adjustments for the age, sex and temporary resident characteristics of practices (Roberts and Harris 1993), a weighting for the proportion of people in the 1991 Census declaring themselves as unable to work due to permanent sickness or disability was applied to calculate health authority allocations (Rice *et al.* 1997a).

Methodology for devolving health authority prescribing budgets to individual general practices is much less advanced. The indicative prescribing scheme sets implicit prescribing levels for non-fundholding practices, but because of the lack of incentives and penalties to encourage compliance on the part of the GPs, the scheme has been criticized and has generally failed to control the rise in costs (Walley *et al.* 1995). Fundholding, although not reducing the total drugs bill, appears to have been successful in reducing the rate of increase of drug costs in participating practices (Department of Health 1994). This appears to be due to the obvious financial benefits to practices of being more conscious of the cost implications of their prescribing patterns.

In the early years of fundholding, allocations to individual general practices were based extensively on a historical cost basis. More recently advice to health authorities has been to allocate prescribing budgets based on a capitation system known as ASTRO-PUs (age, sex, temporary resident originated prescribing units).

These apply weights based on the age, sex and temporary resident structures of practice lists, and are applied to practice populations to derive an overall practice budget. Used in this way, ASTRO-PUs represent a crude adjustment for the demands placed on practices due to readily measured characteristics of the practice list (Roberts and Harris 1993; Lloyd *et al.* 1997).

However, while this method of capitation accounts overall for a reasonable proportion of variation observed in prescribing costs across practices (approximately 25 per cent) (Roberts and Harris 1993: 488), there are wide variations between health authorities and practices. Factors such as out-of-hours services and prescription charge exemptions may account for some of the unexplained variations (Whynes *et al.* 1996). To incorporate such considerations in the budget-setting procedure, initial budgets based on ASTRO-PUs are subject to bilateral negotiation between practices and health authorities to ensure that any special needs a practice may encounter are met. Clearly this practice may give rise to incentives for strategic behaviour and inequity in the sense that allocations are not related to a consistent concept of need.

There is great scope for further understanding the mechanisms behind prescription cost variations, particularly at the practice level, and for developing suitable models to allocate prescribing budgets on an equitable basis. Whether sufficient variation can be explained by relating costs to measures of need at the practice level is central to the issue of devolving budgets equitably.

Research in the area of prescribing is bedevilled by methodological difficulties which need to be addressed before major inroads can be made into suitable resource allocation mechanisms. Some of the difficulties are common to all sectors of health care, and are addressed in more detail below. Further issues of particular concern in relation to prescribing include:

- consideration of practice supply characteristics (for example, is prescribing a substitute for other types of health care?);
- the interface between primary- and secondary-care-led prescribing;
- a lack of standardization of costs and items prescribed;
- patient prescribing history;
- level of generic prescribing;
- level of repeat prescribing.

Primary care: general medical services

HCHS and prescribing account for 90 per cent of NHS expenditure. The major other category of expenditure is GMS. GMS embrace most aspects of primary care, including the provision of GPs and most of their staff. Only a quarter of the overall GMS budget is subject to national cash limits (known as 'Cash Limited' GMS). The White Paper (Department of Health 1997) envisages that only GMS cash-limited expenditure will be included in unified budgets in the first instance. This includes funding of practice staff, premises and computers, but not remuneration of general practitioners. Current guidance issued by the NHS Management Executive for setting GMS budgets to the district authorities states that they are 'to be calculated consistent with the methodology for the reimbursement of non-fundholder costs for GMS staff' (NHS Executive 1996a). Weighted capitation formulae were used in 1997/8 for allocations for Cash Limited GMS to health authorities, based on age, sex and International Classification of Diseases (ICD) chapter stratified consultation rates, developed from an analysis of a survey of individual patients from a sample of practices using the Fourth National Morbidity Survey in General Practice (MSGP4) (Royal College of General Practitioners 1995). There is an additional needs adjustment based on the (under 75) standardized illness ratio. At present, we are not aware of any health authority actively seeking to introduce capitation methods for the allocation of GMS to individual practices.

Summary

Current resource allocation methods consider a number of discrete sectors of health care. Each sector is considered separately, and different methods have been used to derive capitations in each sector. The favoured methodological approach has been, wherever possible, to base allocations on empirical data, in particular seeking to use the national average link between 'needs' indicators and measures of utilization. As a result, data limitations often determine the methods used. Even though sectoral budgets are derived separately (for example, for acute HCHS and psychiatric HCHS), they are often aggregated into a single budget. Usually there is no obligation for budget holders (such as fundholders) to adhere to the individual components of their budget for each sector, so long as they adhere to the total budget.

DEVELOPING WEIGHTED CAPITATION
BUDGETS IN PRACTICE

In many ways the move towards a primary-care-led NHS should make the distinctions between service headings, such as prescribing and fundholding procedures, irrelevant and unhelpful, as a principal objective of the initiative is to encourage GPs to secure the best health care for their patients subject to budget constraints, regardless of the service heading under which the care is found (UK Government 1996). Any partitioning into separate budgets runs the risk of artificially constraining 'rational' assessment by the GPs of the alternatives. Furthermore, a global budget offers no opportunity for GPs to shift expenses to services not covered by their budget. For example, the standard fundholding scheme embraced only routine elective surgery, which accounts for just 20 per cent of HCHS expenditure. There has therefore been an incentive for fundholding GPs to refer patients as emergencies – which lie outside the ambit of their budget – thereby transferring financial liability to the health authority.

The existence of such incentives clearly offers the potential for inefficiencies. In principle, therefore, GP treatment decisions can only be made in an undistorted way if (a) budgets capture *all* expenditure caused by GP decisions; and (b) GPs have complete *freedom* to switch between expenditure headings – that is, separate budgets are not set for specific services. In practice, however, there may be many reasons why this counsel of perfection is neither attainable nor indeed desirable. Among the most important reasons for caution are:

- It may be very difficult to set what are perceived to be equitable global budgets.
- At a strategic level it may be perceived that certain functions (say preventative medicine) could be squeezed out by more urgent health care demands, in which case there may be a case for 'ring-fencing' the associated budget to ensure that GPs do not neglect the service.
- It may be unreasonable to expect general practices to take on certain health care risks such as the treatment of HIV/AIDS for which the associated budget might be held at the health authority or even the national government level.
- More generally, the unpredictable variation in local health care needs may be very high, rendering any budgets meaningless.

- GPs may not have the available information or the decision making skills to make the rational and efficient decisions demanded by the unconstrained budget.
- The management costs associated with devolution may be very high.
- It may be impossible to design satisfactory rewards and sanctions for underspending or overspending budgets.

We nevertheless believe that the devolution of budgets to PCGs is on balance likely to be beneficial, and moreover consider that it is essential that some attempt should be made towards setting budgets for individual general practices. We therefore now consider the practical implications of such a development. The experience of practice-based budgets noted above has highlighted difficulties that were not apparent at the health authority level. These can be summarized as follows:

- The health authority databases of patients registered with GPs usually indicate larger populations than population estimates prepared by the Office of National Statistics. This is the phenomenon known as 'list inflation'.
- There is extremely limited universally available information on individuals – in practice it is confined to age, sex and postcode of residence, leading to the use of small area data as the basis for capitation adjustments.
- With current procedures all patients in a small area are therefore weighted equally, yet there is no reason to suppose that, in general, patients attending a particular practice are representative of the area in which they live (the so-called 'problem of attribution').
- Expenditure variations from expected *per capita* expenditure become very large for small population sizes, such as lists for individual general practices.

In the long run, as patient databases become more reliable and comprehensive, some of these problems may be overcome. However, they present serious obstacles to setting equitable GP budgets for the foreseeable future. We discuss each in turn.

List inflation

Budgets for health authorities are based on contemporary projections of population produced by the Office of National Statistics.

UK population estimates have been the subject of some methodological difficulties, mainly arising from substantial evidence of incompleteness of the 1991 Census of Population, which serves as the basis for current estimates. However, for the purposes of resource allocation to such large areas, the population estimates are generally considered to be adequate.

However, national population estimates are not in general suitable for allocations to smaller areas. Although estimates are produced for local authority wards, these are subject to considerable potential error, particularly when age-specific populations are examined. More importantly, if the general practice is the unit of interest, geographical population estimates are inappropriate, as a practice may draw its patients from a variety of wards, and residents of a specific ward may use a variety of general practices.

Therefore, the unit of population used to set budgets for individual practices or PCGs must be the practice list. These are maintained by health authorities, and at that level, provide very different population estimates from those suggested by the national estimates. GP lists in England are inflated on average by 5.9 per cent, ranging from 28.9 per cent in Ealing, Hammersmith and Hounslow to –8 per cent in Morecambe.

The general view is that the health authority practice lists are unreliable (because of mobility among young adults and delays in removing list members on death and emigration) and could be dramatically improved (although, of course, there will always remain problems in registering immigrants, temporary visitors, the homeless and refugees). In so far as reasonably uncontentious budgets can be set for health authorities, this would not be a source of great concern if the inflation were uniform across a health authority. Practice and PCG could simply be scaled down (or up) to conform to the health authority budget. However, there is evidence of substantial inflation variation within health authorities, with, for example, list inflation ranging from 3 to 27 per cent among individual practices in one London authority. Furthermore, these variations are likely to be even greater within particular age groups, which may exacerbate anomalies in budgets whenever an age-weighted capitation formula is used.

Limited information

The amount of useful information currently universally available about patients on a GP list is minimal, being limited to age, sex and postcode. Its usefulness as a tool for resource allocation purposes is therefore severely constrained. There is no reason why, in principle, GP lists should be subject to such limitations, and the development of the NHS patient number offers the opportunity to ensure that the vast bulk of the population is attached to one, and only one, practice and that more extensive and reliable information is attached to the record. However, any such improvements will pose formidable practical problems and have significant expenditure consequences. The research agenda is to identify the costs and benefits of proposed enhancements.

If the GP list is to be used as the basis of budget allocations, it will in the future be desirable to incorporate as many routine data items as possible into patient records in order to facilitate the development of a sensitive capitation formula. Any item that is included should in principle be:

- useful – an acknowledged risk factor;
- reliable – not subject to major errors;
- practical – readily collected at reasonable cost;
- universal – available for all patients;
- objective – not subject to substantial variations in judgement;
- up to date – capturing contemporary circumstances of the patient;
- free of perverse incentives – in particular, not encouraging GPs to overtreat or undertreat, or to distort reports of health status.

In practice, the range of factors that satisfy these criteria is likely to be quite small. Age and sex clearly satisfy all, and will always form the basis of any system. However, almost all other conceivable items fall down on one or more of the criteria. For example, many measures of health status may be subject to judgement on the part of patient or GP (for example, self-reported measures of health such as limiting long-term illness (Sutton *et al.* 1997)), and may be difficult to keep up to date. Social circumstances, such as living alone, may change from time to time and be difficult to define in any watertight fashion. Economic circumstances, such as employment status are even more difficult to update. One of the more important risk factors may be a measure of past health care utilization. An important research agenda is therefore (a) the extent to which any of these can be used for resource allocation purposes, and what effect they would have on allocations; and (b) whether the use of any of them would induce any unintended behavioural responses on the part of GPs or other health workers.

The problem of attribution

Hitherto, because of the difficulties of obtaining individual data outlined above, British resource allocation methods have used the characteristics of the small area in which an individual lives (rather than that individual's own circumstances) as the basis of a capitation formula. This has many advantages, most notably the vastly increased volume of data that become available as a basis for resource allocation. However, such data bring with them the difficulty that the circumstances of the individual may not be typical of the area in which they live, and that the patients from a small area on a particular GP's list may not be representative of that small area as a whole. This is the 'problem of attribution'.

An associated problem is the adequacy of any small-area data used. Data from the Census of Population are available only every ten years and therefore date rapidly and may suffer from incomplete enumeration. Furthermore, the Office of Population Censuses and Surveys (OPCS) has itself documented the possible bias when using Census data at the smallest area level – the enumeration district, with a typical population of 500 (OPCS 1993). This arises from the problem of random fluctuations arising from small numbers and is exacerbated by the practice of 'Barnardization' (entailing the quasi-random addition of –1, 0 or +1 to all counts except basic population). This problem is especially relevant to use of 10 per cent sample tables, and may mean that data from larger areas (such as wards, with average populations of 5000) may in fact yield more reliable estimates of the aggregate characteristics of individuals living in the small area.

The pitfalls associated with linking small-area data to individuals are known as the 'ecological fallacy' (Selvin 1958), under which associations observed at the area level are wrongly inferred to exist at the individual level. The MSGP4 (Royal College of General Practitioners 1995) contains GP consultation data on all patients (approximately 500,000) registered with 60 participating practices over a one-year period. Socio-economic data were collected by means of a questionnaire administered to each individual which yielded an 85 per cent response rate. Area of residence postcode linkage allowed Census small-area statistics data to be attributed at both the ward and enumeration district level to individual patients.

This permitted an analysis of the assumption that enumeration district data reflected the aggregate characteristics of people living in a district better than ward-level data (Carr-Hill and Rice 1995).

The mean consultation rates for different categories of social class, tenure status and unemployment status across all individuals were shown to display the expected associations. However, when the enumeration districts and wards in the study were grouped according to the social class distribution, the level of owner occupancy or the unemployment rate, there was substantial evidence of the ecological fallacy. Moreover, no significant improvement was detected when moving down from ward to enumeration district level.[1]

Clearly, the extent to which the problem of attribution gives rise to distortions in budget allocations (and consequent incentives to recruit healthy patients from deprived areas) is an important empirical research matter. If the problem of attribution is found in practice to be of relatively minor importance, the need for more comprehensive personal records may be called into question.

Sources of variation from budget

Annual health care expenditure on individuals is highly variable and largely unpredictable. Such variation can be considered under five headings:

1 variation that is predicted by the relevant capitation formula;
2 other variation which is in principle predictable (given the individual's characteristics) but which is not captured by the current formula;
3 variation which is due to clinical practice;
4 variation which is due to local health care prices;
5 variation which is random (that is, for practical purposes unpredictable).

In general, only the first of these sources of variation is captured by the budget. The second, predictable source of variation reflects incompleteness or errors in the current formula. There are always likely to be needs factors that cannot be captured in a capitation formula, and yet which are observable by individual GPs. If GPs are able to predict that expenditure on a particular patient will vary from the associated capitation payment, the potential for 'cream-skimming' arises (Matsaganis and Glennerster 1994). Cream-skimming is the process whereby GPs either seek out patients to add to their lists who are expected to have low costs relative to their capitation payment, or seek to deter or remove from their lists patients whose costs are expected to exceed the associated capitation payment. Although the incentive for cream-skimming exists under most systems of health care, there is no evidence that it has hitherto been a major issue in the NHS, even after the advent of fundholding. However, as the budgetary process starts to encompass a larger proportion of health care expenditure, and if sanctions for overspending were to become more severe, then it may assume more importance.

The third source of variation – variations in clinical practice – should properly be ignored by a resource allocation formula, which seeks to capture some 'standard' set of clinical practices. The fourth source of variation may need to be incorporated into a budget if there exist unavoidable variations in input prices. In England, a complex 'market forces factor' is used to accommodate such variations in hospital and community health services (Institute for Employment Research 1996).

The fifth, unpredictable source of variation can be considered 'random' in the sense that it defies all attempts at systematic modelling. For an individual patient, unpredictable variations from the annual capitation implied by his or her needs rating are likely to be massive. However, as patients are aggregated into populations, positive and negative variations will start to balance each other, so that the unpredictable *per capita* variation from the capitation budget becomes smaller. Such aggregation is known as 'risk pooling'.

At the level of the health authority (with a typical population of 500,000) budget risk arising from the random element of variation is unlikely to be a major consideration. However, at the level of the general practice, with a typical population of (say) 6000, a number of authors have shown that budget risk is likely to be very large (Crump *et al.* 1991). Martin *et al.* (1997) suggest that, assuming cost per case contracts are used, a typical fundholding practice (population 10,000) has a 1 in 3 chance of incurring expenditure more than 10 per cent away from its acute sector budget, compared to 1 in 400 for a population of 100,000. The extent to which extension of the budget to other services would alter these figures will be an important consideration in the new NHS.

Thus, for whatever reason, the actual expenditure incurred by a general practice is very likely to vary substantially from its budget in any one year. This may lead to:

- low spenders 'spending up' to seek to justify their budget;
- high spenders imposing unjustified constraints on treatment and reacting with hostility to the budgeting system;

- patients with identical needs in different practices being treated differently;
- patients with identical needs in the same practices being treated differently depending on the time of year they present (Glazer and Shmueli 1995);
- budget-holding general practices or PCGs negotiating block contracts, thereby transferring the risk to providers;
- budget-holding general practices or PCGs taking out insurance with a third party, resulting in an unproductive outflow of funds from the NHS.

Some of these responses may be severely dysfunctional.

Given the discussion above, variations from budget might be for some or all of the following reasons:

- the budget formula is faulty or incomplete;
- the referral and treatment policies of the practice differ from the average assumed in the budget formula;
- the practice has negotiated contract prices which differ from the average assumed in the budget formula;
- the pattern of disease among practice patients differs unpredictably from the needs-adjusted average assumed in the budget formula.

The managerial implications for each of the four reasons are very different.

Clearly, improvement in the capitation formula could offer some hope of reducing the problem of health needs variation. Evidence from the USA and The Netherlands (Newhouse *et al.* 1989; van Vliet and van de Ven 1992) suggests that one possible way of improving the predictive power of the English capitation formulae would be to incorporate data concerning the pre-existing clinical conditions and past health care use of individual patients. Two major difficulties would be associated with such an innovation. First, it necessitates the development of objective measures of health status which do not depend significantly on clinical judgement. In practice, this may imply reliance on previous health care expenditure. Second, it may offer a perverse incentive to GPs to increase expenditure on individuals in order to secure a higher capitation fee in the future.

However, it is important to recognize that, although the use of a capitation formula is essential, and that some improvement in capitation formulae can be envisaged, no formula – however refined –

can capture all the variations in health care utilization. Rather, Martin *et al.* (1997) argue that unpredictable variations in health care needs (which are beyond the control of GPs) are likely to be the dominant source of variation, suggesting that careful audit of such variations is essential before any managerial action is taken.

In the absence of a perfect prediction of health care needs, there are a number of managerial strategies for handling the inevitable random fluctuations in health care expenditure for small populations (Martin *et al.* 1997). Budgets could be set for periods longer than one year; certain expensive treatments or certain predictably expensive patients could be excluded from the budget; or contracts could be organized to eliminate or share risk. At the same time, if such arrangements totally protect a budget holder, then the GP effectively no longer has any incentive to restrain expenditure, which negates the original purpose of the budget devolution.

TOWARDS A HEALTH CARE USE SURVEY?

Thus far we have considered present allocation mechanisms and some of the practical difficulties encountered using currently available data sources. In this section, we finish by considering how a survey of individual citizens may help to address the methodological problems inherent in current budget development.

It is important to recall that – for practical reasons – budgeting methods in the various sectors of the NHS (such as the acute sector, prescribing and GMS) are currently developed separately, using different methodologies to derive capitation rates in each sector. Even though there is no need for the budget holder to adhere to each sectoral budget, this discrete approach may in principle give rise to methodological problems in determining fair budgets when, as in the NHS, empirically-based capitations are used. The problem arises because there may be significant scope for alternative modes of treatment which imply an element of substitution between sectors – for example, prescribing as a substitute for GP consultations.

Under these circumstances, a clearly better methodology than existing methods would entail basing capitations on the *total* use of NHS resources made by individuals across *all* sectors, thereby accommodating potential substitutions. The method of setting a global capitation health care budget for an individual patient based on that individual's characteristics might then be as follows. There may be certain reliably-measured characteristics of *all* citizens. Let us suppose (purely for illustrative purposes) that they are age, sex, living alone and limiting long-standing illness (ignoring for the moment the difficulties associated with the last two). This might yield a contingency table as illustrated in Table 3.1. Each cell would have a tariff, or capitation amount, associated with it (of course some cells might necessarily be empty). Then a general practice's budget would be determined by multiplying the number of patients in each cell by the associated capitation.

Current methods are based on a hybrid approach. Crude individual characteristics – namely age (and in some cases sex) – are used on a contingency basis, as in this example. However the associated capitation is then adjusted up or down depending on the 'needs' score derived for the small area in which the patient lives. In principle, to use a pure contingency table approach would offer a more scientifically rigorous (and understandable) method for deriving capitations, which eliminates the problem of substitution and overcomes the ecological fallacy. However, this example begs the question: how are the capitation weightings to be derived?

The obvious solution in principle is to undertake a sample survey of individual citizens. This would record all possible personal characteristics of individuals in the sample that could be routinely held by health authorities as part of all patients' NHS administrative records. Thus, apart from routine items such as age, sex and address, data such as long-term illness and recent use of NHS resources might be included. Considerable attention would have to be given to what social data – such as living alone – should be recorded, and what mechanisms for maintaining the database

Table 3.1 Illustrative contingency table of capitations

Age	Sex	With long-term illness		Without long-term illness	
		Living alone	*Not alone*	*Living alone*	*Not alone*
0–14	Male				
	Female				
15–44	Male				
	Female				
45–64	Male				
	Female				
65+	Male				
	Female				

should be used. There would be little point in including data which could not be updated regularly and reliably. The criteria for inclusion, already noted above, would be: usefulness; reliability; practicality; universality; objectivity; timeliness; and freedom from perverse incentives.

The principal task of the survey would be to record all NHS utilization of the individual over the course of (say) one year. (Note that, as we assume we are interested in NHS care only, we omit private health care expenditure.) The survey might seek to capture inpatient, outpatient and community health care, prescribing and primary care consultations. Such data in themselves would of course be invaluable. However, the main intention would be to cost such utilization in order to identify the tariffs to be entered into Table 3.1.

Statistical analysis could then be undertaken to identify which of the individual characteristics are the most important risk characteristics associated with NHS utilization. Here great care would have to be taken to model any important hierarchies in the data (patients within general practices within health authorities). This is particularly important because of the likely importance of supply effects in determining utilization. That is, the magnitude and pattern of utilization might be heavily influenced by the resources available to, and the policies adopted by, the relevant health authority and general practice. It is for this reason that (a) great attention should be paid to the chosen sampling methodology; and (b) modelling techniques which are sensitive to the hierarchical data structure should be used (Rice and Leyland 1996).

The most important risk factors would form the basis of the capitation scheme, and the survey results would be used to identify the weight for each risk class. In this respect it may be necessary to use discrete multivariate techniques to 'smooth' the contingency table. Moreover, the contingency table approach implicitly seeks to model interactions between risk factors. If sample size was too small to secure reliable estimates, it may be appropriate to resort to analytic techniques to identify the impact of each factor independently, along the lines of the synthetic estimation methods used by Benzeval and Judge (1994).

It is important to note that, although probably in practice the most satisfactory approach to deriving capitations, the contingency table approach in itself would not eliminate all of the problems noted above. For example, if patient databases continue to be poorly maintained, inevitable distortions will arise. And there would continue to be fluctuation around any average capitations used in the table, offering a continued scope for cream-skimming. These problems must be addressed via other initiatives, such as improved information systems and careful audit to minimize cream-skimming. Also, the method would still be based on empirical use of NHS resources, and would therefore not accommodate need that is currently unmet (or conversely, inappropriate use of NHS services). There would also be a need for careful treatment of any impact of local supply or utilization as measured in the survey. There are, moreover, numerous details that would need to be resolved before any survey could be implemented, such as a sample survey, the frequency of the actual survey, and how utilization would be measured.

Formidable obstacles therefore stand in the way of implementing such a survey, not least its cost. A great deal of preparatory work would need to be undertaken before embarking on such a project, and there is a substantial research agenda associated with resolution of the methodological difficulties noted above. However, as Carr-Hill *et al.* (1994) emphasize, the potential benefits such methods would yield are enormous, and we feel that they deserve serious consideration. Not least, they would settle once and for all the debate about whether the richer dataset offered by area-level data compensates for the potential distortions to which the use of such data can give rise.

NOTE

1 This type of analysis is a *strict* test of the ecological fallacy because precisely the same individuals were compared using first individual and then small-area data.

REFERENCES

Benzeval, M. and Judge, K. (1994). The determinants of hospital utilisation: implications for resource allocation in England. *Health Economics*, 3, 105–16.

Carr-Hill, R. and Rice, N. (1995). Is enumeration district level an improvement on ward level analysis in studies of deprivation and health? *Journal of Epidemiology and Community Health*, 49, S28–9.

Carr-Hill, R.A., Sheldon, T., Smith, P. *et al.* (1994). Allocating resources to health authorities: development of method for small area analysis of use of inpatient services. *British Medical Journal*, 309, 1046–9.

Crump, B.J., Cubbon, J.E., Drummond, M.F., Hawkes, R.A. and Marchment, M.D. (1991). Fundholding in general practice and financial risk.
British Medical Journal, 302, 1582–4.

Department of Health (1994). Evidence to the House of Commons Health
Committee: *Priority Setting in the NHS: Inquiry Into the NHS Drugs
Budget*. London: HMSO.

Department of Health (1997). *The New NHS: Modern, Dependable*.
London: The Stationery Office.

Emmanuel, C.R., Otley, D.T. and Merchant, K. (1990). *Accounting for
Management Control*. London: Chapman & Hall.

Glazer, J. and Shmueli, A. (1995). The physician's behaviour and equity
under a fundholding contract. *European Economic Review*, 39, 781–5.

Institute for Employment Research (1996). *Labour Market Forces and
NHS Provider Costs: Final Report*. Warwick: Institute for Employment
Research.

Lloyd, D.C.E.F., Roberts, D.J. and Sleator, D. (1997). Revision of the
weights for the age sex temporary resident originated prescribing unit.
British Journal of Medical Economics, 11, 81–5.

Martin, S., Rice, N. and Smith P. (1997). *Risk and the GP Budgetholder*.
(*Discussion Paper 153*). York: Centre for Health Economics, University
of York.

Matsaganis M. and Glennerster, H. (1994). The threat of 'cream-skimming'
in the post-reform NHS. *Journal of Health Economics*, 3, 31–60.

Mays, N., Goodwin, N., Bevan, G. and Wyke, S. (1997). *Total Purchasing:
A Profile of National Pilot Sites*. London: Kings Fund Institute.

Newhouse, J.R., Manning, W.G., Keeler, E.B. and Sloss, E.M. (1989).
Adjusting capitation rates using objective health measures and prior utilisation. *Health Care Financing Review*, 3, 41–54.

NHS Executive (1996a). *General practitioner fundholder budget-setting: the
national framework. NHS Executive Letter EL(96)55*. Leeds: Department of Health.

NHS Executive (1996b). *Financial management and GP fundholding. NHS
Executive Letter EL(96)82*. Leeds: Department of Health.

NHS Executive (1997). *Progress report of the Resource Allocation Group,
1995 and 1996*. (NHS Executive Catalogue no. 96FP0041). Leeds:
Department of Health.

OPCS (1993). *The Use of OPCS Records for Medical Research*. London:
OPCS.

Rice, N. and Leyland, A. (1996). Multilevel models: applications to health
data. *Journal of Health Services Research and Policy*, 1, 154–64.

Roberts, S. and Harris, C.M. (1993). Age, sex and temporary resident orig-
inating prescribing units (ASTRO-PUs): new weightings for analysing
prescribing of general practice in England. *British Medical Journal*, 307,
485–8.

Royal College of General Practitioners (1995). *Office of Population
Censuses and Surveys/Department of Health Morbidity Statistics from
General Practice: Fourth National Study 1991–92*. London: HMSO.

Selvin, H. (1958). Durkheim's suicide and problems of empirical research. *American Journal of Sociology*, 63, 601–19.

Sheldon, T.A., Smith, P.C., Borowitz, M., Martin, S. and Carr-Hill, R.A. (1994). Attempt at deriving a formula for setting general practitioner fundholding budgets. *British Medical Journal*, 309, 1059–64.

Sutton, M.A., Carr-Hill, R.A., Gravelle, H. and Rice, N. (1997). Potential biases in estimating the determinants of medical-care utilisation using self-report measures: an investigation of limiting long-standing illness and general practitioner consultations. Paper presented to Health Economics Study Group (HESG) York: July.

UK Government (1996). *Choice and Opportunity. Primary Care: The Future*. London: HMSO.

van Vliet R.C.J.A. and van de Ven W.P.M.M. (1992). Towards a capitation formula for competing health insurers: an empirical analysis. *Social Science and Medicine*, 34(9), 1035–48.

Walley, T., Wilson, R. and Bligh, J. (1995). Current prescribing in primary care in the UK: effects of the indicative prescribing scheme and GP fundholding. *PharmacoEconomics*, 7, 320–31.

Whynes, D.K., Baines, D.L. and Tolley, K.H. (1996). Explaining variations in general practice prescribing costs per ASTRO-PU (age, sex, and temporary resident originated prescribing unit). *British Medical Journal*, 312, 488–9.

4

LONGER-TERM AGREEMENTS FOR HEALTH CARE SERVICES: WHAT WILL THEY ACHIEVE?

Diane Dawson and Maria Goddard

INTRODUCTION

Longer-term contracts or agreements[1] for health care services were highlighted in the 1997 White Paper (Department of Health 1997) as a way of creating a more stable environment, compared with the 'short-termism' of the internal market. The advantages of a shift towards agreements lasting between three and five years were outlined in the White Paper and subsequently elaborated upon in the 1998/9 *Priorities and Planning Guidance* (NHS Executive 1997). Particular attention has been given to using longer-term contracts as a tool for encouraging collaboration between purchasers and providers, and as a means of achieving stability and long-term planning in the National Health Service (NHS).

There is no technical definition of a 'long-term contract' but, in the economics literature, the term tends to be used to refer to an agreement that covers a sequence of repeat transactions or a single transaction that requires a multi-period production process. It is the opposite of a 'spot' contract. While duration of contract is the key characteristic, there is no theoretical basis for saying how long a contract must be before it is considered 'long term'. The Department of Health has adopted the convention of treating a contract of one year's duration as 'short term' and one of three or more years as 'long term'. We follow this convention as a working definition but note that most examples of 'long-term' contracts in the economics literature are of 15–25 years in duration.

In this chapter we discuss whether the benefits perceived by the government will be delivered by a shift towards longer-term contracting in the NHS. We consider some of the economic issues relating to contract duration in order to draw out the implications of longer-term contracts in the NHS context. In doing so, we draw upon some of the findings of our recently completed study commissioned by the Department of Health. This involved examination of almost 300 NHS contracts and semi-structured interviews with a sample of health authority and trust contracting staff.

We conclude that although longer-term agreements are more consistent with the general policy drift of encouraging collaboration and joint planning, they do not address any of the economic problems for which longer-term contracts are normally proposed. They may not deliver automatically the range of perceived benefits expected by the government and we suggest that, if these issues are seen as important, effort is targeted directly towards achieving them through other means, rather than relying on longer-term contracts as a mechanism.

The chapter is organized as follows. The first section outlines the benefits expected by the government from the current policy developments in contracting. We then consider some of the economic issues relating to the duration, form and nature of contracts, focusing on the importance of long-term *relationships*. The implications of the theoretical issues for the NHS are considered in the next section, and the final section presents our conclusions and summarizes the implications for policy.

EXPECTED BENEFITS OF LONGER-TERM CONTRACTS

The issue of duration of contracts in the NHS is not new. The guidance accompanying the 1989 NHS reforms stated that the previous government expected many block contracts to be three-year rolling contracts with extensions negotiated annually (Department of Health 1989). In almost every year since, central guidance on contracting has encouraged purchasers and providers to consider the use of rolling or fixed longer-term contracts in 'appropriate' circumstances, while noting that annual contracts were the norm (NHS Executive 1992, 1993, 1994, 1996a). Both the previous and the current government have defined the perceived benefits of moving towards longer-term contracts. While the previous government emphasized the competitive advantages associated with longer-term contracts (e.g., encouraging market entry by making it more attractive for trusts to offer new services), the present government has focused on using them as a way of promoting purchaser/provider collaboration. Despite the shift in emphasis, both expect a similar range of benefits to flow from longer-term contracts. The advantages of longer-term contracts outlined in the White Paper (Department of Health 1997) were:

• allowing for longer-term planning for improvements, service changes and investment;
• shifting focus away from cost and volume considerations towards other aspects of performance such as outcomes and quality;
• involving clinicians in agreeing programmes of care;
• reducing the time, effort and resources expended in the annual contracting cycle.

These advantages were reinforced in the 1998/9 *Priorities and Planning Guidance* in which the messages concerning greater involvement of clinicians, better planning and a focus on outcomes and quality were repeated (NHS Executive 1997). The guidance also defined the features the Department of Health expect to see incorporated into longer-term contracts, which include:

• methods for dealing with uncertainty;
• methods for sharing risk;
• methods for dealing with inflation;
• incentives for achieving quality improvements over time.

In particular, central guidance has suggested that the *funding* agreements within longer-term contracts should span more than one year, either being fixed for the contract duration or 'related to a mechanism which can be referred to at agreed intervals during the contract' (NHS Executive 1997).

ECONOMIC ISSUES RELATING TO CONTRACT DURATION

Although the economics and law literature considers the circumstances under which longer-term contracts improve efficiency, it is not immediately clear whether institutional conditions are such that longer-term contracts represent an efficient solution to contracting for health care services. In this section, we discuss just *one* strand of the literature on contract duration, focusing on the nature of contractual relationships and the subsequent implications for the form of contract.[2]

From 'classical' to 'relational' contracting

Much of the law and economics/sociology literature has focused attention on the apparent irrelevance of classical contract law for the form and content of the contracts actually executed by firms. McNeil (1978) used the term 'relational contract' to underline the argument that modern contracts are designed to maintain good working relationships through periods of uncertainty, rather than for the adversarial task of assigning liability for failure to perform. 'Classical' contract law is based on full legal protection for the parties and is relevant only in circumstances when the frequency of exchange is low and all rights and future obligations can be specified in the contract. Non-classical contracts however have three broad distinguishing features as summarized from Campbell and Clay (1992):

1 *Flexibility*: rather than stipulate price and quantity in each period, the contract contains rules/procedures for adjusting price and quantity over time as circumstances change.
2 *Open-endedness*: where circumstances change beyond the limits allowed for in predetermined rules for 'flexibility', the partners agree to what in effect will be renegotiation of the contract.
3 *Extra-legal dispute resolution:* maintaining a good working relationship between the parties is essential to efficient production. Procedures involving legal action, designed to identify blame and assign liability are more likely to harm than to help the relationship.

'Neoclassical' contracts would incorporate a degree of flexibility where both parties acknowledge the contract to be incomplete. The rules/procedures used to adapt to changing circumstances would minimize the likelihood of opportunistic behaviour. This is necessary because although parties recognize they both have a degree of commitment to the exchange, their cooperation is strictly self-interested and trust is limited. Opportunistic behaviour is more likely to occur when one party becomes relatively disadvantaged over time.

'Relational' contracts incorporate the features of open-endedness and extra-legal dispute resolution as they focus on the trust

needed for the parties to commit to an open-ended agreement – an acknowledgement that cooperation between the parties is essential to efficient production and the commitment to finding solutions to problems that permit the relationship to continue over time. These contracts would not contain detailed rules for adjusting automatically price or quantity but would contain provision for renegotiation of the contract when appropriate.

The economic models underlying the alternative forms of contract associate classical contract law with the complete information spot exchange of general equilibrium models, where anonymity of the parties to the exchange is a critical characteristic of efficiency (i.e. 'arms-length transactions'). Neoclassical and relational contracts would reflect the economic structure of small numbers (strategic interdependence) production and exchange under conditions of incomplete information. However, theory yields no prediction about whether the latter categories of contracts will be long- or short-term, only that the economic *relationship* between the parties will be long term. Hence the importance of considering relationships in the analysis of contracts.

Risk sharing and price/activity adjustment mechanisms

The few longer-term contracts observed in other sectors are not fixed price contracts, as costs and nominal prices are normally expected to change over time and in response to unanticipated events. Under a fixed price regime, initial prices would need to be high as they would be front-loaded to reflect potential increases in costs. If this was done imprecisely there would be a strong incentive for one party to breach the contract rather than continue at a disadvantage. At the other end of the spectrum, pure cost-plus contracts allow any increased costs of the provider to be passed directly on to the purchaser in the form of increased prices. The disincentives for efficiency produced by such agreements are well known (Vickers and Yarrow 1989) and the use of cost-plus contracts has declined rapidly in industries such as defence, where they were at one time common (De Fraja and Hartley 1996).

Contracts that do not fall into either the fixed price or cost-plus categories can incorporate risk-sharing mechanisms which provide incentives for agents to cooperate in adapting to changes in circumstances which were not fully anticipated when the contract was negotiated. However, the longer the duration of contract, the higher the likelihood that conditions will change and unanticipated events will occur before the contract has ended. Such events may alter the return to each party and reallocation of that risk may be achieved through the use of price or quantity adjustment rules which adjust automatically the value of the contract to each party. The economics literature suggests two distinct roles for these risk-sharing mechanisms:

1 The bilateral monopoly literature focuses on minimizing the use of resources to renegotiate contracts when *events outside the control of the parties* to the contract change the value of the contract. Examples include changes in the price of raw materials or changes in consumer demand. In the absence of risk sharing, these events would open the window for opportunistic behaviour. The risk-sharing arrangement would be reflected in a price or quantity adjustment rule that adjusted the financial value of the contract to each party in a way which reflected a jointly recognized 'fair share' of the new contract value (see Blair and Kaserman 1987 for an example).

2 The principal-agent literature stresses the role of risk sharing as producing incentives for each party to act in ways that will minimize the *deviation* of cost and demand conditions from those the parties would have agreed to had they known of future conditions at the time the contract was originally agreed. This gives each party the incentives to manage risk efficiently. It implies a pricing structure that 'rewards' efficient risk management and 'penalizes' inefficient management (see Chalkley and Malcomson 1996 for examples).

In the short run this distinction may be obvious – an increase in raw material prices is exogenous, while a rise in unit costs due to poor inventory control is endogenous. In the long run the distinction is blurred as one wants firms faced with a rise in raw material prices to have an incentive to change production processes and thus minimize the effect of the price change on profits. The reason for maintaining the distinction when discussing risk sharing is that it relates to the distinction between 'fairness' and 'efficiency', both of which can be important in sustaining the relationship between buyer and seller in a bilateral monopoly. The rise in raw material prices will reduce the profitability of the joint enterprise of the two parties *even if* the producer responds in an efficient manner. Is it 'fair' for that loss to be borne solely by the reduced profits of the producer, as in a fixed-price contract, or should the buyer share the loss by accepting a larger fall in profits than would have occurred with the fixed-price contract?

This traditional view of risk sharing raises three issues that we return to later when discussing the NHS. First, when the adjustment of contract value is via a semi-automatic price or quantity adjustment, there is an implication that the financial value of the contract becomes open-ended. The value of the contract for date t+1 is unknown at the time of agreement because it depends on whether events activate the risk-sharing rule that adjusts contract values or if the 'rewards' for successful risk management are greater or less than any 'penalties'. Ceilings can be used to limit the extent of upward movement in price, but if the ceiling is so low it is always likely to be hit, it will be in effect a fixed-price contract with negligible automatic risk-sharing properties. If there is to be genuine automatic risk-sharing and if these agreements are to become binding on the budgets of the parties, then both need access to capital markets, equity capital or financial reserves of sufficient size to absorb changes in contract values that result in expenditure exceeding current income.

Second, it is not always obvious which party is in the best position to manage particular risks. Returning to the example above, it may be that in the face of the higher raw material prices the strategy to minimize the loss of profitability of the joint enterprise would be for the buyer to change marketing activity and promote a redesigned product that used fewer of the more expensive raw materials. Where this situation is likely to arise, *ex ante* allocation of risk may be inefficient and what is needed is a means of encouraging cooperative behaviour.

Third, if theory suggests that risk-sharing adjustments to contract values may contribute to efficient performance, would we expect to observe these principles being applied in the public sector? To apply these risk-sharing rules *across the years* may not be consistent with annual, cash-limited budget allocations where the real change from one year to the next is unpredictable and failure to balance the budget may be penalized – i.e. in the public sector.[3] The historic argument against allowing public sector organizations malleable budgets is centred on a perception of the incentive structure. It has been argued that because public sector organizations cannot go bankrupt, individuals have an incentive to be 'over-optimistic' in forecasting the future outcome of present plans. A budgetary regime that does not allow a unit to obtain funds now against some future expected outcome is designed to minimize the social cost of this behaviour. However, the Treasury does not tend to believe a public sector organization when managers say that if only they are allowed to spend more now, they will find savings in the future. One therefore observes that virtually all budgets for production in the public sector are annual and cash limited, with very little temporal virement. This reflects the presumption that on average such limited budgetary flexibility will produce more efficient outcomes than would otherwise be the case.

The chancellor has recently announced that government departments are to have budgets set for each of the next three years (HM Treasury 1998). The intention is to break from the annual public expenditure round where departments bid against each other (and against the Treasury) for incremental resources. There has been no suggestion that the statutory requirement for trusts to break even on an annual basis is to be changed though there has been a marginal increase in the amount of any 'underspend' that can be carried forward into the next financial year. There has been no mention of granting a power to spend in excess of the budget for the current financial year in anticipation of funding to be made available in the following financial year. The degree to which a three-year cycle will genuinely reduce uncertainty for health authorities and trusts about their income over a three- to five-year period will only be apparent after the system has operated for several years. However, it is difficult to believe that budgets will not continue to be affected by the same sort of policy initiatives that we currently see announced during each financial year, which are often accompanied by changes in finance. Examples from the past year would include initiatives to deal with winter pressures, waiting lists and breast cancer.

The approach to risk sharing agreed by the contracting parties will be reflected in the price/quantity adjustment mechanisms adopted. Those which tackle the issue of changing the financial value of a contract over time can be classified as redetermination or renegotiation provisions (Crocker and Masten 1991). The former establishes prices by a formula which takes the form of either a 'definite' or 'indefinite' price escalator. Definite price escalators allow for predetermined increases in price and are fairly uncommon in longer-term contracts, as they do not allow consideration of changes in factors thought to influence price and are therefore quite inflexible. Indefinite price escalators specify the process by which price changes are to be agreed, usually linking contract prices to changes in the price of variables indicative of general changes in market conditions. At the simplest level, contract value could be linked to the market price of the good, but this assumes the good is homogenous and there is a spot market with which to make price comparisons. Another variation would link contract price to changes in the price of substitute goods, hence reflecting opportunity cost (e.g., the price of gas linked to the price of oil). Finally, cost-plus mechanisms adjust the contract value to reflect changes in supplier costs, but may not provide good incentives for efficiency. As the contractual environment becomes more complex or uncertain, and as a result it becomes difficult or costly to obtain and certify information about the future environment, *redetermination* clauses will become difficult to design and enforce. *Renegotiation* then becomes the norm and parties will not set out in advance how agreements on prices will be reached but will negotiate mutually acceptable terms each time a change in circumstances arises.

This analysis suggests that when examining contracts in the NHS we want to know if there are differences in the mechanisms used to allocate risks in long- and short-term contracts, whether some mechanisms appear to be more successful than others, and whether the financial regime of the public sector affects the approach to risk sharing.

Contracts and relationships in the private sector

There has been a tendency to identify 'relational contracts' with long-term contracts on the grounds that in a world of incomplete information, long-term relationships are likely to be more profitable than 'arm's-length' transacting. Trust and reputation play a greater role in contractual arrangements that are repeated over time and thus the hypothesis that long-term relationships are likely to be more efficient is probably correct. However, long-term relationships do not *necessarily* involve longer-term contracts. The critical distinction is whether anonymous/arms-length transactions are likely to produce outcomes as efficient as cooperation between transactors who recognize their mutual dependence. If cooperation is expected to be more efficient, we would predict its emergence irrespective of duration of contract: we are as likely to see the relevant behaviour whether the world is one without formal contract, with short-term contracts or with long-term contracts.

In much of the private sector, the duration of contract is less of an issue than the duration of *relationships*. A recent study of the engineering and kitchen furniture industries in three countries revealed that the majority of all firms had long-term relationships with their largest customers: 80 per cent of British firms had been dealing with their largest customer for more than 5 years and almost 40 per cent for more than 20 years (Arrighetti *et al.* 1997). However, rather than having long-term contracts with guarantees of future price and quantity built in, most firms tended to contract on a short-term basis either order by order or through a 'framework' or 'requirements' contract under which buyers place orders as required. The British firms, in particular, placed a high degree of emphasis on personal contacts and informal understandings of the basis on which they conducted their business. The authors state that: 'a commonly expressed view was that the success of the relationship depended on how well the exchange proceeded from the point of view of the parties, not on the form of the agreement' (Arrighetti *et al.* 1997: 182). They quote a UK supplier as saying: 'we don't have long-term contracts. We do have long-term relationships' and 'long-term relationships have very little to do with pieces of paper' (p. 186).

Many firms saw advantages in retaining the flexibility of short-term contracts and stressed some of the difficulties of making hard guarantees in the long term. However, although the majority were happy to have shorter contracts within the framework of a long-term relationship, a few did see some advantages in having long-term contracts with guaranteed volume, mainly in terms of allowing them to make firm commitments in buying supplies. This was seen as particularly important when the supplier operated in a volatile and competitive market. In the context of the NHS, this is unlikely to apply to many trusts as the majority of their income will be more or less guaranteed by their main purchaser. However, of more relevance was the view that long-term *relationships* were important as a means of focusing on product quality, innovation and development. Longer-term framework agreements (which do not commit finance) were seen as one way of developing this focus.

Research on private sector contracting has shown that the nature of contracts and of contractual relationships is influenced heavily by the social and institutional environment. Many studies have shown how extra-legal sanctions, unwritten rules, social pressures and norms are used to manage relationships based on trust and reputation, rather than reliance on rigid contract terms (e.g. Macaulay 1963; Beale and Dugdale 1975; Burchell and Wilkinson 1996; Arrighetti *et al.* 1997).

This strand of analysis suggests that rather than being considered in isolation, the issue of contract duration in the NHS should be viewed within the context of the relationships between purchasers and providers. In the NHS, does the form and content of the contract reflect the reality of the relationship? Do short-term contracts reflect short-term relationships?

IMPLICATIONS FOR LONGER-TERM CONTRACTS IN THE NHS

Duration of NHS contracts

There appears to be some confusion about the prevalence of longer-term contracts in the NHS. The Department of Health has reported that despite the absence of official obstacles to prevent parties entering into longer-term contracts, the annual contracting cycle has been dominant and the vast majority of contracts are for one year (NHS Executive 1996b). Hence the guidance aimed at encouraging the use of longer-term contracts. However, some survey evidence has suggested that purchasers and providers were already using longer-term contracts (Raftery *et al.* 1996). We offer an explanation for this apparent confusion in the final section. (As stated in the introductory section of this chapter, there is no technical definition of a long-term contract. For our empirical work we adopted the Department of Health convention of treating a contract of three or more years as 'long-term'.)

In our sample of 106 contracts from six health authorities,[4] we found that the majority of contracted activity in five of the health authorities is currently organized under agreements spanning three years. In these health authorities, where annual contracts are used, they tend to be for small sums and with providers outside the authority boundary. All the health authorities with longer-term contracts stated that they had been using them for some time and not as a response to the more recent policy announcements. The other health authority currently uses only annual contracts but expects to be moving towards three-year agreements. In the sample of five contracts supplied by the NHS Executive, three covered a three-year period, one a two-year period and one a five-year period. The latter was written to ring-fence resources at a mental health trust to effect the transfer of patients with learning difficulties into the community over this period. Tables 4.1 and 4.2 summarize the findings. Of the 177 contracts from GP fundholders, only one specified a duration greater than one year.

Table 4.1 Contract duration: – number/proportion of contracts of different duration from 106 health authority contracts

Health authority	3-year	3-year rolling	1-year	Other	Notes
1 **n=50**	All bar 1 main contract	None	Most small contracts	2-year rolling for 1 main contract	2-year rolling was with a main provider but year 2 was to be reviewed following results of acute services review
2 **n=29**	None	All 9 main contracts with the exception of some specific named services within the 3-year contract with the provider	All small contracts with the exception of 3 small acute contracts which were 3-year rolling. One year contract for some specialist health promotion and for open access occupational therapy within a 3-year contract with trust	2-year rolling for 'mainstream' health promotion	The terms 3-year and 3-year rolling appear to be used interchangeably. The core contract terms refer to all contracts as 3-year rolling but some of the contract documentation has 3-year written on it. The services for which there were 1-year contracts within a 3-year general trust contract were either due to be reviewed, put out to tender or retracted
3 **n=9** **(example only)**	All 4 main contracts	See next column	Four contracts stated they were 1-year 'within the context of a 3-year rolling contract'. 1 annual contract with provider outside health authority	None	One example of small contract with provider outside health authority was supplied but all others follow the same format, i.e. annual

Table 4.1 Continued

Health authority	3-year	3-year rolling	1-year	Other	Notes
4 **n=5** **(examples only)**	All 4 main contracts. One small contract with provider outside health authority	None	None	None	One example of small contract with provider outside health authority was supplied but all others follow the same format, i.e. 3-year
5 **(example only)**	None	All main contracts	None	None	One example only was provided but all other contracts are in the same format
6 **(n=13)**	None	None	All contracts	None	All contracts were annual in this health authority, but 2 with community trusts stated that there was an intention to move towards a 3-year rolling contract with annual review

Note: n = number of contracts

Table 4.2   Contract duration in isolated sample of longer-term contracts

Contract description	Duration	Notes
Health authority and mental health trust	5-year	Refers to a single contract with a mental health trust which ran from 1992 to 1997 in order to effect a transfer of patients with learning difficulties to the community
Consortium of purchasers and acute trust	3-year	For provision of cardiac services only
Health authority and community trust	2-year rolling	For provision of community health services excluding specific parts of service covered by different contracts
Three health authorities and acute trust	3-year	For provision of all acute services
Health authority and community trust	3-year	For provision of mental health services. Draft of general terms only

Risk handling in the NHS and price/adjustment mechanisms

Despite the fact that the majority of patient activity was included in three-year contracts, the *financial value* of these contracts was almost always renegotiated annually. The obligation on trusts to break even each year is reflected in the contracts in the form of highly detailed rules for adjusting and renegotiating activity in-year and for adjusting contract values. These clauses are designed to help both parties stay within their annual budget constraints. They inform the parties of the adjustments that are acceptable when conditions change (e.g. reduce elective work if an increase in emergency work would otherwise threaten to breach total cost agreements). While these triggers for adjustment of contract value *in-year* were common for acute services, within our sample of contracts there were few examples of rules for automatic adjustment of contract price *between* years. Table 4.3 summarizes the details of just three contracts (all from the sample provided by the NHS Executive) which contained rules for adjusting contract value *across* years.

Central guidance makes it clear that the Department of Health wants to see contracts moving away from providing for annual negotiation of finance and activity to three- to five-year agreements on finance (NHS Executive 1997). It does not say how this is to be done, only that: 'the funding agreement is either fixed or related to a mechanism which can be referred to at agreed intervals during the contract' (NHS Executive 1997).

A fixed price agreement would not be consistent with the argument in the same guidance for more risk sharing. It therefore appears that the guidance is referring to redetermination mechanisms like those found in some of the long-term contracts in the energy sector as in this hypothetical example: 'the purchaser agrees to automatically adjust payment in line with changes in spot gas prices within the limits of +/–4% of prices at the date of signing the contract; if prices go outside the limits, the terms of the contract are to be re-negotiated'. This is very similar to the wording of existing NHS contracts where floors, ceilings and triggers operate in-year to manage annual contract value. Extending this type of 'automatic' price adjustment mechanism between years would only contribute to the objective of 'reducing time spent' each year negotiating finance if the ceilings and floors were rarely reached, and the likelihood that the parties would have to meet to renegotiate was thus reduced.

At present, the annual renegotiation of contract finance centres on:

- The change in the purchaser's budget which will be composed of any change in the formula allocation from the region, any inflation allowance, any real growth and any additional funding for specific services (all determined on an annual basis by the Treasury, Department of Health and region).
- 'Cost pressures' of providers which can be (roughly) broken down into (i) legislation/government policy changes; (ii) changes in costs of usual activities; and (iii) new developments favoured by providers.
- Purchaser priorities for new developments.

Table 4.3 'Rules' and principles for adjusting price and activity over time in 93 contracts

Health authority	Price?	Activity?	Notes
1	Annual renegotiation. One contract states the 'anticipated' cash limit for following year and lists factors to be considered when setting it next year (inflation, changes to non-recurrent funding in health authority). All other contracts say this year's activity and price to be used as a 'baseline' for future negotiations	Core contracting terms state that 75% and 50% of year 1 activity is guaranteed as a minimum in years 2 and 3 respectively. These terms apply to most main providers	
2	Annual renegotiation. Contracts with main providers state that both parties recognize the 'preferred status' of the other and thus expect the provider to ensure the prices it offers are as least as favourable as to others who may wish to purchase the same services (i.e. other health authorities, GP fundholders etc.). If during the contract the provider offers or sells the services to a third party at prices lower than those in the contract, the health authority expects to be notified and normally offered the same terms	Annual	The price clause is similar to the 'most favoured nation' clauses contained in longer-term contracts in the private sector in some industries (e.g. gas). Such clauses have been viewed by some as potentially anti-competitive devices, but by others as an efficient means by which price adjustments can be made to reflect changing economic circumstances, as it is assumed that new prices relate to changes in costs or demand which would otherwise be difficult to track. It is not clear that this is the reasoning behind the health authority clause

Table 4.3 Continued

Health authority	Price 'rules'?	Activity 'rules'?	Notes
3	Annual renegotiation. One contract with a main provider states that funding for the following will include consideration of additional posts and extra theatre lists, and the recurrent nature of unfunded inflation. However, it states that this is 'unlikely' to involve any additional cash increase over current year	Annual	
4	Annual renegotiation. States that this will reflect the recurring financial baseline with amendments made for inflation, costs of additional activity and 'agreed' in-year cost pressures	Annual	Contracts with non-local providers state that the annual renegotiation will reflect service changes which may arise as a result of acute service reviews taking place in those areas. This presumably reflects the difficulty of devising even a general indicator of the factors likely to impact on price and activity during a period involving substantial service shifts. Additionally, the health authority is likely to have far less control over the shifts occurring in distant areas than it does within its own boundaries
5	Annual renegotiation to reflect agreed changes in quantity, quality and finance	Annual	

Renegotiation of contract price would normally represent only small changes in year-on-year expenditure for a main contract. Except where there has been prior agreement to move a block of services, the annual negotiations between a purchaser and their providers centre on how to divide the *change* in income between providers to deal with cost changes of existing services (which are likely to differ by provider) and how much can be invested in new developments with different providers. In our sample, trying to distinguish between changes in the cost of existing services and new developments in the acute sector was the most frequently cited problem of the annual financial negotiation.

The annual financial margins of change are so small that they create apparently contradictory messages for those who want longer-term financial agreements. First, for all main contracts, it would be easy to draft contracts that guaranteed, say, 95 per cent of the current budget of £Xm for each of the next five years. This might look more like a longer-term financial agreement than the present contracts but would in fact represent no change. Annual negotiations are not about moving large parts of contracts but about the allocation of any *extra* money allowed by the Treasury each year. Second, although annual negotiations are over marginal resources, small numbers are of disproportionate importance – the ability to redirect 0.5 per cent of the budget is the only way a purchaser may have of affecting the pattern of service development and delivery. Similarly, a trust deficit of 0.5 per cent of the budget is treated as a serious financial difficulty unless a feasible recovery plan is in place. With margins this tight, neither party is usually willing to commit themselves to pricing rules that would remove the discretion to negotiate marginal expenditure and revenue each year.

In our sample, all purchasers said they could live with a pricing rule that automatically gave providers the national inflation adjustment, but only one purchaser was willing to go further and offer all providers an increase in line with the total increase in their budget. This is the only contract pricing rule that would serve the purpose of eliminating annual renegotiation of contract prices. All other purchasers felt that growth money was there to implement purchaser priorities and not to simply be handed over to finance provider priorities. The purchasers with the strongest commitment to strategic planning and those involved with trusts in metropolitan service 'reconfigurations' were the most likely to oppose a pricing rule that automatically gave providers a percentage of growth money.

From interviews it was clear that contracting parties have developed some mechanisms to improve the management of the risks they face and thus reduce the 'hassle' of annual financial agreement, but none saw the possibility of reducing them to pricing rules that could be incorporated into three- to five-year financial agreements. One health authority had produced a matrix of relevant costs that allowed a provider to alter in-year casemix without requesting additional funding. Another was trying to develop more robust definitions of cost pressures in order to further separate discussion of cost changes from new developments. For that authority, a cost pressure is a change in the cost of a service that is not associated with a change in quality or quantity. This would make a pay increase or a change in junior doctor hours a cost pressure, but the introduction of a new drug with improved therapeutic properties for treating an already treated condition a new development. In these circumstances it is not clear what the *Priorities and Planning Guidance* (NHS Executive 1997) means by 'risk sharing' and 'managing risks'. In the academic literature, the first term is used to indicate that the health authority and trusts would share the extra costs. Incentives are strengthened as neither party's budget would bear the full burden of the change in staff costs or the cost of introducing the new treatment. However, health authorities are cash-limited public sector organizations. The only way they can 'share' the cost with a trust is to reduce their reserves or forgo preferred service developments elsewhere. In the US literature on risk sharing, the assumption is that the payer (the employer or government) agrees to depart from strict capitation payment and adjusts payment to partly reflect actual costs (see Frank *et al.* 1995 for an example of 'soft capitation'). A health authority is not in a position to do this across all providers.

Public sector budgets, cash limited for each financial year, ordinarily contain a 'contingency reserve'. The contingency reserve is an important mechanism for managing in-year financial risk so as not to breach the annual cash limit, but such reserves are not useful for carrying risk between years. The tradition within the public sector has been to approach risk sharing in a discretionary, rather than a rule-based, way. Each tier holds back part of its fixed budget as a contingency reserve before passing the remainder on to the next tier. When unforeseen events arise, the higher tier decides, often on an ad hoc basis, whether and on what terms to contribute to the financial problems of the unit below. In several interviews, individuals pointed out that each year there was not only uncertainty about their formal allocation but even more uncertainty about the various forms of non-recurrent funding that might be made available during the year via regional offices – in effect, their receipts from the regional, departmental and Treasury contingency reserves.

Contractual relationships in the NHS

Contracts between NHS parties are not legally binding and are legally enforceable only if they involve a private sector provider (Allen 1995). Disputes are dealt with not through the courts but rather through internal arbitration or conciliation processes at a regional level, with the secretary of state acting as final conciliator in pre- or post-contract disputes (NHS Executive 1991). The latter option has rarely been used in practice (Mchale *et al.* 1995). On the surface, NHS contracts thus appear similar to the relational contracts outlined earlier. However, there may be some question about the degree to which the form of the contract corresponds to the reality of the nature of the relationships between parties in the NHS, as the latter may not *necessarily* be based on goodwill and trust.

Interviewees were asked what they understood by the term 'long-term contract'. While two said anything longer than one year was a long-term contract, the overwhelming majority said that as long as finance was negotiated on an annual basis, their contracts were short term. One trust executive referred to their three-year contracts as '*a sham*'. He argued that the three-year contracts were there to show commitment but both parties already knew they must continue to work together. Others felt there was some value in 'showing commitment' but agreed that the annual cycle of agreeing finance and activity was what most parties considered the core of contracting. When asked whether her contracts were long or short term, one contract manager replied she thought it an irrelevant question as the *relationship* with her main purchaser was obviously long term: '*Where else can they go?*'. The duration of the contract did not matter.

It is not clear that acknowledging the relationship as long term was likely to engender the cooperative relationship discussed in the relational contracting literature. Those negotiating on behalf of the health authority often saw trusts as trying to increase their share of resources, while trusts often felt they had a right to a 'fair share' of any growth money received by the health authority, irrespective of whether there was a difference in priorities. There was no agreement as to what constituted 'fair shares' of the resources annually made available by the Department of Health.

It has been argued that long-term contracts would reduce uncertainty where services are to be restructured. Our research suggested that health authorities and trusts often develop non-contractual frameworks to agree and implement policies of service development and structural change. It would appear a matter of indifference, or more likely of local convenience, whether these arrangements are referred to or included in contract documentation. There was considerable variation in what people in different health authorities considered relevant to include in the paperwork of the contract – as opposed to appearing in other documents. For example, one health authority had a five-year rolling strategic plan and each year particular points for action were agreed with each of its contracting trusts. Neither the strategy nor the points for action during the current year appeared in contracts. Another included the equivalent strategic points for action within the contract documentation. In both cases the parties to the contracts had planning periods longer than the duration of their contracts, and significantly longer than the annual renegotiation of the financial value of the contracts.

Several interviewees said they did not see contracts as the appropriate place for detail of their strategic plans. In future they expect to put this information in the local Health Improvement Programme (HImP), not in a longer-term contract/agreement. This view of the rather limited role of contract occasionally emerged when discussing service specifications. In some contracts service specifications were no more than lists of procedures, in others we found detailed clinical protocols included as service specifications. The same contract would have highly detailed service specifications for some services but not for others. A number of those interviewed treated service specifications as marginal or irrelevant to contracting. In one health authority where effort went into producing a complete set of service specifications three years ago, they are now ignored. If a problem arises, the clinicians sort it out with the health authority. It was considered that achieving change in clinical practice was an ongoing process of dialogue – '*an organic process*'. The important thing was to work out protocols with clinicians: 'pulling all this together in a service specification is bureaucratic' as one interviewee put it.

The contracting process was seen as peripheral to the process of raising clinical standards and moving to longer-term contracts would make no difference. The government would appear to share this view as have established national institutions such as the National Institute for Clinical Excellence (NICE) and the National Commission for Health Improvement as key instruments for bringing about changes in clinical standards.

CONCLUSIONS AND POLICY IMPLICATIONS

The lack of longer-term *financial* agreements coupled with frequent use of longer-term frameworks for planning investment and service developments is probably at the root of the confusion about the extent to which long-term contracts are used in the NHS. It was clear from our interviews that contracting is seen as a narrow financial activity – a longer-term contract is one that settles financial arrangements for a period of three years or more. Long-term planning and strategy are not necessarily carried out within this narrow contracting framework and our research indicated that in most cases parties to NHS contracts had planning periods longer than the duration of their contracts and significantly longer than the annual round of financial renegotiation. Four- to five-year financial frameworks were used to explore the financial implications of service development strategies. A five-year, and in one case a ten-year investment planning horizon was used where purchasers and providers were negotiating changes in infrastructure. Use of longer-term plans for investment and service development was not inconsistent with annual renegotiation of prices and activity. Most of the expected benefits of a move to longer-term contracts are at present being realized by use of arrangements *other* than contracts. We found no evidence to support the view that a movement to longer-term contracts with financial redetermination clauses (the proposed change that *would* be significantly different from present practice) would contribute to the objectives of better planning, more clinician involvement and improved clinical standards.

Economic theory and the evidence from the NHS suggest there is limited scope for revising the current longer-term agreements to incorporate redetermination clauses which adjust price and activity automatically over time. Changes in contract value are currently achieved via annual renegotiation and this is appropriate within the current financial system with its stress on annually-balanced budgets and cash limits. A three-year expenditure cycle for central government departments may reduce some uncertainty for health authorities about their budgets for the next three years, but a firm three-year budget for the Department of Health does not mean a firm three-year budget for a health authority. The most obvious sources of change would be changes to the capitation formula, changes in the proportion of funds distributed by criteria other than capitation and new policy initiatives from the Department of Health. Trusts face even more sources of income variation as purchasing budgets are devolved to primary care groups (PCGs).

When trying to assess the impact of moving to a three-year public expenditure round it is useful to distinguish between the effect on forward planning and the effect on managing financial risk across years. The three-year cycle may well enable public sector organizations to make better guesses about the real value of expected budgets in each of the next three years. However, that information does not make them better able to absorb the financial risk of committing in year one to pay a predetermined share of a contingent cost that may arise in year three due to change in the price of a drug, introduction of a new therapy, a change in demand or any other 'unplanned' event that affects cost. Because of the relatively smaller size of PCG budgets, we would expect the between-years financial risk of redetermination clauses to be even greater for PCGs than it is perceived to be for health authorities.[5]

We conclude that the present system has already evolved to encompass many of the activities which the Department of Health wishes to encourage through their new policy (e.g., joint longer-term planning and strategy), and in this sense the impact of requiring longer-term agreements will be neutral. However, we would advise a cautious approach to the implementation of rigid rules for longer-term financial agreements, as this would deliver few benefits while forcing purchasers and providers into an activity which may have substantial resource implications as they try to cope with the increase in financial risk.

NOTES

1 The Department of Health uses the term 'agreement' rather than contract in most recent guidance. However, in this chapter we use the terms interchangeably. NHS contracts are not legal documents, so substituting the terms makes little difference.

2 There are many other themes and issues which arise in relation to the economics of contracting which are not discussed here. Our research

covered a number of topics and the results will be published elsewhere in future.

3 This is not to imply that the financial regime of the private sector will always accommodate variable priced contracts. Firms reliant on bank finance with little equity capital would not be able to enter into such contracts. The rarity of examples of private sector contracts with long-term price adjustment rules suggests the problem may simply be *relatively* more serious in the public sector.

4 See Appendix for a description of the sample.

5 See Carr-Hill, Rice and Smith (Chapter 3) for a discussion of funding PCGs.

APPENDIX: SELECTION OF HEALTH AUTHORITIES, GP FUNDHOLDERS AND INTERVIEWEES

Selection of health authorities/GP fundholders

The duration and scope of the project did not allow for the collection of all contracts from all health authorities. We therefore decided to limit our sample to two regions outside London from which we would choose a number of health authorities and GP fundholders. As all regions were likely to provide a good cross-section of health authorities with different characteristics, we chose two regions whose proximity would limit cost and time involved in fieldwork associated with the project. The following criteria were used to select health authorities within these regions:

- Population: an indicator of size.
- Revenue budget: an indicator of size/purchasing power.
- Number of main provider contractors: an indication of the number of contracts to be examined.
- Number of general practices (fundholding practices): examining the ratio would give an indication of the relative purchasing power of health authorities and GP fundholders.
- Acute/community expenditure split (expressed as percentages): included partly because the nature of the contract may vary depending upon whether the main provider is largely acute or community service-based.

There were 24 health authorities in the two regions. Eight health authorities were initially selected (allowing for a 25 per cent non-response/non-compliance rate) and approached to participate in the study. All of the GP fundholding practices within each selected health authority area were also approached to participate in the study.

We requested copies of *all* contracts from the health authorities and GP fundholders in the study, explaining that although the project focused on longer-term contracts, part of the scope was to assess the extent to which longer-term contracts were used and that we required annual contracts for comparative purposes.

Response

Although six health authorities agreed to send us their contract documentation, there was substantial variation in the documents which were seen as being part of the actual contract. For example, some health authorities sent us every service specification to which they refer in contracts, while others sent us only the contract schedules or one or two specifications as examples. Some health authorities had 'core' documents which contained details of their financial and contracting requirements which applied to all contracts; others had separate details for each provider. Although this may reflect nothing more interesting than the amount of photocopying that the health authorities were willing to undertake on our behalf, we believe some of it represents a genuine variation in what is understood by 'contracting' at both the health authority and trust level in terms of the range and nature of the activities that are included as part of this process.

Two health authorities sent us 'representative' examples of their standard contract documents, rather than all the contracts, as they stated that the format and all the terms and conditions were identical in every contract with their main providers. One health authority supplied us with examples of main contracts and examples of those with distant or marginal providers.

In total, we received 106 separate health authority contracts. Additionally, the NHS Executive supplied us with some examples of longer-term contracts they had collected via a trawl around regional offices, which added five more to our sample.

The response from GP fundholders was less favourable. This may have in part been due to the cost of photocopying (although we did offer to reimburse practices for this) but also because they believed the health authority held copies of all their contracts and would send them to us in one batch. Although we did follow this up, it became clear that if the contracts were indeed held at health authority level, they were not all located in one place and we were unable to find anyone who could supply copies at the health authority level. Thus we had to rely on the responses from the GP fundholders. In total, 47 practices responded and sent 177 contracts. Again, many of them said all their contracts followed an identical format, so sent only a single example. A preliminary analysis of the fundholding contracts led us to expect that gathering further examples would not add substantially to the project and thus we did not attempt to send reminders.

Interviews

Interviews were held with staff from each health authority in our sample (we included the health authority with one-year contracts for comparative purposes) and from a trust with which the health authority contracted. The trusts were selected as being a main provider of services to the health authority and also as representing a spectrum of experiences. Two were mental health trusts, two were non-teaching acute and two were teaching acute. The individuals interviewed varied in terms of their position as we asked for someone who was involved in the contracting process with the specific health authority/trust in question. In general, the individuals in both trusts and health authorities tended to be directors/assistant directors of planning, commissioning or contracting.

REFERENCES

Allen, P. (1995). Contracts in the NHS internal market. *Modern Law Review*, 58, 321–42.

Arrighetti, A., Bachman, R. and Deakin, S. (1997). Contract law, social norms and inter-firm co-operation. *Cambridge Journal of Economics*, 21, 171–95.

Beale, H. and Dugdale, T. (1975). Contracts between businessmen: planning and the use of contractual remedies. *British Journal of Law and Society*, 2, 45–60.

Blair, R. and Kaserman, D. (1987). A note on bilateral monopoly and formula price contracts. *American Economic Review*, 77, 460–3.

Burchell, B. and Wilkinson, F. (1996). *Trust, Business and the Contractual Environment*, Working Paper Series 35. Cambridge: ESRC Centre for Business Research, University of Cambridge.

Campbell, D. and Clay, S. (1992). *Long-Term Contracting: A Bibliography and Review of the Literature.* Oxford: Oxford University Press.

Chalkley, M. and Malcomson, J. (1996). Contracts for the National Health Service. *Economic Journal*, 106, 1691–701.

Crocker, K.J. and Masten, S.E. (1991). Pretia ex machina? Prices and process in long-term contracts. *Journal of Law and Economics*, 34, 69–99.

De Fraja, G. and Hartley, K. (1996). Defence procurement: theory and UK policy. *Oxford Review of Economic Policy*, 12, 70–88.

Department of Health (1989). *Contracts for Health Services: Operational Principles.* London: HMSO.

Department of Health (1997). *The New NHS: Modern, Dependable.* London: HMSO.

Frank, R., McGuire, T. and Newhouse, J. (1995). Risk contracts in managed mental health care. *Health Affairs*, 14, 50–64.

HM Treasury (1998). *Stability and Investment for the Long Term.* Cm. 3978. London: HMSO.

Macaulay, S. (1963). Non-contractual relations in business: a preliminary study. *American Economic Review*, 45, 55–69.

Mchale, J., Hughes, D. and Griffiths, L. (1995). Disputes in the NHS internal market: regulation and relationships. *Medical Law International*, 2, 215–27.

McNeil, I. (1978). Contracts: adjustment of long-term economic relations under classical, neo-classical and relational contract law. *Northwestern University Law Review*, 72, 854–905.

NHS Executive (1991). *NHS Contracts: Guidance on Resolving Disputes* (EL(91)11).

NHS Executive (1992). *Review of Contracting in Guidance for the 1993/4 Contracting Round* (EL(92)79).

NHS Executive (1993). *Review of Contracting – Guidance for the 1994/5 Contracting Cycle* (EL(93)103).

NHS Executive (1994). *1995/1996 Contracting Review: Handbook* (EL(94)88).

NHS Executive (1996a). *Planning and Priorities Guidance 1997/98* (EL(96)45).

NHS Executive (1996b). *Seeing the Wood, Sparing the Trees*. Leeds: NHS Executive.

NHS Executive (1997). *NHS Priorities and Planning Guidance 1998/99* (and Appendix 1 on longer-term agreements) (EL(97)39).

Raftery, J., Robinson, R., Mulligan, J. and Forrest, S. (1996). Contracting in the NHS quasi-market. *Health Economics* 5: 353–62.

Vickers, J. and Yarrow, G. (1989). *Privatisation: An Economic Analysis*. London: MIT Press.

5

SHAPING UP TO IMPROVE HEALTH: THE STRATEGIC LEADERSHIP ROLE OF THE NEW HEALTH AUTHORITY

Brian Ferguson

INTRODUCTION

The role of the health authority in the United Kingdom National Health Service (UK NHS) has been the subject of debate for many years, heightened by the reforms of 1989 and 1997 (Department of Health 1989; Department of Health 1997). Pre–1989 there were 192 old district health authorities (DHAs) in the 14 regional health authorities in England. During the 1990s there has been a gradual reduction in the number of health authorities: in 1995/6 there were around 110 DHAs with populations ranging from 92,000 to over 900,000 (NAHAT 1995). In 1997/8 there were 100 health authorities in the eight English regions (IHSM 1997), on average covering populations of about 450,000 people (Ferguson and Smith 1997). Another important trend has been the merger of DHAs and family health services authorities (FHSAs) to create unified authorities responsible for integrating services across primary and secondary care.

Such structural changes have resulted in fewer, larger health authorities with wider roles and responsibilities. The rationale for this evolution during the 1990s was partly to counterbalance the increased power of hospital trusts in the internal market. Not surprisingly this has led to situations of bilateral monopoly in many geographical areas, undermining the notion that competition would drive improvements in efficiency. In addition, the merger of DHAs and FHSAs was based on the rationale that integrated care would only be achieved if historical boundaries between care sectors disappeared.

WHAT IS THE HEALTH AUTHORITY?

The objective of this chapter is to examine the long-term role of the health authority in view of recent major policy developments. The 1997 White Paper (Department of Health 1997) provides some clues as to the new strategic role of the health authority: service planning is back in vogue if not in name, and there are some obvious parallels to the 1989 reforms – for example, in the health needs assessment role. But what will the health authority be as an organization?

Health authorities do not directly provide health care, and most of their direct purchasing role has been devolved to primary care groups (PCGs). While regional offices exist, health authorities do not have an explicit regulatory role, although in practice this task may indeed lie with health authorities locally. The process of conciliation in the NHS will remain, at least in the short term, the responsibility of regional offices.

The health authority has no line management responsibility for hospitals which provide health care services. It has statutory responsibility for the development of PCGs, but many of the players in these new groupings are independent contractors in the NHS – for example, general practitioners (GPs). The health authority is partly the advocate of the consumer, but where does that leave community health councils (CHCs)?

In truth, the health authority of the future will have many and diverse roles, but it remains difficult to describe the health authority in organizational terms. It will not be a provider, a purchaser (except for specialist services) or an explicit regulator – so what will it be?

A useful starting point is to explore some of the legal considerations.[1] The NHS is, in law, part of the services of the Crown, which 'is one of the most curious departments of English administrative law' (Wade 1971). Since the inception of the NHS, duties have been imposed on various bodies (such as the old regional hospital boards) which 'are probably not *legal* duties at all, in the sense that they can be enforced by legal process' (Wade 1971, original emphasis). For example, the opening words of the National Health Service Act (1946) state that: 'It shall be the duty of the Minister of Health

... to promote the establishment in England and Wales of a comprehensive health service'.

The Health Authorities Act (1995) completed the 1989 NHS reforms, creating the new unified health authorities following the merger of DHAs and FHSAs. The Act placed a duty on these authorities 'to take the advice they need to fulfil their functions from doctors, nurses, midwives and other persons with professional expertise in and experience of health care'. Although these examples of duties are imposed by statute, 'it seems plain that it must be by political rather than legal means that they are to be enforced' (Wade 1971: 157–8). This distinction between administrative and political accountability is reinforced in a paper discussing the accountability of Total Purchasing Pilots (TPPs) (Dixon *et al.* 1998), which as formal subcommittees of health authorities were subject to the same accountability mechanisms (which will also be the case for the emergent PCGs). The Secretary of State is formally accountable to Parliament for the performance of health authorities, and in turn health authorities are 'downwardly accountable' to the public – for example, via the need for open health authority meetings and the statutory responsibility for having local functioning CHCs.

Through such mechanisms, and as public bodies within the NHS, health authorities can therefore be viewed as the statutory 'agents'[2] of the Secretary of State for Health, and will be held to account via the political process and the usual remedies of public law (Wade 1971). Where there is an application for judicial review, it is likely that cases will hinge upon procedural issues concerning *how* a decision is made, rather than the content of the decision itself. Dixon *et al.* (1998) highlight the important aspect of *clinical* accountability as an additional dimension in the NHS, since health professionals are accountable for their clinical behaviour to their respective professional bodies. This aspect of accountability will assume considerably more importance with the development of clinical governance arrangements, which in practice will be overseen by the health authority in its new role.

THE DEVELOPING ROLE OF THE HEALTH AUTHORITY

The 1997 reforms gave health authorities a clear strategic leadership role which is highly consistent in tone with the evolution of government policy through the 1990s:

Health Authorities will give strategic leadership on the ground in the new NHS. They will lead the development of local Health Improvement Programmes which will identify the health needs of local people and what needs to be done to meet them. Health Authorities will work closely with NHS Trusts, the new Primary Care Groups, Local Authorities, academic and research interests, voluntary organisations, and the local community in devising this new strategic approach to the planning and delivery of health care.

(Department of Health 1997, para. 4.1: 24)

Given that the 1997 White Paper (Department of Health 1997) is set within the context of the same medium-term priorities for the NHS (NHS Executive 1997) as those under the previous administration, this consistency is hardly surprising. The increased emphasis upon wider determinants of health, the underlying evidence base, quality standards, public involvement and multi-agency working largely reinforce trends which were occurring anyway. What, then, is radically different about the 1997 White Paper?

Before addressing this question it is important to summarize the envisaged future role of the health authority. The overarching 'leading and shaping' role contains a number of key tasks, which can be summarized as two distinct, related roles:[3]

1 To develop an all-inclusive Health Improvement Programme (HImP) reflecting important health needs and addressing important health care service issues, with commonly agreed objectives, standards and targets across partnership organizations.
2 To develop PCGs and monitor their pace of change, ensuring appropriate resource allocation mechanisms are in place to facilitate this within a clear accountability framework.

The first of these represents the long-term *raison d'être* of the health authority: the strategic planning role aimed at improving health in agreed national and local priority areas. The second area is at least in theory a time-limited role, if PCGs progress quickly through the four levels described in the 1997 White Paper (Department of Health 1997).

The future role of the Health Authority will continue to involve the resource allocation element, and indeed certain functions to support PCGs can be expected to remain with the health authority.

However, the central rationale for the existence of health authorities must hinge upon the first of these major roles.

It is argued that there are four ways in which the latest reforms signal a *radical* shift in policy emphasis with respect to the role of the health authority. First, and perhaps least tangible, is the shift in the power base back towards health authorities. The 1989 reforms offered NHS trust providers significant capital and labour market freedoms and the possibility – if not the financial incentives ultimately – to behave entrepreneurially, seeking to maximize income from different purchasers, forging alliances with private sector providers, pricing competitively, raising quality standards to attract 'business', and so on. The 1997 reforms, however, placed the health authority in a clear 'leading and shaping' role, embodied within the HImP.

The HImP signals a return to service planning with its comprehensive coverage, including: the most important health needs; the main health care requirements of local people; and the range, location and investment required in local health services to meet identified needs. The responsibility for developing this three-year planning framework lies with the health authority which, although it must undertake this collaboratively, will ultimately be held to account for meeting targets outlined in the HImP. Additionally, it is clear that health authorities will be able to hold others to account in ensuring delivery of the NHS contribution.

The second radical change in emphasis is the statutory accountability of PCGs to health authorities. The White Paper outlines four levels at which PCGs might operate, and it is unclear to what extent and at what pace PCGs will be expected to progress from Level 1 through to Level 4. While PCGs remain at Levels 1 or 2, they will be constituted formally as subcommittees of the health authority, with the chairs of PCG boards being directly accountable to the chief executive of the health authority (NHS Executive 1998d).

At this stage most of the evidence regarding the level at which PCGs will operate is anecdotal. Early development work has focused upon the size and configuration of PCG groupings, with more recent guidance (NHS Executive 1998e) concentrating on issues of process such as the composition of PCG boards. It is not clear what degree of enthusiasm exists among GPs to develop the commissioning role of PCGs beyond Levels 1 or 2. Similarly, it is unclear how much pressure will be exerted from central government to progress towards primary care trust (PCT) status.

The HImP represents the framework within which all of the

relevant organizations must operate to meet important health targets. Health care professionals within PCGs will not be able to make independent commissioning decisions *which are inconsistent with the agreed HImP*, one aim of which will be to ensure that patients on the lists of all GP practices are treated equitably, in the sense that they are part of the same commissioning framework. (Thereby ending the two-tier system of fundholding/non-fundholding and potentially unequal access to health care resources.)

Third, a major change for the health authority is the devolution to PCGs of direct purchasing for all primary and secondary care services. Over time it is envisaged that health authorities will retain the direct purchasing function for specialist services only. In practice, however, it is less clear at what pace PCGs will develop through the different levels. Experience from the evaluation of TPPs (Goodwin *et al.* 1998) suggests that PCGs will inevitably develop at different speeds: for example, large multi-practice pilots were reported as needing more time for organizational development. This suggests that health authorities will retain the direct commissioning role for longer in the case of some PCGs, although the expectation is that ultimately they will largely relinquish this role.

Finally, health authorities will have reserve powers to ensure that major investment decisions – such as capital developments or new consultant medical staffing appointments – are consistent with the HImP. This is potentially a radical step, reinforcing the shift in the balance of power to the health authority, assuming that the reserve powers are used effectively. 'Purchaser support' for major investment decisions could actually become a real lever for ensuring that change takes place when it is required, and equally for preventing changes which are not considered necessary by all parties to the HImP.

There is a fifth way in which the White Paper is radical, and although not relating directly to the health authority's role, it is critical nevertheless. This is the 'extension of corporate governance from financial to clinical matters' (Black 1998: 297). The White Paper contains a set of proposals for ensuring that the performance management framework gives a stronger emphasis to issues of quality, including proposals for the establishment of a National Institute for Clinical Excellence (NICE) and a National Commission for Health Improvement. Ministerial statements have reinforced the new statutory duty for quality for which officers in PCGs and trusts will be held accountable (Department of Health 1998c).

Through the HImP, health authorities will have a central role in ensuring that the outputs of NICE are used to inform decision making on the basis of the best available evidence. A key role of the health authority will be to ensure that appropriate frameworks exist for developing clinical governance in primary and secondary care. In practice the expectation is that this will be achieved through the HImP 'determining local targets and standards to drive quality and efficiency in the light of national priorities and guidance, and ensuring their delivery' (Department of Health 1997, para. 4.3: 25). National service frameworks, initially focusing on cancers, heart disease and mental health, are one major source of priorities for the HImP.

HEALTH AUTHORITY OBJECTIVES

Remarkably little has been written about the formal objectives of health authorities, an understanding of which is critical to predicting behaviour arising from any set of reforms. Clearly the objectives of any large organization are complex and multidimensional, compounded by the existence of principal-agent relationships. Leaving aside the problems arising through what will inevitably be imperfect agency relationships, it is worth exploring what these objectives are likely to be following the latest NHS reforms.

Health authority objectives will reflect a combination of inputs from the non-executive members and the executive directors (officers) of the authority. Overall goals will translate into strategic and operational objectives which at least in theory will be reflected in the individual objectives of all health authority staff. Given this filtering of information throughout the organization, the most accurate reflection of health authority objectives is likely to be contained in the personal objectives of the chief executive, which will be influenced by the views of non-executive members, including the chair of the health authority. Analogously, as Black (1998: 298) notes in relation to the new statutory duty for quality and the development of clinical governance: 'making trust chief executives personally responsible for the clinical performance of their services might prove to be just the incentive needed'.

A key constraint for health authorities is the need to maintain financial control (Griffiths 1998). Although it appears that the annual budget-setting round will move to a three-year cycle (*Financial Times* 1998), health authorities will nevertheless be subject to a relatively tight budget constraint requiring careful in-year financial monitoring. The devolution of comprehensive budgets to PCGs will almost certainly mean that health authorities exercise *more* financial control in the face of greater perceived risk. The statutory accountability of PCGs for their commissioning decisions inevitably means that health authorities cannot absolve themselves of responsibility for the use of resources once those resources have been allocated.

The high-level objective of health authorities is to improve the health of their resident populations. Increasingly it is recognized that this requires a multi-agency, intersectoral approach to tackle the root cause of health and social problems, which can only be affected marginally by the health care sector. Health authority chief executives will be careful to ensure that they are held to account on realistic objectives and targets, which will focus on delivering what the NHS can contribute to these wider health and social problems, albeit within increasingly consistent frameworks and shared priorities (Department of Health 1989; Department of Health 1998a; Department of Health 1998b). In practice, therefore, the high-level objective of improving health will be proxied by objectives which health authorities can reasonably influence in day-to-day practice. These objectives could include:

- developing and maintaining a strategic overview of health and health care;
- avoiding adverse publicity;
- establishing good working relationships with partnership organizations;
- enhancing the regional/national prestige of the health authority;
- assessing health needs and planning services accordingly;
- allocating resources equitably;
- setting and monitoring performance targets;
- overseeing clinical governance arrangements;
- improving the evidence base upon which commissioning decisions are made;
- listening and responding to the views of the public.

These objectives are neither exhaustive nor mutually exclusive – for example, avoiding adverse publicity can be achieved partly by establishing good working relationships with GPs, hospitals and local authorities. They are largely process objectives, illustrating the difficulty in specifying measurable, tangible, outcome-based objectives. The new *National Framework for Assessing Performance* (NHS Executive 1998c) contains many indicators which are aimed at providing a more 'rounded' view of performance, but in practice these will indicate direction of travel towards improved quality of care rather than health outcomes.

The political dimension should not be underestimated. The weight attached to different objectives by health authority chief executives will vary depending upon the latest ministerial pronouncements. If the key measure of performance is announced to be a reduction in the size of the waiting-list pool or average waiting times, then considerable emphasis will be placed on achieving this objective. Political goals change frequently and will have a direct impact on the *weight* placed on different process objectives. Arguably, however, the above list of objectives would remain robust in terms of the health authority's long-term role, since all are central to the development of the HImP and the discharge of its statutory duties.

These require that health authorities develop relationships and coordinate work across a range of organizations. Also required is a careful and systematic approach to prioritization decisions; accountability for such decisions will have to at least be informed by the available evidence base if clinical governance is to be implemented successfully. Planning the range and location of services in partnership with other organizations, and identifying the underlying investment required, are major challenges for the new health authorities in meeting the above objectives. In addition, the whole issue of measuring impact must be addressed through the performance assessment process, interpreted broadly to include aspects of quality as well as financial measures.

Developing financial strategy to support the HImP and ensuring equitable resource allocation to PCGs will remain central elements of the health authority's role. Issues around resource allocation and financial accountability have been discussed in more detail elsewhere (Bevan 1998), drawing upon lessons from the evaluation of TPPs. It is the new focus – upon accountability for quality of clinical care – which is considered in more detail in the remainder of this chapter. This requires a fundamental shift in thinking and culture in the NHS, recognizing that:

- long-term relationships must be developed with partner organizations based on common objectives;
- the evidence base can at least partially inform prioritization decisions;
- equity considerations may conflict with approaches based on efficiency criteria;

- managing changes in (clinical) practice is inherently complex;
- there will be many barriers/constraints to the change process.

Developing relationships and coordinating work across organizations

The health authority's new role can be characterized as leading the development of health strategy. Hickson *et al.* (1986) note that strategic decisions involve numerous parties within and outside firms, whereby the more parties are involved, the greater the likelihood of serious conflicts of interest. This insight is highly relevant to the NHS from even a cursory glance at the different partners with which health authorities have to engage in developing their HImPs: 'NHS Trusts, Primary Care Groups, other primary care professionals such as dentists, opticians and pharmacists, the public and other partner organisations' (Department of Health 1989, para. 4.7: 26).

The strength of the White Paper proposals (Department of Health 1997) lies in the recognition that the development of such relationships takes time and commitment from all sides. As Besanko *et al.* (1996: 754) point out, however, commitment 'presumes some stability in the firm's strategic environment, so that the firm can persist in its strategic activities long enough to recoup its investments'. In the context of the NHS, the health authority ('the firm') can only 'recoup its investments' (in time and resources to develop the necessary relationships) if a long-term view is taken of the strategies required to improve health. What is not intrinsic to the NHS is any degree of stability in the 'strategic environment', which is heavily dominated by political influences. Health authorities will have to adopt a robust position with regard to their long-term objectives and not be deflected off course by changes in rhetoric and labels. For instance, improving the quality of health care delivered can only be achieved if this is viewed as a long-term objective towards improving health, to which all partnership organizations are committed.

The potentially conflicting interests of different organizations will have a direct impact on the objectives of the health authority, since in improving the high-level objective of pursuing the health of its resident population, account will have to be taken of the objectives of those organizations. In formal terms there is a significant externality problem by which the ability of the health authority to pursue its objectives will be influenced heavily by the behaviour of organizations. Indeed, it could reasonably be argued that the health authority can *only* achieve its high-level objective if the interests of other organizations can be aligned with its own. Although not stated in formal economic terms, this is the rationale behind the HImP and the policy guidance that all parties must be in agreement regarding the content of the Programme.[4]

This intended alignment of objectives can perhaps be seen most explicitly in the guidance on establishing PCGs (NHS Executive 1998e). The initial step of establishing Level 1 and 2 PCGs will involve operating these as subcommittees of the health authority, reinforcing the statutory accountability element stated in the White Paper (Department of Health 1997). Indeed, the chief executive of the health authority is the accountable officer 'and must ensure that proper arrangements are in place for ensuring that the Primary Care Group operates within the authority it has been delegated' (NHS Executive 1998e, para. 30: 11). In effect the PCG will operate as the agent of the health authority.

There is not space to consider the conflicting objectives and incentives even *within* PCGs: suffice to say that an individual PCG is itself not a homogeneous unit, since it represents the views of a wide range of practices and health care professionals. Also relevant will be the attitudes of different health authorities, to the extent that a 'command and control' or a *laissez-faire* approach is taken towards the development of PCGs. *A priori* it would be expected that PCGs would be constrained as subcommittees of the health authority (confirmed by experience from the evaluation of total purchasing – see Dixon *et al.* 1998), although in practice this will depend on behavioural factors and the extent to which the objectives of different organizations can be aligned.

Prioritization decisions

There is strong evidence from case studies that health authorities will have as a key objective the avoidance of adverse publicity. A recent case (Dyer 1998) concerned the treatment of multiple sclerosis patients with interferon beta, whereby the High Court ruled that North Derbyshire Health Authority had acted unlawfully in denying a patient drug treatment:

> Mr Justice Dyson stated that the Health Authority had knowingly imposed what was in effect a blanket ban on the use of the drug, *despite guidance in an NHS circular on making it*

available through hospitals. A blanket ban was the very antithesis of national policy, whose aim was to target the drug at patients who could most benefit from the treatment.

(Dyer 1998: 146, emphasis added)

What this reinforces is that cases in which health authorities' decisions are called into question will hinge upon procedural issues concerning *how* a decision is made, rather than the content of the decision itself. In this instance the judgement appears to hinge on the extent to which the health authority followed guidance contained in the relevant NHS circular. In other words, the imposition of what was in effect a blanket ban on the use of interferon beta[5] was viewed as being at odds with the stated national policy of targeting the drug on the basis of 'capacity to benefit'. The content of the decision – that is, whether the individual in question who was denied treatment would actually have benefited from the drug – appears to have been of secondary importance to the judgement.

The rights and wrongs of this case are not for debate here. What is interesting is the conflict of objectives faced by health authorities. *If* in the interferon beta case North Derbyshire Health Authority could have proved beyond all reasonable doubt that the patient who was denied treatment would in fact *not* have benefited from the drug – citing evidence from several hypothetical randomized controlled trials (RCTs) – then presumably the judge would still have found against the health authority, on the basis that its actions were at odds with national policy guidance. In reality, health authorities will inevitably compromise their high-level objective of improving health at the expense of avoiding such adverse publicity.

A second example reinforces the difficulties which arise for purchasers in the absence of evidence from well-designed RCTs. This was highlighted by the debate on sleep apnoea in the *Lancet* and the *British Medical Journal*. The case is instructive because it highlights the important distinction between the efficacy (largely the concern of the individual clinician) and the effectiveness (largely the concern of the purchaser) of treatment. In the *Lancet* article, Stradling (1997) frequently refers to the efficacy of continuous positive airways pressure (CPAP) in the management of patients with obstructive sleep apnoea (Stradling 1997).[6] In the *British Medical Journal* two months later, Wright *et al.* (1997) reported the results of a systematic review of the effectiveness of CPAP. The authors concluded that: 'there is a paucity of robust evidence for the clinical and cost-effectiveness of CPAP in the treatment of most patients with sleep apnoea' (Wright *et al.* 1997: 857). Despite the vigorous defence of CPAP by Stradling – who argued that North Yorkshire Health Authority had in effect 'misused evidence-based medicine' by advising local GPs that there was 'doubt as to the clinical significance of sleep apnoea and of benefit from nasal CPAP' (Stradling 1997: 201) – the two positions are not irreconcilable.

One position is arguing that sleep apnoea is efficacious for some patients. The other position is based on the wider consideration of whether the health effects of nasal CPAP for patients with obstructive sleep apnoea are sufficiently important to justify significant investment. That is, what are the clinical and cost-effectiveness arguments for giving priority to CPAP as opposed to all of the other competing priorities faced by the health authority? Given that the systematic review concluded that 'the evidence for a causal association between sleep apnoea and other adverse health outcomes is weak' (Wright *et al.* 1997: 857), it is reasonable to question whether nasal CPAP should be funded in preference to other interventions. For example, the review proposes RCTs of CPAP versus effective weight reduction programmes. From the patient's perspective, this may be desirable given the 'unpleasant aspects of this nightly treatment [nasal CPAP]', as recognized by Stradling himself (1997: 201).

This debate highlights a common theme from many systematic reviews of research evidence: *the absence of good evidence is different from saying that a treatment does no good.* It also raises the fundamental question of how far cost-effectiveness evidence should be taken into account in the commissioning decisions which health authorities and PCGs will have to make. The immediate policy implication of the North Derbyshire Health Authority interferon beta case was that: 'Those health authorities in a similar position to North Derbyshire will now need to review their policies. If additional money is to be spent on interferon beta, it will mean taking cash from some other sources'. (Dyer 1998: 146, quoting Stephen Thornton, chief executive of Cambridge & Huntingdon Health Authority).

In short, health authorities which attempt to take into account evidence based health care (EBHC) in their commissioning decisions, however rational and well-intended, run a substantial risk of adverse publicity which outweighs the possible benefits of explicit rationing. It is not surprising that the present government, while advocating strongly the use of EBHC (to be reinforced through initiatives such as NICE and the National Commission for Health

Improvement), has stopped short of a call for explicit rationing. This is despite a relatively recent London conference, where in open debate a multi-disciplinary audience of doctors, patients and health service managers voted overwhelmingly in favour of the motion that 'the government has an obligation to take a lead in rationing' (Kennedy *et al.* 1997: 147).

The issue will not disappear and several cases have highlighted the dilemmas faced by health authorities. Recent examples include the use of statins (lipid-lowering drugs) in the primary and secondary prevention of ischaemic heart disease. Freemantle *et al.* (1997: 826) describe the Standing Medical Advisory Committee (SMAC) guidance on the use of statins as a 'case of misleading priorities', since it fails to link costs and benefits (effectiveness) information. Regardless of the merits or otherwise of the SMAC guidance, the question for health authorities will be at which groups of patients statins should be targeted, on the grounds of both appropriateness and *cost*-effectiveness. Similarly, the dilemma faced by the Department of Health in the absence of a systematic process for the economic evaluation of new drugs is highlighted by the indecision over how to deal with the introduction of Sildenafil (Viagra), culminating in interim guidance (NHS Executive 1998b) advising health authorities not to support the drug's provision at NHS expense.

All of these examples highlight the same fundamental dilemma: what incentives are there for health authorities to inform their own and PCGs' commissioning decisions with the best available evidence on clinical and cost-effectiveness? The answer lies potentially in the implementation of initiatives on clinical guidelines, national service frameworks and the new emphasis on clinical governance. These provide the incentive to place quality at the heart of the health care agenda. There will be a need, however, for the NHS Executive to explore in great depth the socio-legal implications of commissioning decisions *which will increasingly be based on the work of bodies such as NICE*. The implications of implementing such work sit somewhat uneasily with the government's commitment that GPs' clinical 'freedom to refer and prescribe remains unchanged' by the introduction of PCGs (letter from Alan Milburn to Dr John Chisholm 1998).

Chief executives of health authorities, both in their traditional role and as the accountable officers of PCGs, will need to be reassured that a consistent approach will be taken (if necessary by the courts through the process of judicial review) to reviewing commissioning decisions which are based on nationally available evidence of clinical and cost-effectiveness. The absence of much case law in the area of health care prioritization decisions does not help in this respect, given that legal precedent will presumably be the key determinant in judging the outcome of specific cases. The position of health authorities is akin to that of hospital trusts which face rising patient expectations and possible litigation over individual clinical decisions – hence the incorporation of risk management activities into the wider clinical governance frameworks being developed by trusts. Health authorities and PCGs will face parallel considerations in the decisions which they take at a population level, strengthening the argument for a consistent accountability framework which supports evidence-based commissioning decisions.

Equity considerations

The unquestioning application of EBHC in the context of improving health is an unsatisfactory description of the health authority's role for several reasons, one of which is that equity considerations are typically ignored by such an approach. The EBHC movement is based on a belief that health will be improved (or maximized) if decisions are made on the basis of robust clinical and cost-effectiveness evidence.[7] That is, allocative efficiency in the health care sector will be enhanced. This, however, does not deal with the distribution of health benefits across different groups of society.

Harrison (1998) notes that an approach based on maximizing total health gain may well produce different results from an approach which gives greater weight to the distribution of health benefits (the classic efficiency/equity trade-off). It is important to bear in mind that some notions of equity treat health care as partly an end in itself, a principle which is embodied in the founding principle of the NHS ('equal access for equal need regardless of ability to pay'). The evidence-based approach is underpinned by the criterion of (cost-) effectiveness, and would clearly be at odds with an approach based on the principle of equal access to health care being the predominant criterion for resource allocation.

The efficiency/equity trade-off in health care is hardly new, but raises two important issues for health authorities in their new role. First, if they are to take seriously the issue of patient and public involvement, equity considerations may have to be given more weight than would be implicit in the evidence-based approach. Policy formulation will need to consider both efficiency and equity, but the question of whose views should count as to the respective weights should be the subject of debate with local populations. Second, there will be a strong political imperative for health authorities to give prominence to equity considerations in their role as allocators of resources to PCGs. This will be required to avoid any repeat of the claims after the 1989 reforms that GP fundholding led to a two-tier system of access to waiting lists and 'cream-skimming'. Health authorities will have to ensure a fair process of local resource allocation, and frequently this will involve a more process-orientated interpretation of equity (e.g. equity of access to hospital services) than an approach based on maximizing health or ensuring some notion of equitable outcome for equal need.

It is also worth noting the caveat that:

> the evidence-based approach, dominated by a focus on health outcomes from health care interventions, overlooks the notion that society is not a 'level playing field'. Policies aimed at maximising health outcomes ... risk redeploying resources inefficiently and in ways which systematically favour those groups with favourable 'prospects for health'.
>
> (Birch, 1997: 556)

Health authorities in their future role cannot afford to ignore this, and must balance the need for an evidence-based approach against the other criteria which decision makers and the public consider to be important.

It is a timely reminder (Birch 1997) that making health care decisions on the basis of the best available information is simply one normative position which can be taken. If the distribution of health benefits is made more unequal by overemphasizing such an approach, then health authorities will be judged to have failed in delivering at least some of the wider social goals of the latest NHS reforms. The encouragement of joint strategies between health and social care will reinforce the need to consider alternative paradigms such as 'entitlement' or the 'rescue principle' (Harrison 1998), which are likely to lead to different policies than those based solely on considerations of clinical and cost-effectiveness.

Changing clinical practice

If the shifting balance of power towards purchasers is to bring about real benefits to health authorities' resident populations, then changes in culture have to be achieved throughout different care settings. The implementation of EBHC involves the application of important principles, but it is naive to assume that simply collecting and disseminating scientific evidence will bring about the necessary changes in behaviour. Even where the evidence has been reviewed systematically, there often remain disagreements about the nature of the evidence and the conclusions drawn by those undertaking the reviews, as well as about the validity of recommendations in local circumstances. The Walshe and Ham (1997) survey of the impact of selected *Effective Health Care* bulletins is instructive in this respect. For example, in the bulletin which recommended the use of transurethral incision of the prostate (TUIP) in the treatment of benign prostatic hyperplasia, the authors found that the vast majority of clinicians working in urology services did not agree with the bulletin's recommendations. Not surprisingly, therefore, the survey found that only 12 per cent of trusts planned to change their practice accordingly and 'virtually no Health Authorities had incorporated this recommendation [to use TUIP as the preferred operation of choice] into their contracts with providers of urology services' (Walshe and Ham 1997: 27).

This does not necessarily mean that this particular bulletin's conclusions were incorrect. It does illustrate, however, the near-impossible task of changing clinical practice if the evidence is insufficiently robust. A further criterion is perhaps the extent to which the evidence meets with accepted clinical practice. This is a controversial area, since there is no universal definition of what is 'accepted practice', and there is a danger that efforts to challenge accepted clinical practice on the basis of sound evidence meet with resistance for the wrong reasons. This reinforces the conflict between the use of population-derived data from systematic reviews and the use of such information for helping clinicians make decisions with individual patients. As health authorities and PCGs begin to implement national service frameworks and the findings from NICE, this tension needs to be recognized and managed carefully in discussions with local providers.

There is no single solution to the issue of bringing about desired changes in clinical practice. However, certain structural and process changes in the health care system may help. First, a move away from the annual contracting round, with agreements increasingly based on a longer-term strategic view of service configuration, will hopefully shift attention towards quality of care and health outcomes, and away from the 'head counts' of finished consultant episodes and client contacts. Second, the process of integrating research evidence, routine information analysis, clinical guidelines, education and training, clinical audit and service specifications (and the structures in health authorities and trusts to support these) should ensure that a coordinated approach is taken to implementing clinical governance. Third, coordination of health authority and PCG commissioning should help to integrate work at the interfaces between primary, secondary and community care (in particular if health authority and local authority decisions can equally be coordinated). Viewing care in this genuinely integrated way is not typical in the NHS, despite years of rhetoric about 'seamless care' and 'integrated care packages'.

Finally, and perhaps most important, basing the purchaser/provider relationship on cooperation rather than competition (Goddard and Mannion 1998) could have far-reaching effects in attempting to develop a common, evidence-based approach. This process would be assisted by the involvement of key clinicians in drawing up service agreements. It seems eminently sensible that local experts in particular fields should be involved in a process which is intended to bring together many diverse aspects of 'quality', including the local implementation of national guidelines.

Barriers to change

Even where the research evidence is considered robust and results valid in a local context, routine information systems are often inadequate. For example, obtaining accurate and timely casemix analyses from hospital data remains problematic. Variations in practice between hospital clinicians – an inevitable feature of practice and differing caseloads/casemixes – remain largely 'not talked about'. The White Paper (Department of Health 1997) refers to the need to identify 'poor clinical performance' at an early stage; doing so will require a greater sharing of information between purchaser and provider and a more open dialogue about individual clinician performance. A major barrier to making progress in this area is the paucity of existing hospital coding systems to ensure accurate diagnostic and procedure code data.

There are limits to evidence-based health care. At its worst it has been described as 'cook-book medicine' (Hayward 1994). Guidelines should be perceived as precisely that: guidance based on recognized best practice, but with an understanding that they have to be tailored to the needs of individual patients. The blind application of guidelines and protocols makes the false assumption that medicine is an exact science – for example, that diagnosis is always accurate and not subject to bias or uncertainty.[8] Even where an accurate diagnosis has been made, there remain many factors influencing the individual clinician's decision – for example, the probability of particular outcomes, the valuation of possible different outcomes and the willingness to live with a degree of risk (McKee and Clarke 1995). A key problem is that, in advance of providing treatment to a particular patient, likely outcomes can only be expressed in terms of probabilities applicable to a defined population. The outcome for an individual patient is uncertain, and the nature of probability distributions is such that there will almost certainly be one patient who will benefit from a treatment which the research evidence has 'proved' to be ineffective for a defined population.

All of these arguments are valid, but should not be used as an excuse for health authorities and PCGs to avoid an evidence-based approach. If specific treatments are undertaken for particular patients where the evidence base is weak, there should nevertheless be good reasons for doing so. It is also in trusts' interests to deal with this process explicitly, with hospital risk management and clinical audit programmes seen as integral to the emerging clinical governance agenda.

The issue of patient expectations is closely related to the areas of clinical uncertainty and risk management. The 'health care information industry' runs the risk of increasing patient expectations still further. More and more people will gain access to relevant sources of information on the Internet, information which can be used to influence or challenge the clinical decision. Clinicians, and hospitals in general, will be fearful of litigation and the development of an integrated approach to clinical audit, clinical effectiveness and risk management is essential. There will be situations where individual patients demand treatments which are of uncertain, unproven benefit. Problems will inevitably arise if one clinician has provided such a treatment for one patient and another patient is denied similar treatment. As far as possible, there should be consistent use of guidelines and accurate recording of information (e.g. diagnosis, patient characteristics and risk factors), together with an effective audit process, to minimize the degree of uncertainty in the exercise of clinical judgement. The health authority will have to tread a fine line between providing the best information to patients to allow genuinely informed choice about preferred courses of treatment, and supporting providers and other purchasers in managing expectations where the evidence base is weak.

Achieving improvements in the quality of care is only one aspect of performance on which health authorities and trusts will be judged. There is considerable scope for conflicting incentives in practice, as the following passage illustrates:

> the much criticised Efficiency Index rewards needless clinical activity and punishes watchful waiting . . . some of these perverse incentives to ineffective clinical practice need to be removed. Ideally, new measures which recognise and reward effective clinical practice should be put in their place.
>
> (Walshe and Ham 1997: 34)

Where health authorities face clearly conflicting incentives – for example, where a relatively ineffective treatment is not being reduced and finished consultant episodes in the relevant specialty are rising, this needs to be detected and recognized within the new performance assessment framework (NHS Executive 1998c). In practice it is unclear how new indicators of NHS trusts' financial performance, such as the National Schedule of Reference Costs (NHS Executive 1998c), will be used alongside indicators of quality to produce broader measures of efficiency, and how the possibility of conflicting incentives will be resolved.

NOTES

1 For an excellent discussion of the whole issue of public law and health service accountability, see Longley (1993). In addition, Allen (1997) focuses upon the legal framework of the NHS internal market, with an informative discussion of the nature of NHS 'contracts' and the process of conciliation in the resolution of contractual disputes.
2 Although not in the legal sense of the term 'agent', since there is no legally binding contract of agency between them (Allen 1997).
3 See Department of Health (1997, para. 4.3: 25) for a fuller description.
4 The consistency in style and tone of the latest social services White Paper (Department of Health 1998b) is helpful in this respect.
5 The health authority adopted the policy that the drug would not be made available outside a clinical trial, and continued to refuse payment when informed that a proposed national trial had been postponed indefinitely.
6 As a result, Stradling (1997: 201) concludes that CPAP is simple and 'unarguably technically effective', and that 'there is abundant evidence for the efficacy of nasal CPAP'.
7 The weight attached to cost-effectiveness information by proponents of

evidence-based health care will differ according to disciplinary background.
8 There is not space here to rehearse all of the important arguments on this subject. An excellent summary is provided in McKee and Clarke (1995), 'Guidelines, enthusiasms, uncertainty, and the limits to purchasing'.

REFERENCES

Allen, P. (1997). Legal framework of the NHS internal market. In B.A. Ferguson, T.A. Sheldon and J.W. Posnett (eds), *Concentration and Choice in Healthcare*. London: *Financial Times* Healthcare.

Besanko, D., Dranove, D. and Shanley, M. (1996). *Economics of Strategy*. Chichester: John Wiley.

Bevan, G. (1998). *Resource Allocation Within Health Authorities: Lessons from Total Purchasing Pilots*, National Evaluation of Total Purchasing Pilot Projects Working Paper. London: King's Fund Institute.

Birch, S. (1997). As a matter of fact: evidence-based decision-making unplugged. *Health Economics*, 6, 547–59.

Black, N. (1998). Clinical governance: fine words or action? *British Medical Journal*, 316, 297–8.

Department of Health (1989). *Working for Patients*. London: The Stationery Office.

Department of Health (1997). *The New NHS: Modern, Dependable*. London: The Stationery Office.

Department of Health (1998a). *Modernising Health and Social Services: National Priorities Guidance 1999/00–2001/02*. London: Department of Health.

Department of Health (1998b). *Modernising Social Services: Promoting Independence, Improving Protection, Raising Standards*. London: The Stationery Office.

Department of Health (1998c). *NHS to Have Legal Duty of Ensuring Quality for First Time – Milburn*. Press Release, Monday 13 April.

Dixon, J., Goodwin, N. and Mays, N. (1998). *Accountability of Total Purchasing Pilot Projects*, National Evaluation of Total Purchasing Pilot Projects Working Paper. London: King's Fund Institute.

Dyer, C. (1998). Ruling on interferon beta will hit all health authorities. *British Medical Journal*, 315, 146.

Ferguson, B.A. and Smith, P. (1997). Health care financing in the United Kingdom National Health Service. In A. Stepan (ed.) *Finanzierungssysteme im Gesundheitswesen: ein internationaler Vergleich*, pp. 89–110. Vienna: Manz.

Financial Times (1998). Blair to scrap annual public spending round, 24 April.

Freemantle, N., Barbour, R., Johnson, R., Marchment, M. and Kennedy, A. (1997). The use of statins: a case of misleading priorities? *British Medical Journal*, 315, 826–8.

Goddard, M. and Mannion, R. (1998). From competition to co-operation: new economic relationships in the National Health Service. *Health Economics*, 7, 105–19.

Goodwin, N., Mays, N., McLeod, H., Malbon, G. and Raftery, J. (1998). Evaluation of total purchasing pilots in England and Scotland and implications for primary care groups in England: personal interviews and analysis of routine data. *British Medical Journal*, 317, 256–9.

Griffiths, S. (1998). From health care to health. *British Medical Journal*, 316, 300–1.

Harrison, S. (1998). The politics of evidence-based medicine in the United Kingdom. *Policy and Politics*, 26(1), 15–31.

Hayward, J. (1994). Purchasing clinical effectiveness. *British Medical Journal*, 309, 823–4.

Hickson, D.J., Butler, R.J., Gray, D., Mallory, G.R. and Wilson, D.C. (1986). *Top Decisions: Strategic Decision-Making in Organisations*. San Francisco, CA: Jossey-Bass.

IHSM (Institute of Health Services Management) (1997). *Health and Social Services Yearbook 1997/98*. London: IHSM.

Kennedy, I., Levvy, G., Macara, S. *et al.* (1997) Dear Mr Dobson . . . *British Medical Journal*, 315, 147.

Longley, D. (1993). *Public Law and Health Service Accountability*. Buckingham: Open University Press.

McKee, M. and Clarke, A. (1995). Guidelines, enthusiasms, uncertainty, and the limits to purchasing. *British Medical Journal*, 310, 101–4.

NAHAT (National Association of Health Authorities) (1995) *NHS Handbook 1995/96*. Tunbridge Wells: JMH Publishing.

NHS Executive (1997). *Priorities and Planning Guidance for the NHS: 1998/99* (EL(97)39). London: DoH.

NHS Executive (1998a). *Reference Costs: A Consultation Document*. London: DoH.

NHS Executive (1998b). *Sildenafil (Viagra)*, (Health Services Circular 158). London: DoH.

NHS Executive (1998c). *The New NHS Modern and Dependable: A National Framework for Assessing Performance – A Consultation Document* (EL(98)4). London: DoH.

NHS Executive (1998d). *The New NHS Modern and Dependable: Developing Primary Care Groups*, Health Service Circular 139. London: DoH.

NHS Executive (1998e). *The New NHS Modern and Dependable: Establishing Primary Care Groups*, Health Service Circular 065. London: DoH.

Stradling, J. (1997). Sleep apnoea and the misuse of evidence-based medicine. *Lancet*, 394, 201–2.

Wade, H.W.R. (1971). *Administrative Law*. Oxford: Clarendon Press.

Walshe, K. and Ham, C. (1997). *Acting on the Evidence: Progress in the NHS*. Birmingham: NHS Confederation.

Wright, J., Johns, R., Watt, I., Melville, A. and Sheldon, T. (1997). Health effects of obstructive sleep apnoea and the effectiveness of continuous positive airways pressure: a systematic review of the research evidence. *British Medical Journal*, 314, 851–60.

6

ECONOMICS AND PUBLIC POLICY: RESEARCH AND DEVELOPMENT AS A PUBLIC GOOD

Tony Culyer

INTRODUCTION

The research and development (R&D) supported by the National Health Service (NHS) (most of which is also done within NHS institutions) has intriguing characteristics. Three were highlighted by Arrow (1962) but may be added to. Attributes of R&D considered here are:

- it is a public good;
- it has considerable potential for supplier-induced demand (induced, that is, by the suppliers of R&D rather than the suppliers of health services);
- there are all-pervading information asymmetries;
- there is some joint production in health care and R&D;
- funding comes from a diversity of sources having both complementary and competing objectives;
- the output and value of R&D is inherently uncertain;
- the measurement of outcome is in its infancy;
- R&D is, moreover, largely undertaken within non-profit institutions whose motivation and efficiency is poorly understood and whose behaviour is difficult to predict.

Each of these issues merits an essay in its own right. Here, the focus will be on these factors as elements that have helped to shape the recent arrangements established by government for supporting R&D in the NHS.

In the 1990s two major developments had a dramatic impact on the organization and character of research in and for the NHS. One was the creation in 1991 of the Research and Development Strategy for the NHS (Department of Health 1991). The other was the task force report on supporting R&D in the NHS (Culyer 1994), which led to a substantial overhaul of the methods by which R&D in and for the NHS is funded at the institutional level. Both grew out of concerns with the arrangements that preceded them and both provide illustrations of practical ways in which the demand and supply of a public good (R&D) can operate within a quasi-market structure designed *a priori* to optimize output. This chapter begins by outlining the particular analytical characteristics of R&D in health care which are common to all systems. It then describes the particular UK arrangements that preceded the new developments and the evidence for their unsatisfactory working. The new arrangements are then described and discussed. Finally, there is a preliminary assessment of their working – it is as yet too soon to attempt a comprehensive assessment of their cost-effectiveness.

THE SPECIAL CHARACTERISTICS OF R&D IN HEALTH CARE

Publicness

While some R&D undertaken within the NHS is largely private rather than public in character (for example, that supported by pharmaceutical firms) much else has the characteristic of 'publicness'. It has been a long-standing convention in the NHS that 'commercial' research (such as that funded by pharmaceutical firms) should cover its full costs and receive no public subsidy. While there are issues concerning the identification of these 'full' costs, the role and finance of such R&D is not discussed in this chapter, whose focus is on that research which has a public-good character.

The classic definition of a public good is that by Samuelson (1954: 387): 'Each individual's consumption of such a good leads to no subtraction from any other individual's consumption'. A similar definition can be found in Samuelson (1955: 350): 'Each man's consumption of it . . . is related to the total . . . by a condition of equality rather than of summation'. Thus, a public good, if provided for one, is also provided for all (though each may attach a different utility to it).

This defines the purely public end of what is often a spectrum or degree of 'publicness' and 'privateness', in which intermediate points are characterized by some diminution of others' consumption, though by less than the amount consumed by another (as when a public facility becomes congested), or when there are relatively few who value the good highly enough to want to consume it under any circumstances (as when the public good is essentially local in character). It also makes plain that the character of publicness is a technical characteristic of the good in question rather than an artefact of the particular arrangements in existence for its production and distribution. It is the technical character of the demand for the good rather than its production that defines publicness. The idea that a public good can be defined in terms of exclusion (Musgrave 1959) is somewhat different, though also demand-based. It defines publicness (or a 'social want') in terms of whether a consumer can be excluded from the benefits of a good by not being required to pay a contribution or price towards it (Musgrave 1959: 9). Later, another (supply-based) definition given by Musgrave is those goods whose 'inherent quality is such that they cannot be left to private suppliers' (p. 43). Samuelson's technical definition (1954) is that used here.

R&D in health care, whether biomedical or applied social science, has the characteristics of a public good. Once done, it is available to society as a whole at zero additional marginal cost of production (though accessing and using it is costly), and the use of it by one 'consumer' does not diminish the 'amount' left for others to use. Its benefits accrue to a wide variety of individuals and institutions: most directly to those who manage and deliver health care but, more ultimately, to the consumers of health care themselves. While it is possible to establish exchangeable property rights in the information produced by R&D through intellectual property rights and patents, in general this has not been seen as desirable in the case of NHS supported R&D. This is on the grounds that publication is one of the major mechanisms through which quality control is exercised via peer review, and because future research productivity is dependent upon what has gone before. Even when the outcome of research commissioned by a public body, such as the Department of Health or the NHS, is held privately by the commissioners, it retains its technical demand-side character as a public good. The fact that some are excluded from its use through secrecy about its existence or through intellectual property right constraints on its dissemination reflects social artefacts that in no way detract from the technical character of the good.

R&D approximates, therefore, to the 'pure' end of the spectrum of publicness. Several problems immediately arise out of this publicness of R&D. One is that mechanisms for revealing the (public) demand for R&D are required. A second is the creation of mechanisms for valuing and prioritizing the R&D projects and programmes to be supported and to determine the appropriate level of resourcing each should have. A third is the determination of the overall resource commitment to NHS R&D in general. Crossing all of these issues is a more fundamental one: should the broad character of the mechanisms for solving these problems be a central mechanism, or should there be substantial devolution of demand mechanisms in, for example, the form of quasi-markets in which the demand side is revealed by local commissioning agencies such as health authorities or regional offices of the NHS Executive?

Supplier-induced demand

A second characteristic of health care R&D is the dominant role traditionally played in it by researchers themselves. The suppliers of R&D have a practical role in formulating the demand for R&D, – for example, by sorting questions into those that are researchable and those that are not, in developing protocols, in commissioning work, and in assessing the quality of what is done. Many may also have a shrewd appreciation of the kind of work that is needed in the NHS, through long acquaintance with its working. On the other hand, researchers also have their own research agendas and this provides the potential for supplier-induced demand. They tend to have a preference for curiosity-driven research, have in mind the criteria of their immediate peers in such matters as promotion in universities and hospitals, and most would prefer to set their own standards of excellence to having standards thrust upon them. They are also likely always to want 'more' regardless of whether 'more' would be optimal from any wider social perspective. These values lie deep within the academic culture, doubtless partly driven by the liberal values of universities, forged largely in the nineteenth century. Another reason is that there has never been any systematic way in which the ultimate funders of university research can direct the ways in which generic research funding is used towards, for example, the government's perceptions of what was most needed in social research.

One expects the research community, as suppliers of R&D, to induce demand whenever they can, and to give it a bias towards the particular agendas they have as curious people and people with careers to promote. It therefore becomes important to ensure that the mechanisms for revealing the NHS demand for R&D, and for supplying it, are not contaminated by factors and interests that are not relevant in determining the optimal supply of this public good. Such mechanisms must also be without prejudice to the wider public interest in having free institutions with a major part of their activity devoted to programmes of work determined by academic priorities.

Information asymmetries

Information asymmetries are all-pervasive in health care R&D. One kind – the ability to distinguish between an important question and an important *researchable* question – has already been mentioned. Managers may be good at the former and researchers bad at it; researchers are usually good at the latter and managers bad. Each possesses specialized information that the other does not. Another asymmetry is that between commissioners and doers of research. Doers will generally have a better idea of the character of the detailed work they will be doing, and of its quality, than commissioners. This asymmetry can give rise to inefficiencies from both sides. Without mechanisms to overcome the problem, commissioners may commission poor work (and may not even recognize poor work when it is done); researchers may use the information gap between them and their commissioners to pursue interests which are contrary to those of the commissioners but nonetheless at their expense.

Joint production

A fourth characteristic of R&D in health care is joint production. This is particularly prevalent in research that uses patients. The patient in a research institution is there to receive care, funded as a frontline service. The research will often require additional or specially varied patient treatment packages, arising solely because of the research. The issue then arises: are the costs of treatment costs of research or of patient care? The problem is directly analogous to the classic textbook example of wool and mutton: is the cost of the sheep's fodder the cost of the wool or of the mutton? There is no analytical answer to this question – though the question of the cost of an additional kilo of meat or wool may be answerable.

Arbitrary decisions about the appropriateness of R&D cost esti-mates, like those for service costs, need to be avoided. The solution consists in the development of methods of cost accounting that do not distort decisions about either care or research, and that do not provide systematic incentives for strategic, self-serving behaviour by the various players in the system. Although direct analytical solutions to this problem may elude us, it ought in principle to be possible to design institutional and behavioural arrangements that produce the desired outcomes. In the case of private goods, the jointness of wool and meat production does not prevent a solution that in most cases probably approximates to the optimum or at least a second-best optimum. The question then arises whether a quasi-market arrangement might not achieve something similar for NHS R&D.

Multiplicity of funding sources

Health-related R&D is usually funded by a multiplicity of sources. In the UK, these include government departments, the Higher Education Funding Councils, the NHS itself, industry, research councils (mainly the Medical Research Council and the Economic and Social Research Council), and a large number of medical research charities. Each typically has specific objectives which differ. For example, some emphasize the 'science' end of research, others more applied health services research, others will not sup-port cancer-related R&D; while others *only* cancer-related R&D. The availability of a wide variety of different sources for funding research is a protection for research institutions having a (wise) policy of diversifying their funding sources. However, there is no automatic mechanism through which complementarities between funders can be addressed (even obtaining information about differ-ent funders' plans is a highly costly activity) and no means of identi-fying overlaps, duplications and gaps in coverage. This is partly a problem of information production and dissemination (itself a public good) and partly a problem of coordinating mechanisms.

Uncertainty of outcome

All research is beset by uncertainty as to the outcome. The project may not 'work'. The researchers selected may not be sufficiently skilled to complete their task. On the upside, research projects may also yield useful outcomes that were not anticipated. Again, a mechanism is therefore required that is not excessively risk-averse, nor short term in the thinking it encourages, and that maximizes the chances at reasonable cost of the work achieving its set objectives.

Measurement of outcome

The measurement of outcome – especially of ultimate outcome which, in the NHS, is the benefit to patients – is hard to characterize and calibrate. It may not always be possible to identify 'success', especially when research is very long term or devises new algorithms for (say) planners and managers. Mechanisms are therefore required to enable judgements about outcomes to be made as best as is possible under the circumstances – making them as near to the ultimate benefit as possible and using intermediate outcomes that are themselves useful and which may be good indicators of likely final benefit. Ultimately, one expects the value of R&D outcomes to determine (assuming that R&D resources are efficiently allocated) the overall level of resource commitment to NHS R&D, which is currently running at something under 1.5 per cent of the total.

Non-profit institutions

R&D is usually performed in non-profit institutions like hospitals and universities, whose internal mechanisms for supporting research may be quite primitive (even absent) and which certainly vary enormously from institution to institution. A mechanism is therefore also needed that systematically provides incentives for the effective internal organization and management of research in institutions.

All R&D systems have to confront and resolve these problems.

R&D IN THE NHS PRIOR TO THE CHANGES OF THE 1990s

The NHS Research and Development Programme was the direct result of the House of Lords Select Committee on Science and Technology report, *Priorities in Medical Research* (House of Lords 1988). This advocated the creation of a National Health Research Authority, with a broad brief that included health services research, which was regarded both by the Select Committee and the government as a neglected and deprived area but one of importance for the conduct of public policy. Both felt that the NHS lacked mechanisms for identifying and meeting the NHS's needs for R&D and that, while much research ought to continue to be science-led, there had developed an imbalance in the pattern of research taken as a whole. The Select Committee sought a special health authority in order to keep R&D at arm's length from the Department of Health. The government's response to the report (Department of Health 1989) was to integrate the R&D function within the Department of Health, the NHS Executive and the (then) regional health authorities. It proposed the creation of a new senior post of chief of research and development with a support staff. The new post of director of research and development was created, whose task, as described in the government's *Response* (Department of Health 1989), was to advise the NHS Management Executive (as it was then called) on the priorities for NHS R&D, to manage a programme of R&D to meet identified needs (especially the effectiveness and efficiency of health services) and to disseminate R&D results to managers and clinicians in the NHS. The key parts of the House of Lords recommendations and of the government's response clearly hinged on the publicness of R&D, especially developing mechanisms for revealing the NHS's demand and ensuring that resources for R&D were not hijacked by 'purely' academic and clinical interests.

By 1993, the main elements of the NHS R&D strategy had become clear. It had six objectives, of which the first was 'to contribute to the health and well-being of the population through the conduct and application of relevant and high quality research' (Department of Health 1993: 2). It had also established six structural features of its way of working: national and regional infrastructures for identifying and prioritizing NHS R&D requirements; the initiation of major programmes of work on priorities identified by the central R&D committee as being important to the NHS; a quasi-market mechanism for commissioning R&D via contracts; the development of strategic alliances with other health research funders; a dissemination strategy; and a strategy for research training and career development. The director of R&D had established a central R&D committee, with representatives from the research community, the NHS and (later) consumers of NHS services. Regional programmes attuned to the perceived R&D needs of the regions had been developed from the previous regional arrangements, under regional directors of R&D.

The central programme had two basic elements: a set of national priority areas, each time-limited, on a dozen or so topics (such as mental health, cardiovascular disease and stroke, and cancer) and the Standing Group on Health Technology Assessment – a permanent group operating a programme that directly addressed the central concerns of effectiveness and cost-effectiveness. It was hoped that this would be an engine for generating major culture change in the NHS by promoting a more critically aware pattern of professional service delivery based, wherever possible, on reliable evidence about 'what worked' and at what cost. To begin the task of disseminating this work and other relevant research, the Cochrane Centre at Oxford and the NHS Centre for Reviews and Dissemination at York were established, a process now being taken much further under the new government's policies for the NHS. A national project register, containing information on all R&D of interest to the NHS, was begun (though its subsequent development has been painfully slow). Similarly slow has been the development of mechanisms addressing the training implications of the R&D programme and the capacity requirements of the research community if the needs identified by the programme are to be met (Baker 1998).

The central committee had had several discussions on the definition of R&D but, apart from determining that 'development' ought not to include the service development work conducted by hospitals and others as a part of their normal processes (and which was not, therefore, 'public'), agreed to go no further than define some criteria for funding NHS R&D. These criteria were that funded work should: be designed to provide new knowledge considered necessary to improve the performance of the NHS in enhancing the nation's health (a dimension of publicness); be designed so that the results will be of value to those in the NHS facing similar problems outside the particular locality or context of the project (publicness); follow a clear, well-defined protocol (quality control); have clearly defined arrangements for project management (quality control); have the clear intention to report the findings that are open to critical appraisal (publicness and quality control) (Department of Health 1993).

It was also agreed early that the character of R&D in the NHS was such that final decisions about priorities and commissioning could not be substantially devolved (e.g. to health authorities). This was partly on the grounds of their skill to do the job, partly because of the limited national availability of skills and their highly unequal geographical spread (and the likely demands that would be placed on the people possessing them), and partly because NHS R&D was seen as a public good whose benefits flowed primarily to the entire country.

The commissioning mechanisms used by the R&D strategy are well-illustrated by the work of the Standing Group on Health Technology Assessment (Department of Health 1997d). This supervises the work of six advisory panels, covering the acute sector, diagnostics and imaging, pharmaceuticals, population screening, primary and community care, and methodology. Each panel has academic and NHS membership, observers from the Medical Research Council, Department of Health and the NHS Executive, and each is in the process of acquiring 'consumer' members (who were trialed successfully in the methodology panel!). The potential for consumer participation is discussed in Department of Health (1998). The presence of the methodology panel, and its success in getting a large number of projects funded, is testimony to the breadth of view taken as to the implications of NHS R&D as a public good. The work of this panel is now explicitly addressed to methodological issues across the entire gamut of the R&D programme, whose solution is seen as beneficial to it. It might be seen as a kind of meta-public good devoted to the production of public goods needed in the production of public goods!

Each panel conducts an annual consultation exercise within the Department of Health, the NHS Executive, NHS management, NHS clinicians (including nurses and professions allied to medicine), and the academic community to elicit proposals (1800 in 1997). They are then further sifted by the secretariat in discussion with panel chairs into a total of about 100 topics. These researchable proposals are then further developed, through an iterative process, into 'vignettes' by the secretariat describing the nature of the work required, its likely results, its likely benefits to the NHS and its likely costs. These are then reviewed by each panel, scored into three categories (A: top priority for which proactive methods will be used to commission the work if public calls for bids are not adequate; B: middle priority for which proactive methods will not be used; and C: priority but not to be funded out of the current year's budget). At this stage, the possibility of external or joint support is explored (e.g. with the Medical Research Council) and bids for the work are then sought through an open public bidding process.

The other major departure innovation resulted from the acceptance by the government of the recommendations of the task force report (Culyer 1994) on how best to fund the infrastructure for research in institutions. In 1993, the principal sources by which the R&D of teaching hospitals was funded were diverse and problematic. The largest single source of specific project funding was industry – though there was considerable variance in the quality of this work. There was also the Department of Health's service increment for teaching and research (SIFTR) – the main source of R&D infrastructure support for teaching hospitals but oddly a function of undergraduate student numbers rather than research students or research. This is the principal means through which the secretary of state's statutory obligation to support research in the NHS was fulfilled, a task which has usually been interpreted as an obligation to support Medical Research Council projects in the NHS, and was based on earlier attempts to estimate the cost of: teaching in hospitals (Culyer *et al.* 1978). Other sources were non-SIFTR (the support for a few teaching hospitals with no medical undergraduates); the specially negotiated annual research support for the London postgraduate hospitals; some specifically 'tasked' (earmarked) money for academic general practice research; and the 'own account' research undertaken by hospitals from within the resources provided for them for patient care (research whose quality was often unknown and whose total size of funding was quite unknown). This system had 'growed' like Topsy, mostly as a consequence of problems as they arose. It was medically dominated; it was institution-focused (to the neglect of community-based NHS practice); it was arbitrary (e.g. tying funding to undergraduate numbers); it could not be used as an instrument for enhancing quality or encouraging a focus on the needs of the NHS; there were complaints from researchers that the funding was not actually supporting research; it was impossible to account for it, or to hold anyone *to* account for it; the quality of some of the work supported was alleged to be poor; and it amounted, for the most part, to a general subsidy to institutions (Culyer 1994). Moreover, SIFTR, non-SIFTR and the special arrangements for the London postgraduate hospitals were all very institutionally focused streams of funding. Not only did they exclude all community-based R&D, which was odd since the community had become increasingly the location of health care, but they provided no means of support for partnerships between institutions. For a comprehensive account of the perceived faults of the previous systems, see Culyer (1995, 1998).

Following the introduction of the internal market for patient services, a further problem had arisen for secondary care providers who engaged in 'own account' non-commercially funded research. Since their prices incorporated the costs of such research, they were increasingly at a competitive disadvantage as health authorities and fundholding general practitioners (GPs) sought the least-cost packages from their service contracts. This led to fears of a substantial squeeze on R&D and that 'own account' research funding (though its quality was largely unassessed) would be driven out. The research community in such institutions had made very public its concerns at the one-sided way in which the newly established market was prejudicing R&D in the absence of any corresponding quasi-market structure for R&D. However, and conversely, there were also indications that institutions whose research was relatively well supported were subsidizing patient care prices. The mechanisms then extant afforded little protection against either hazard.

What replaced this miscellany of *ad hoc* measures was radical (see Department of Health 1996a, 1996b, 1997a, 1997b, 1997c). First, the general source of all funding for both the R&D programme itself and the infrastructure support became a levy, along with several others, on health authorities. Since this was a stream of funding that they had never received before, this step alone left them in a financially neutral state. However, it did make clear the opportunity cost of R&D within the system and gave the health authorities, for the first time, a direct stake in the R&D spend. Since a principal function of health authorities is to assess the need of their communities for health care, from now on they had an incentive to identify their R&D needs in pursuit of this function.

Second, a new national forum was created at which all the principal players in the R&D system (the universities, the Higher Education Funding Council for England, the NHS Executive, the relevant research councils, the medical charities and industry) were represented and which could address common issues on both the demand and the supply sides and offer advice both to the NHS director of R&D and their own constituencies.

Third, a new bidding system was introduced to replace SIFTR, non-SIFTR and the special arrangements for the London postgraduate hospitals. Not only institutions could bid for this stream of funding but also consortia – the latter opportunity being particularly directed at community-based service providers with R&D capability, to enable them to collaborate both with other similar groups to achieve scale economies and with established centres of excellence to enhance quality.

Two types of time-limited contract were introduced, called portfolio and task-linked. The first was designed for large institutions with predictable need for Medical Research Council and other non-commercial research support and which has the general form of a block grant with relatively little specific monitoring of specific components or outcomes, thus minimizing contracting costs. The second format was designed for institutions or consortia of community-based practices whose quality and track record was more difficult to ascertain and whose R&D objectives were more tightly negotiated. Over time, institutions may be expected to move between these two types of support, depending on performance and scale of activity. A set of ten criteria was established (Department of Health 1997a: 4–7) for evaluating bids relating to expected flows of non-commercial external support, the quality of research management and the relevance of the bidders' plans to the needs of the NHS. The assessments (where available and relevant) of clinical departments in medical schools collaborating with trusts in the Higher Education Funding Council for England's research assessment exercises were also borne in mind.

The bidding guidance also made clear the public good nature of the activity which it was intended the levy should support. An elaborate system of regional evaluation followed by central arbitration to ensure consistency in the application of the criteria and to make marginal adjustments in the light of expected productivity was developed and applied. The task force had recommended that the changes be introduced without serious destabilization of existing recipients of previous streams of funding. Final allocations were agreed with NHS regional directors. Had this pledge not been honoured, funding shifts between institutions would have been larger than turned out to be the case in the first round of the new system in 1997/8. Doubtless greater shifts of funding will occur in the future as the responses of institutions and consortia to the advice of regional directors of R&D is assessed, in the light of institutions' achievement of their own stated R&D goals, and as the amount and quality of information about the uses to which the funding is put is accumulated over time. The mechanism thus placed the articulation and quantification of demand in the hands of the NHS Executive on behalf of the NHS, created a national competition between R&D suppliers for the resources, and instituted a set of incentives for institutions to manage their R&D work more efficiently.

The introduction of the new system replacing SIFTR and the

other diverse funding sources had been preceded by an accounting exercise in which all recipients declared all their non-commercial sources of R&D income and accounted as far as possible (and with some fairly heroic assumptions in the case of joint costs) for existing R&D expenditures. This exercise was accomplished with a minimum of (detected) gamesmanship and served as the benchmark against which to judge the subsequent movement of funds. While the exercise had inherently arbitrary aspects, perhaps the most important feature of the new system is that it does not rely on central judgements about the costs of research against the costs of teaching or the costs of patient care. Instead it requires bidders both to set out what they intend to achieve, with measurable outcomes, and their own estimates of what it will cost. Instead of a system requiring central judgements as to what R&D will actually cost, and without any indication of the outcomes and their value that the resources will enable, the new system attempts to establish a well-designed quasi-market, with the ultimate judgements about the value of public-good outputs being made by the director of R&D advised by the central R&D committee, the reasonableness of the costs being judged by central and regional experts, and plenty of scope for individual institutions to display their own initiative and set their own priorities in the light of what they know to be the broad priorities set by ministers.

The new system also provides the protection from the service commissioning processes that R&D requires, as health service commissioners seek to minimize their contract costs. The protection is not absolute but depends on the quality and relevance of R&D work. However, the new mechanisms no longer require hospitals to fund their own R&D out of service contract income. For the first time there is a rational opportunity for institutions to increase their infrastructural funding – and, indeed, some have succeeded in doing just that.

THE NEW R&D STRUCTURE: OVERVIEW

Overall funding for medical and health-related research in England amounts currently to about £3299 million per year. Of this, industry (primarily pharmaceuticals) contributes about £2 billion (an extremely 'round' estimate!), research charities £340 million, the Medical Research Council £278 million and the Higher Education Funding Council for England £190 million (medical schools). The

Department of Health and the NHS contribute £491 million, of which £65 million comes from the Department of Health and £426 million from the NHS.

The new arrangements for NHS R&D (both NHS funded R&D and NHS support for the non-commercial R&D funded by others) are shown in Figure 6.1. R&D in the NHS is now comprehensively managed by the director of R&D on the advice of the central R&D committee. There are two broad divisions into which the work is divided: that funded directly by the Department of Health and that funded out of the R&D levy.

On the left of the Figure, directly funded R&D falls into two categories: work commissioned by the Department of Health as a part of its policy development activity (usually determined by ministerial priorities and directly related to political judgements of the public good need for relevant R&D). This is the policy research programme, which includes social care research as well as health and health services research. Second from the left are a miscellany of other centrally funded R&D activities such as the specific

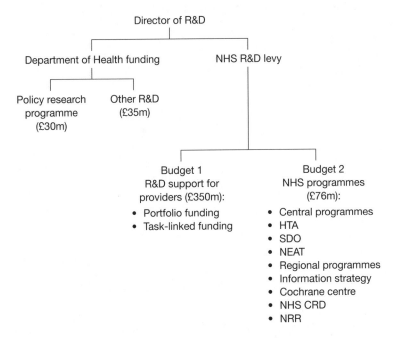

Figure 6.1   Department of Health R&D and NHS R&D strategy

programme managed by the High Security Psychiatric Hospitals Commissioning Board. On the right are the activities supported by the R&D levy. 'Budget 1' is the new form of support for NHS providers – the new single stream that replaces SIFTR, non-SIFTR, and so on, which is available through the processes described in the form either of portfolio or task-linked Funding. 'Budget 2' funds the NHS R&D programme, which now consists of three central programmes where the scope of publicness is NHS-wide: the health technology assessment programme (HTA) under the standing group, and two new programmes also with standing groups in service delivery and organization (SDO), and new and emerging applications of technology (NEAT). The regional programmes support work that is also national in its publicness but of lower general priority while being of particular regional concern, and the information strategy consists of the Cochrane Centre, the NHS Centre for Reviews and Dissemination (CRD), and the National Research Register (NRR), formerly the National Project Register. Yet to be determined are the way in which workforce capacity development will proceed and the manner of the integration of the whole of this activity with the National Institute for Clinical Excellence (NICE).

INTERACTION BETWEEN THE DEMAND AND SUPPLY OF THE PUBLIC GOOD

A (Samuelsonian) public good like R&D is defined in terms of its demand-side characteristics. The publicness of R&D is, however, compounded by supply-side matters which policy needs also to address if the amount produced is to be optimized.

Health-related R&D is located principally in universities and hospitals or practices associated with universities. Universities are independent non-profit private organizations in the UK (though heavily dominated by their principal funder – the state) which pursue agendas that are their own and, in the case of research, are largely determined by the preferences (values) of researchers themselves. Unfortunately, the economic theory of institutions such as universities is poorly developed and offers little in the way of guidance (for an early contribution to this still thin field see Culyer 1970). Academic freedom is jealously guarded and, even when research projects are commissioned by external bodies, researchers typically seek to promote their own priorities as far as possible on the back of such sponsorship. This creates tensions requiring trading-off in the commissioning process and, for the most part, the Department of Health and the NHS R&D programme have seen their own interest as also being served by helping to ensure the continuation of a vibrant research community that is not entirely and exclusively driven by the needs (whether short or long term) of the NHS. There is thus not only scope for bargaining as to the terms under which research projects are undertaken (for example, many have included training components) but also a degree of long-term mutual interest.

More difficult is the issue of the efficiency with which universities manage their research activity. Most universities adopt a 'bottom-up' approach in which the research priorities of institutions are derived from the preferences of the researchers themselves, and the resource and support structures provided are those preferred by the same group. Until the advent of the research assessment exercises of the Higher Education Funding Councils, however, there was typically little thought given to the management and support of research within institutions, little sharing of good practice, and remarkably little attention given to the career interests of an increasing proportion of staff who were funded by external research support grants with a limited life. (Most, for example, have taken the view that the life of the employment contract should be the same as the life of the support grant.) Research management and support in hospitals was substantially worse and many claiming a serious commitment to R&D lacked a senior manager and support staff to develop strategies through which it could be made to flourish.

Even since the advent of the research assessment exercises, many institutions have been slow to improve their internal support strategies. Much of the specific reaction has been tactical rather than strategic (for example, finding ways of excluding research-inactive staff, or tactically playing with the units of assessment in which staff are reported). So, one set of issues for a major public programme of R&D concerns the efficiency and quality of the management of R&D in institutions. There are few levers to be pulled to affect the supply side, though the financial incentives built into the way in which research assessment exercise results are used by the Funding Councils provide a mechanism for promoting and rewarding quality, and the operation of the portfolio and task-linked mechanisms in the case of Budget 1 allocations (or future transfers between Budget 1 and Budget 2) will provide similar levers for the NHS in the future.

More intractable in the short term is the issue of research workforce capacity. Universities seem to be able to change their practices only slowly in response to changes in the ways in which
demand is revealed. Despite the widespread recognition of specific
skill shortages and notwithstanding the availability of funding for
research that depends upon these skills, the system has been slow to
respond. The NHS's own financial support for education and
training has largely ignored these problems and policy towards education and training, including continuing professional development, has been developed in an almost entirely separate way from
R&D, despite their manifest interdependence. That is to say, the
effective use of R&D results in actual clinical and managerial practice depends upon there being a service workforce that is capable of
assimilating new information and interpreting it in relevant ways in
the daily context of people's work, and the production of the R&D
itself is dependent upon there being a sufficiently well-trained
R&D workforce capable of meeting the demand for R&D, and on
the scale at which it is demanded. There are many complex issues
involved here. For example, ensuring that, in general, NHS staff
have a good appreciation of relevant R&D outcomes and how they
may be best utilized in the service. NHS staff should be able to
articulate the ways in which prospective R&D might further their
own work and clinicians' roles in R&D should be enhanced (these
roles cover a range from the provision of patient 'material' for
research, through collaborative work with other researchers, to
managing their own research programmes).

In the long term some sort of equilibrium may be established.
Unfortunately, the R&D agenda for the NHS is large, growing, and
is demanding of a high order of professional skill. Left to the
'market' – that is, left to institutions to respond to their perceptions
of the changing nature of demand – adaptation to change is likely
to be slower than it need be. A higher priority is required to be
given to the development of mechanisms that might speed the
process up. This would have to include the better identification of
R&D workforce capacities centrally and regionally, the collaborative funding of both the training and the jobs, and changes in university cultures regarding the employment status and career
development of 'limited term' research staff.

In research-oriented hospitals there is some evidence of a major
culture change in the way that R&D is perceived and supported
(Arnold *et al.* 1998), almost entirely in response to the economic
incentives provided by the new funding system in the form of

Budget 1 culture change. It has also been facilitated through the agency of NHS Executive regional directors of R&D and, perhaps more importantly, through the establishment of directors of R&D in hospitals (largely as a result of the creation of the new system). Such highly personal connections that facilitate supply responses to the demand for a public good should not be underestimated for their potential impact, especially when coupled with powerful financial incentives and performance monitoring against openly stated criteria. These methods used for the research-orientated hospitals could be applied with better effect to the universities.

CONCLUSIONS

This chapter has analysed NHS R&D as a Samuelsonian public good, whose demand ought to be revealed by those with the technical competencies to do so (for example, to distinguish the researchable from the unresearchable) and those with political legitimacy (that is, representing the public interest – the need of the NHS for knowledge). It has identified other characteristics of R&D that further compound the problems in securing appropriate and timely delivery: the fact that supplier-induced demand may distort the optimal pattern; the presence of important information asymmetries; the jointness in production between research, education and patient service delivery; the multiplicity of research funders; the inherent riskiness of research; the subtlety of the output of research and its lack of amenability to sensible measurement and valuation; and that it is typically produced by private non-profit organizations called 'universities'.

The structure developed in England for dealing with these problems has been described. Its principal character is that it has a strong demand-side focus and it has yet to develop truly effective means of ensuring a short- to medium-term supply-side responsiveness. This may be partly due to our imperfect understanding of the way in which hospital and university 'firms' respond to changes in their environment (or can be encouraged to respond), and partly due to inherent characteristics of universities as self-governing communities of scholars. The new mechanisms have the character of a quasi-market, in which demand is determined through various public agencies and widespread consultation, and contracts are placed with research supplying institutions (universities and hospitals). This mechanism replaced a more centrally planned but actually quite chaotic model which, even if it had been simplified and better co-ordinated, was inherently incapable of addressing key issues such as the 'cost' of R&D in hospitals, the value of research output, and the marginal value of the overall programme. These issues ought to have determined the overall public budgetary commitment to R&D in the NHS. The exploration of the supply side and the interaction between demand and supply are two key research issues for the future.

REFERENCES

Arnold, E., Morrow, S., Thuriax, B. and Martin, B. (1998). *Implementing the Culyer Reforms in North Thames: Baseline and Initial View of Impact*, preliminary report. Brighton: Science and Technology Policy Research Unit.

Arrow, K.J. (1962). Economic welfare and the allocation of resources for invention. In R.R. Nelson (ed.), *The Rate and Direction of Inventive Activities*, Princeton, NJ: Princeton University Press.

Baker, M. (1998). Taking the strategy forward. In M. Baker and S. Kirk (eds), *Research and Development for the NHS: Evidence, Evaluation and Effectiveness*, 2nd edn, pp. 9–24. Abingdon: Radcliffe Medical Press.

Culyer, A.J. (1970). A utility-maximising view of universities. *Scottish Journal of Political Economy*, 17, 349–68.

Culyer, A.J. (1994). *Supporting Research and Development in the National Health Service: A Report to the Minister for Health by a Research and Development Task Force Chaired by Professor Anthony Culyer*. London: HMSO.

Culyer, A.J. (1995). Supporting research and development in the National Health Service. *Journal of the Royal College of Physicians of London*, 29, 216–24.

Culyer, A.J. (1998). Taking advantage of the new environment for research and development. In M. Baker and S. Kirk (eds), *Research and Development for the NHS: Evidence, Evaluation and Effectiveness*, 2nd edn, pp. 53–65. Abingdon: Radcliffe Medical Press.

Culyer, A.J., Wiseman, J., Drummond, M.F. and West, P.A. (1978). What accounts for the higher costs of teaching hospitals? *Social and Economic Administration*, 12, 20–30.

Department of Health (1989) *Priorities in Medical Research – Government Response to the Third Report of the House of Lords Select Committee on Science and Technology*, Cm 902, London, HMSO.

Department of Health (1991). *Research for Health*. London: HMSO.

Department of Health (1993). *Research for Health*. London: HMSO.

Department of Health (1996a). *The New Funding System for Research and Development in the NHS – An Outline*. London: Department of Health.

7

THE PERFORMANCE FRAMEWORK: TAKING ACCOUNT OF ECONOMIC BEHAVIOUR

Maria Goddard, Russell Mannion and Peter C. Smith

 INTRODUCTION

The publication of the 1997 White Paper *The New NHS: Modern, Dependable* (Department of Health 1997), and its Scottish and Welsh equivalents, signalled a fundamental change in the way that the National Health Service (NHS) is to be managed. The new NHS is to be 'based on partnership and driven by performance' (Department of Health 1997, para. 1.3). The government's 'third way' is neither an attempt to return to the centralized command and control systems of the 1970s, nor a commitment to retaining the competitive internal market system of the 1990s. The stated intention is to build upon the strengths of each, creating a more collaborative service with economic relationships based on partnership and cooperation. Whereas the internal market reforms gave competition the central role in securing performance, the key instrument for managing the NHS in the future will be the provision of quantitative information, in the form of a new national performance framework. Proposals for the nature and content of the framework were issued for consultation in January 1998, providing more detail on the broad intentions outlined in the White Paper (NHS Executive 1998).

In general, the new approach to managing the NHS is to be

Department of Health (1996b). *NHS Support for Non-commercial Externally Funded Research and Development.* London: Department of Health.

Department of Health (1997a). *Strategic Framework for the Use of the NHS R&D Levy.* London: Department of Health.

Department of Health (1997b). *Department of Health and NHS Funding for Research and Development.* London: Department of Health.

Department of Health (1997c). *R&D Support Funding for NHS Providers.* London: Department of Health.

Department of Health (1997d). *The Annual Report of the NHS Health Technology Assessment Programme 1997: Identifying Questions, Finding Answers.* London: Department of Health.

Department of Health (1998). *Research: What's in it for Consumers?* London: Department of Health.

House of Lords Select Committee on Science and Technology (1984). *Priorities in Medical Research* (HL Paper 54). London: HMSO.

Musgrave, R. (1959). *The Theory of Public Finance.* London: McGraw-Hill.

Samuelson, P.A. (1954). The pure theory of public expenditure. *Review of Economics and Statistics*, 36, 387–9.

Samuelson, P.A. (1955). Diagrammatic exposition of a theory of public expenditure. *Review of Economics and Statistics*, 37, 350–6.

welcomed. However, in developing the performance framework, it is essential to have a proper understanding of the strengths and limitations intrinsic to the use of performance indicators for securing management control in the NHS. A key issue which has so far been largely ignored in the White Paper and the consultation document is the impact of performance indicators on behaviour. If it is to have any effect, publication of performance data must lead to changes in behaviour of NHS organizations and staff. Yet there is little appreciation in the official documents of the complex behavioural consequences that may arise as a result of the collection and dissemination of performance data. In addition to having the predicted impact on behaviour, the potential exists for performance management systems to produce unintended and possibly dysfunctional consequences which may be damaging to the NHS.

This chapter summarizes the theoretical issues and the results of previous research in this topic. It then uses some of the findings from a recently completed study to illustrate the sort of unintended side-effects that occur within the current system of performance management, which may in principle be replicated in the new system in future. We conclude that careful attention needs to be paid to the potential for unanticipated side-effects. The possibility of such consequences does not invalidate the principle of seeking to develop a workable performance framework. However it does suggest that much more attention than is evident in the consultation document must be directed at how the proposed data are to be disseminated and used within the NHS.

The chapter is arranged as follows. The next section provides an overview of the new performance framework as set out in the White Paper. We then set out a theoretical model of the performance measurement process. The following section summarizes the key research findings from attempts to introduce comparable measurement schemes in the public sector. This is followed by a brief outline of the aims and methodology of a study funded by the Department of Health of the information used to assess NHS trusts (Goddard *et al.* 1999). The next section summarizes some of the findings of this study relating to the unintended and dysfunctional outcomes of performance indicators, and makes some suggestions for a range of strategies to offset some of the unanticipated consequences described. The final section outlines a number of policy recommendations relating to the future development and implementation of the national performance framework.

THE NATIONAL PERFORMANCE FRAMEWORK

The White Paper (Department of Health 1997) and the consultation document (NHS Executive 1998) outline the six key areas of performance on which the national framework will focus:

1 *Health improvement: the aim of improving the general health of the population.*
2 *Fair access: to health services according to need irrespective of geography, class, ethnicity, age or sex.*
3 *Effective delivery of appropriate health care: the aim of providing effective, appropriate and timely health care which meets agreed standards.*
4 *Efficiency: the use of NHS resources to achieve best value for money.*
5 *Patient/carer experience: the way in which patients and carers view the quality of treatment and care that they receive.*
6 *Health outcomes of NHS care: assessing the direct contribution of NHS care to improvements in overall health.*

Targets for progress against these six areas are to be built into: the performance agreements between NHS Executive regional offices and health authorities; local Health Improvement Programmes (HImPs); accountability agreements between primary care groups (PCGs) and health authorities; and the agreements between PCGs and trusts. The measures used to assess each of these dimensions will be constructed in the light of responses to the consultation document. It is expected that the performance framework will replace the purchaser efficiency index in 1999.

The proposals for assessing and managing the performance of the NHS are to be welcomed on a number of grounds. Specifically, they represent an improvement on existing arrangements because they:

- focus on the health aspects of performance rather than only on finance and activity issues;
- focus on equity issues;
- focus on patient experience;
- acknowledge the contribution of other agencies besides the NHS to health outcomes;
- focus on the population or client group rather than solely on providers;
- focus on the local as well as the national level.

More generally, the increased emphasis to be placed upon performance measurement in the NHS is to be welcomed. Excessive reliance on markets to secure improvements in health services is misguided. Successful performance management is likely to require a far more sensitive set of instruments than a competitive market, and a good system of performance measurement must form an essential component of that set.

THEORETICAL CONTEXT

It is probably simplest to think of the performance measurement process as one of *feedback*. Figure 7.1 outlines a very simple model encapsulating the essence of this process. Certain aspects of the organization are measured. These are analysed and interpreted in the light of environmental influences and organizational objectives. Finally, some sort of action results which alters the nature of the organization. The process then continues.

Many of the consequences of this system of feedback are likely to be intended and helpful. For example, publication of data relating to waiting times for elective surgery, in association with substantial political attention to the issue, has undoubtedly contributed towards an improvement in certain aspects of waiting times within the NHS. Less certainty however, can be attached to the broader consequences of such measurement. For example, at various times it has been claimed that the emphasis on very long waits has led to increased emphasis within NHS trusts on relatively minor

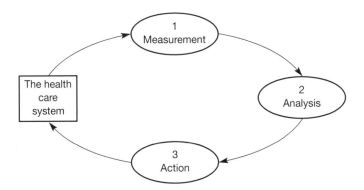

Figure 7.1 A model of the performance measurement process

procedures at the expense of more urgent surgery, and that the emphasis on elective surgery has resulted in the diversion of resources from activities for which equivalent performance measures do not exist.

Thus the net effect of any single performance measure (or set of measures) on the NHS as a whole may be quite complex to evaluate. In particular, it is clearly important to look well beyond any improvements in the measure itself in order to determine whether publication of the measure is on balance beneficial. In this section we therefore summarize a variety of ways in which unintended side-effects can arise from performance management systems. The discussion considers these effects under the three headings represented in Figure 7.1: measurement, analysis and action.

Measurement stage

Any measurement system will to some extent be *partial*. If it is intended to affect the behaviour of managers, clinicians and other workers, it will require incentives to pay increased attention to the measured, and therefore conversely less attention to the un-measured. This may induce tunnel vision, or the neglect of un-measured aspects of activity.

A slightly different danger is that of *fragmentation*. Many outcomes from health care depend on the collaboration of a variety of other organizations, both within and outside the NHS. The eventual outcome therefore depends on the joint efforts of these agencies. It may be quite challenging to devise measurement schemes which can capture the contribution of each agency to outcome, and there is a danger of sub-optimization, in the sense that agencies are driven towards pursuing their own performance criteria with little regard for joint outcomes.

Almost all measures are *short term* in their perspective. Yet current measures may reflect the outcome of years' of health care activity, and therefore cannot be attributed solely to current activity. And current activity may affect future outcomes, which are not captured in current performance measures. Special attention will therefore have to be given to activities which have long-term health outcomes.

Although there may be universal agreement that a particular phenomenon is an important aspect of NHS performance, there may be numerous *instruments* for capturing the phenomenon of interest. For example, existing measures of waiting time choose to focus on exceptionally long waits, but there is no reason why this particular aspect of waiting should necessarily be addressed. Yet the choice of one instrument in preference to another may have profound implications for organizational behaviour. There is a danger of encouraging *measure fixation* if managers pursue strategies which enhance their success in terms of the reported measure, rather than focusing on the underlying objective.

It must be remembered that the collection of many indicators of performance will rely on the cooperation of front-line NHS staff. If their rewards are to any extent dependent on the data they report, there is of course a constant danger of *misrepresentation* in one form or another. Finally, it is important to bear in mind that health care is a dynamic, ever-changing activity, and that technologies and needs change very quickly. There is therefore a danger of *ossification*, and any performance measurement scheme therefore needs to be constantly reviewed to ensure that it captures current priorities.

Analysis stage

Health care performance data are often immensely difficult to interpret. Many measures reflect the outcome of a complex interaction of factors, such as environment and deprivation, which may have a profound impact on the measure which is outside the control of the NHS. Careful analysis may therefore be required to ensure that the *contribution* of the NHS to the chosen performance measures is correctly identified. In practice, the analysis of performance data is in its infancy, and the potential for faulty inferences may be large (see Chapter 8).

Action stage

The impact of a performance measurement scheme will depend on the rewards, punishments and incentives implicit in its design. At one extreme, if no appropriate incentives are put in place, the data produced may be largely ignored and produce no meaningful action. At the other extreme, the livelihood of managers and health care professionals may depend crucially on reported measures, leading to the potential for excessive attention to reported performance (as opposed to patient outcome), and misrepresentation.

Furthermore, certain types of measure may be susceptible to *gaming* on the part of health care professionals. This phenomenon was endemic to the Soviet Union, where year on year improvement was the usual performance measure. Managers had little incentive to achieve good results in the current year because in all probability their future targets would be based on the new level of attainment, leading to the need for increased effort in the future.

PREVIOUS RESEARCH ON BEHAVIOURAL RESPONSES

This section summarizes the limited amount of research evidence available in relation to the behavioural impact of performance data publication. A more detailed account can be found in Nutley and Smith (1998).

Publication of performance data has little purpose if it is not to have some impact on the behaviour of the health care organization. The nature of the feedback that organizations receive from interested parties following publication is therefore a key influence on subsequent managerial and clinical actions. Such feedback might be formal, as in the case of the peer review organizations advocated by the US Health Care Financing Administration (HCFA), which are intended to offer a 'non-punitive' interpretation of results. Or the feedback might be more haphazard and informal, as for example in the *Patient's Charter* initiative in the United Kingdom (UK). Here data are exposed in the public arena, from which a variety of political pressures might emerge. Indeed the implications of feedback may be very different depending on whether or not data are made public. For example, Conway *et al.* (1995) describe a feedback system in Maine, in which data are shared in confidence with clinicians in order to retain their support for the project.

As noted above, intrinsic to the feedback process is the system of punishments and rewards attached to the performance measurement scheme. These are likely to be largely implicit and difficult to define, but may nevertheless be of immense importance. In concrete terms, performance rankings might affect budgets, bonuses and job security, while less tangibly they are likely to influence staff morale and recruitment. In the USA a surgeon's poor league table rating might lead to loss of livelihood. Moreover, a potential problem in the feedback process is the existence of contradictory messages. For example, the US Health Quality Improvement Initiative emphasizes consensus, collaboration and non-antagonistic feedback. Yet Nash (1995) points out that the HCFA are also basing accreditation and payment decisions on performance data, a conflict which may undermine many of the benefits of feedback.

While undoubtedly of central importance, the nature of the feedback process and the associated reward structure are intrinsically difficult to study, and there has been a notable lack of research on the impact of performance publication within the health care sector (Rosenthal and Harper 1994; Nash 1995). Any user of health care performance data is likely to need supporting material to help interpret the results. This might take the form of supplementary data or of expert help. For example, Goldman and Thomas (1994) describe how hospital specific mortality rates provided a screening tool which led on to a focused medical records review in outlier providers; Nelson *et al.* (1995) report the use of supporting data in the form of 'instrument panels'; Finlan and Zibrat (1994) describe the impact on clinical practice in one hospital of comparative data provided by the US Joint Commission on Accreditation of Health Care Organizations; and Moller *et al.* (1994) describe how a consortium of providers have set up a study group to examine outcome measures in paediatric cardiac care. However, in general there has been little examination of the mechanism for feeding information back to hospitals and clinicians. Most schemes appear to rely on a vague hope that providers will 'do something' in response to the data. Yet evidence from the broader UK public sector suggests that – in the absence of formal feedback procedures – little change may occur.

One of the key concerns about many performance measurement systems, and particularly report cards, is that they are backward-looking, judgemental and poor motivational devices. Greene and Wintfield (1996) conclude that by the time the data are published, users of the report cards can have little confidence that the ratings are still applicable. As a response to these concerns, some authors like to think of performance indicators in terms of the instrument panel of an aircraft or car (Jackson 1995; Meekings 1995). The focus is then on providing real time, on-line monitoring which is action oriented. Although Nelson *et al.* (1995) illustrate the instrument panel concept by reporting on work in the Dartmouth-Hitchcock (US) health care system, it is not generally clear how these principles can be translated to the health care setting.

More generally, few studies have sought to evaluate in any comprehensive way the behavioural ramifications of publication. The obvious means of judging the impact of a performance measurement scheme is by examining its apparent impact on performance.

Such exercises may however be tautological, in the sense that the yardsticks used to evaluate the scheme may be precisely the same potentially imperfect instruments of measurement used in the scheme itself, which may be subject to the problems of partiality, distortion and incompleteness we have noted above. Thus, the previous UK government proclaimed the success of the *Patient's Charter* by citing improvements in the length of time patients waited for inpatient admission, the *Charter's* prime performance measure (UK Government 1995). Yet there are many other aspects of NHS health care on which the *Charter* is silent, but which may have been adversely affected by the emphasis on waiting times.

In the same way, Chassin *et al.* (1996) cite a notable decline in risk-adjusted mortality associated with the New York report card scheme. However, Greene and Wintfield (1996) argue that the phenomenon may be more a function of an increase in the reporting of risk factors than a real improvement in surgical outcomes. And Ghali *et al.* (1997) note that similar improvements in risk-adjusted mortality were found in Massachusetts, which did not publish mortality data. Naive examination of apparent improvements in reported performance is therefore inadequate, and much more complete evaluation, seeking to identify any side-effects of performance publication is needed.

In this context, Smith (1993) examined the impact on maternity managers of a single, well-established performance measure – the perinatal mortality rate. He identified seven potentially dysfunctional consequences of publication of these data, and found compelling evidence that some had indeed materialized. For example: managers were concentrating on perinatal mortality at the expense of other dimensions of performance; maternity units were paying less attention than previously to the effects their actions might have on other parts of the health service; long-term outcomes were being given less attention than hitherto; and there was some suggestion that doctors' reporting of the timing of mortality may have been influenced by the definition of perinatal mortality (which excludes the first 28 weeks of pregnancy).

Thus, the feedback phase of the performance measurement process clearly requires more attention. As Stewart (1984) points out for the broader public sector, in examining the accountability relationship it is important to consider both the giving *of* an account (the publication of performance data) and the mechanisms available to hold organizations *to* account. The accounts provided to stakeholders within health care systems need to meet their varied interests and be communicated in a language which makes sense to them. There is then a need for mechanisms with which to hold service providers to account. The strengthened role of external audit bodies is one means of achieving the latter. Where a market exists for health care services, it may be possible for patients and purchasers to vote with their feet and choose providers on the basis of reported performance. However, within a publicly-provided system there is also a clear need for transparent democratic processes for holding providers to account.

In summary, whatever the system of health care, simply reporting performance is unlikely to be sufficient to secure improvements.

AIMS AND METHODS OF STUDY

The aim of the research funded by the Department of Health was to investigate the types of information used to assess the performance of NHS trusts. A major element in the research was the exploration of the kinds of 'soft' or informal information used alongside more formal measures of performance. The results of this will be reported elsewhere. However, we also sought to identify any unintended and dysfunctional behavioural consequences of current performance measures. Although the study was based on experiences with the current set of performance measures, it is of relevance to the new framework for two reasons. First, many of the indicators proposed will be the same as (or very similar to) those used currently (e.g. waiting times); second, the principles relating to behavioural responses will apply to a range of measures which have characteristics similar to those considered, even if the specific measures differ.

The research was based on case studies of eight trusts. Two NHS Executive regional offices were approached and senior staff responsible for provider finance and performance were asked to nominate four hospitals exhibiting what they considered to be a wide range of performance. We limited the choice to district general hospitals, in order to make our sample as homogenous as possible. The chief executive of each of the selected trusts was contacted and invited to participate in the research.

Within each trust, semi-structured interviews were undertaken with the chief executive, the medical director, a nurse manager and a junior doctor.[1] One junior doctor did not attend for the interview, so we undertook a total of 31 interviews within trusts. In addition, we interviewed the finance director of the local health authority for each trust (the trust's main purchaser). We asked the finance director to include any other relevant staff in the interviews and in half the cases additional people attended, mainly from a health development or commissioning background. At the regional offices we interviewed staff responsible for provider finance and performance. These external organizations added a further 10 interviews to the dataset and thus in total the study is based on the results from 41 interviews.

THE UNINTENDED CONSEQUENCES OF PERFORMANCE INDICATORS

Following Smith (1995), we report the findings on unintended consequences of performance indicator schemes under the following headings:

- *Tunnel vision*: concentration on areas that are included in the performance indicator scheme, to the exclusion of other important areas.
- *Sub-optimization*: the pursuit of narrow local objectives by managers, at the expense of the objectives of the organization as a whole.
- *Myopia*: concentration on short-term issues, to the exclusion of long-term criteria that may only show up in performance measures in many years' time.
- *Misrepresentation*: the deliberate manipulation of data including 'creative' accounting and fraud so that reported behaviour differs from actual behaviour.
- *Gaming*: altering behaviour so as to obtain strategic advantage.

We consider these below in turn, taking into account the range of views received from different organizations and from people at different levels within the trusts.

Tunnel vision

There was clear recognition by staff at all levels that current indicators did not give a 'rounded' view of the performance of a trust and that their specific focus often diverted attention from equally legitimate (but unmeasured) aspects of trust performance:

If you set ten performance indicators what this will do is encourage the trust to perform on these ten and not be too bothered about anything else.

(Health authority finance director)

It [the current system of performance indicators] cannot possibly give a rounded view because they are only a handful relative to the whole spectrum that goes on in a trust.

(Trust medical director)

There is no point in only trying to manage what you can measure. You have to be imaginative about other things and work out ways of trying to assess them.

(Trust chief executive)

The current priority given to waiting times targets was frequently cited as diverting attention and resources away from other important spheres of trust performance. Indeed it is apparent that a vast amount of effort and resources are devoted by health authorities and trusts to ensuring they meet the targets and some clearly feel it is money which they would prefer to spend elsewhere. In some cases, those responsible for ensuring the target is met will use a range of tactics to ensure they achieve the correct results, sometimes at the expense of other priorities. Examples of both the time and effort involved and the sort of tactics employed at trusts to ensure targets are met included:

- a senior person in one health authority spending the majority of their time chasing the trust about individual patients on the waiting list who have to be treated in order to avoid a breach of the standards;
- treating all the cataract patients on the list in order to reduce the numbers at a relatively modest cost, while leaving people requiring more expensive operations on the list;
- removing long waiters, regardless of their medical condition;
- putting people on the 'pending list' (a waiting list for the waiting list) rather than on the official waiting list;
- the employment of 'hello nurses' in accident and emergency (A&E) departments in order to ensure the five-minute waiting time target is met.

In such cases, staff feel they have been pressured to 'manage the waiting lists rather than the patients' and that changes have been made 'not to improve the quality of care but to improve our ratings' (Trust medical director).

The propensity for tunnel vision may be associated with the particular management style of a trust: 'We are not performance indicator driven but I know that you could go to others and it would all be about performance indicators. The trust we are merging with couldn't be more different in that respect. They would say ... if you cannot graph it or put a number to it, it doesn't exist' (Trust medical director). Clearly, the introduction of a wider range of measures, including clinical indicators, will offset to some extent the common complaint that the current system leads managers to focus only on the process-orientated measures at the expense of more important things which may not be measured (or measurable).

The lack of measures relating to outcomes, compared with the number focusing on process and activity, was mentioned frequently in our study. The piloting of clinical indicators and the proposals for the national performance framework were therefore welcomed by most staff. However, difficulties in finding good comparators and methods for dealing with casemix were seen as potential problem areas. Given the perceived limitations, some clinicians advocated that clinical outcome measures should be supplemented by process measures of clinical activity such as the recording of 'near misses'. The use of evidence-based guidelines and 'clinical pathways' were also thought to be important in augmenting outcome measures.

Adding new measures may therefore reduce the extent to which people focus only on demonstrating success using a small number of measures, but too *many* measures may also induce dysfunctional consequences, particularly if it becomes a 'juggling' act to try to focus on them all. For example, when asked about the new proposals for performance management, one health authority finance director reported that even without the addition of the new indicators he felt there were too many. No one could be expected to do well on them all and thus it would result in a considerable waste of time and effort as people tried to discover what the 'real' key indicator was.

Sub-optimization

Sub-optimization can occur where there is a lack of congruence between personal incentives and the global objectives of the organization. This was one of the key aspects of performance which we addressed in our study and we will be reporting on this in detail elsewhere in future. However, in brief, we found that although each trust had corporate objectives, these objectives were not always aligned with the specific incentive structures for different staff within the organization. In particular, it was clear that it was often difficult to align the trust financial objectives with specific clinical priorities. In order to address this problem, all of the trusts were attempting to actively engage medical staff within the management process to facilitate clinical 'ownership' of the major strategic financial and administrative issues facing the organization. This was thought by some respondents to be a particularly difficult task when a trust was in a serious financial position and clinicians were expected to cooperate in service reductions:

The trust objectives as a whole are business-type objectives. What I'm trying to do now is get enough information to turn them into more clinical objectives . . . What I want [is for the clinicians] to own the decisions and own the outcomes.
(Trust chief executive)

One of the key reasons why this organization has failed is because the clinical staff, junior and senior, have largely been disengaged from the management process. So part of the work we have been doing to address our financial deficit has not just been to take a substantial amount of money out of the cost expenditure, it has also been to bring clinicians into the heart of the management process.
(Trust chief executive)

Interviews with the junior doctors also revealed a lack of congruence between their own personal objectives – which were largely related to getting a good reference for their next job – and those of the trust in general. Indeed, many of them reported little detailed knowledge of the formal performance management system at all: 'I don't have much to do with performance indicators. They don't impact on my work. I haven't seen the [clinical indicators] at all' (Junior doctor). Although there were some exceptions where junior doctors did realize they had to see patients within a certain length of time in order to comply with *Patient's Charter* demands, most saw themselves as being distant from the formal systems of performance assessment.

Another example of sub-optimization identified by senior staff was the potential for a lack of congruence between the incentives or objectives of different agencies responsible for provision of health care within a local community. The most commonly cited example of this was 'bed blocking', which can occur as a result of lack of agreement about responsibilities of health and social services.

Aside from trying to promote ownership of objectives by clinical staff by involving them in the setting of targets, other strategies for dealing with sub-optimization were discerned. We found that setting devolved budgets and undertaking individual performance review or formal appraisal schemes were the two main mechanisms for transmitting trust-level objectives down to staff at various levels within the organizational hierarchy. Additionally, some trusts had used comparisons with clinical services in other trusts to combat professional challenge of corporate objectives: 'We've only been able to break into the professional dominance by challenging such things as staffing levels based on benchmarking at other Trusts . . . We've also maintained a professional nursing support group where senior nurses can express their views about skill mix, etc.' (Trust chief executive).

Myopia

There was a general feeling among our respondents that many of the current performance indicators are short term in nature and actions taken now may not show up in indicators for several years:

> I think short-termism has been a major problem in the performance management culture of the NHS – for example, the fact that there has been until recently the requirement to make income and expenditure balance each year. Now we have failed to do that and we have been treated like lepers for doing so. But when you are going through major change any private sector enterprise would not just look at one year's results but achievements against a five-year plan.
>
> (Trust chief executive)

In fact, most of the respondents in our sample were fairly optimistic about this. Although they felt that they were sometimes being pushed to deliver short-term targets (e.g. reductions in management costs) without a view to the longer term, there was some recognition that sometimes the short-term picture will be poor but that this was acceptable if it produced a better long-term outcome. For example, regional office staff recognized that some trusts had performed poorly in terms of their financial duties but that this was not a concern as it was to be addressed through the longer-term financial strategy. As long as the use of supplementary and softer information remains as a complement to the hard performance indicator data, this may not become a significant problem in the future.

The perspective of those people responsible for taking actions which influence long-term outcomes will be influenced by the likelihood that they will still be in post when the outcomes are revealed. For example, some of the trust chief executives in our study had inherited a very poor financial or clinical situation from the previous post holder and it may be the case that some of the actions taken previously would not have been taken if the post holders had anticipated they would be around to face the consequences. As one chief executive who had recently taken over a poorly performing trust stated of his predecessor: 'The last guy got out of here before it hit the fan. Timing is all'.

Longer employment contracts may encourage behaviour which takes account of the impact of current actions on future targets. Alternatively, ensuring that at least some reliable and appropriate process measures are included in a performance management system would provide an early signal of whether behaviour was likely to produce the desired long-term outcomes in the future.

Misrepresentation

Misrepresentation is the deliberate manipulation of data so that reported behaviour differs from actual behaviour. The scope for misrepresentation of data within a trust environment is particularly broad because many of the data used to measure performance and hold staff to account are under the direct control of those staff. A mixed picture emerged in our study, with some people citing specific instances of misrepresentation (either by them personally or by others), while others said they were confident this did not happen within their organization. Examples of 'creative measurement' cited included:

- double counting of finished consultant episodes (FCEs) when a patient is referred to another consultant within the same hospital;
- excluding the least favourable when calculating results – e.g. not including outpatient clinics where a consultant was sick or was called to casualty so that the 30-minute waits were achieved;

- changing the order in which the codes for procedures undertaken on patients are entered – for example, the pressure to achieve a low rate for dilation and curettages (D&Cs) can encourage staff to enter the D&C as the second, rather than the primary procedure undertaken on a patient because only the first code is included in the returns.

Some of this manipulation is undertaken because people are keen to give the impression they are meeting the targets, and the degree of flexibility involved in recording and reporting the data makes this possible without them having to resort to outright lies. Most people said they felt they were 'massaging' data rather than misrepresenting it and that all they were doing was presenting themselves in the 'best possible light'. There was some evidence that health authorities and trusts sometimes collude in this, especially when the NHS Executive is taking a tough line with failures to meet targets.

> . . . you look for ways that you can conspire with the health authority to give them what they want to hear up there. In a way it minimizes your pain and maximizes their gain.
>
> (Trust finance director)

> Yes we definitely did that [collude with the local trust to misrepresent efficiency index figures]. The only way that health authorities were gaining resources was to show that they were increasing care in areas that they were not. But what we felt was that once you start fiddling the figures you have to keep a consistent message year on year and it gets further away from reality.
>
> (Health authority finance director)

Thus there is an incentive to just ensure the information is reported in such a way as to give those on the ground a 'quiet life'. Similarly, some health authorities noted that although they were pleased that their local trusts met the *Patient's Charter* standards, they could not help wondering whether this was an accurate reflection of what actually went on at ground level or whether the trusts were skilled at ensuring the data were recorded in a way that gave the right results: '. . . they are very good at demonstrating they are very good at meeting the *Patient's Charter*, but that doesn't mean they have met the spirit of what you are trying to achieve' (Health authority finance director).

Paradoxically, because there has been a tendency to provide

additional finance for those failing to meet the waiting-times targets, there is also sometimes an incentive for trusts to misrepresent their data in the opposite direction, extending their waiting times in order to obtain additional funds. Some trust chief executives noted that it was relatively easy to 'extend' their waiting lists in order to provide a good argument for a share of extra funding (especially central funds).

Although many examples of misrepresentation were supplied, others in our sample stated that even though they knew they could distort the information, they chose not to, either because they felt it was dishonest or because they feared detection. For example, one medical director said he had been approached by a casualty consultant about reducing the number of people who were sent home rather than admitted, as, if they admitted them, the patients would count as extra FCEs, hence boosting their activity data. The medical director declined on the grounds that this was poor clinical practice and that they would bound to be detected. Others felt it was wrong to cover up a problem by fiddling the figures, as the root cause of the problem would then never be tackled. In addition, many of the junior medical staff were not even aware of the current measures, so they were certainly not in a position to undertake a great deal of data manipulation.

Misrepresentation of data can also arise when those responsible for reporting do not place sufficient importance on it, because they feel the measures are not valid and are not therefore willing to devote effort to ensuring the data are valid. A particular example of this was revealed in our interviews when a medical director admitted that he had 'scandalized' his junior colleagues by suggesting that: '. . . we save ourselves five hours and make the figures up'. In this case, the indicator for patients' complaints required the trust to use a different classification system for the returns to the NHS Executive than the system they were using for returns to the purchaser. The medical director felt justified in having a guess rather than going through a bureaucratic process, as he did not feel they were doing it for gain (other than saving time).

An additional aspect of data misrepresentation which does not involve the deliberate manipulation of data relates to the general quality of the data used to compile the measures. A number of respondents mentioned the 'garbage in–garbage out' issue whereby they felt that although the measures may be acceptable in principle, in practice the data used to compile them were so poor and subject to so many errors or distortions that they felt no confidence in the figures that came out at the end. For example, in relation to the proposals for national reference cost schedules, a number of purchasers remarked that they had already tried cost benchmarking and had identified significant problems using it just on a local basis. One problem is caused by the difficulties in ensuring the cost data used by trusts are comparable and measure the same thing. Even if the data are gathered on a healthcare resource group (HRG) basis and are supposed to follow central guidance on methodology, the results of the exercises raise more questions than answers. In the words of one health authority director of finance: 'there are clouds and clouds of smokescreens around the differences – you cannot just say, you [the trust] are twice as expensive as the other'.

A similar point was made in relation to the waiting times data by another health authority and also in relation to the discrepancies in what is actually counted as a day case or an inpatient stay in some of the trusts. It was clear that without a lot of effort on the part of those monitoring the indicators, the results themselves were not very useful when the quality of the data used to produce them was questionable. Many of the indicators proposed in the new framework will rely on data which are similarly subject to a degree of interpretation or are of variable quality.

One possible way of reducing the extent of misrepresentation is to increase audit activity in order to detect it, and to penalize those responsible. However, the costs of any increased monitoring and audit would have to be weighed up against the benefits. Providing incentives to record data honestly and consistently may also reduce misrepresentation, although it was clear from our study that it was not always obvious where the 'blame' for this behaviour would rest. For instance, although the doctors or nurses might record information truthfully, the data could be 'massaged' further up the management line by those who gain from apparent good performance. Conversely, even if senior staff discourage misrepresentation, if those responsible for providing the data have no faith in the measures, the incentives may not be sufficient to motivate them to ensure the accuracy of the data is maintained. The key is to find a balance by ensuring that those responsible for collecting, recording and reporting the data (which includes the most junior staff as well as the senior executives who are held to account for performance) believe the measure is reasonable and worthwhile.

Gaming

The most frequently cited example of gaming concerned the efficiency index. Respondents indicated they would be reluctant to achieve high gains one year for fear that they would be expected to deliver the same or higher gains in the future. This ratchet effect was a common feature of the former Soviet economic system where managers were 'punished' for good performance by having higher standards set in the subsequent year's plan. Where this occurs managers have little incentive to increase productive efficiency and reduce organizational slack. In our study, there was some acknowledgement that all parties knew that gaming went on and acted accordingly. Frequently an analogy to participating in a 'game of chess' was made. One trust in the study which started out performing very well on the efficiency index tables saw that there was little scope for matching these achievements in the following years so decided to reduce performance in certain areas so that they could get credit for improving performance at a later stage:

> In the second and third year [of the efficiency index] we began to realize that simply working our staff harder and keeping the wage bill down was not necessarily the right way to go. So we then had a plan of sliding down the table and accepting that our position on the table would get worse, because everyone wants to get better and slide up the table.
>
> (Trust medical director)

However, some trusts pointed out that it had become easier over time to reach an agreement with the health authorities about the need to moderate future demand for efficiency gains if they had managed to achieve high gains in a particular year (especially if this was due to a specific service reconfiguration which would not be repeated the following year). Some felt that the game playing wasted a lot of time and effort and that they preferred to avoid it if they could. Although the efficiency index is due to be replaced, it is worth noting the problems above as they will relate to any system in which the current performance target is based on past performance.

The financial regime in which trusts operate was also felt to encourage some gaming. It was noted that trusts which fail to meet their financial duties will often get 'bailed out' by the region and thus there may be an incentive to fail to meet these targets – not in a spectacular way which would attract a great deal of attention, but sufficient to allow overspending without penalty. One trust used the example of a neighbouring trust which had managed to get five-star ratings on the *Patient's Charter* targets by overspending and would not be required to meet their deficits the following year. Similarly, those who fail to meet waiting times targets are more likely to receive a share of the extra waiting list funds made available from central resources than those who have already achieved the targets.

One strategy for minimizing gaming is to use a range of performance measures rather than just one which may be easily gamed. Although there are currently a range of indicators for the NHS, a great deal of emphasis has been placed on achievement of the efficiency target and as this is also sometimes linked to explicit rewards for senior staff it is therefore not surprising that gaming has focused on this specific indicator. Although the efficiency index is to disappear, it is important to ensure that the reward structure for meeting any targets is flexible enough to respond to managerial efforts which contribute towards improvements in future targets as well as the achievement of current targets. Development of benchmarks of performance which are independent of the organization's past behaviour can also help to minimize the gains from gaming. Although comparative analysis of performance brings a different set of problems, if managers understand that their future targets will not be influenced to any great extent by current performance, they are more likely to seek out opportunities to improve their performance.

SUMMARY AND POLICY RECOMMENDATIONS

In this chapter we have outlined the importance of ensuring that attention is paid to the potential unintended and dysfunctional consequences induced by any system of performance measurement. It is clear that performance measures do not always effect the desired changes in behaviour. The unintended consequences of some measures may actually encourage people to behave in ways which are directly contradictory to what was expected. Although respondents were referring to the current indicators which may be changed in the future, many will be similar to (or in some cases, the same as) existing indicators. Moreover, there is no reason to expect substantially different behavioural responses even for completely new indicators.

Techniques to mitigate some of the specific unintended consequences highlighted by respondents have been suggested and it is also possible to identify ten general strategies which address the dysfunctional outcomes, as noted by Smith (1995). The first four strategies address a large number of problems, and so are likely to be applicable in most situations:

1 involving staff at all levels in the development and implementation of performance measurement schemes;
2 retaining flexibility in the use of performance indicators, and not relying on them exclusively for control purposes;
3 seeking to quantify every objective, however elusive;
4 keeping the performance measurement system under constant review.

The importance of the next three strategies is more dependent on the particular aspect of performance being measured, being most relevant when objectives are poorly defined and measurement of output problematic:

5 measuring client satisfaction;
6 seeking expert interpretation of the performance indicator scheme;
7 maintaining careful audit of the data.

The final three strategies are designed to address specific difficulties – myopia, misrepresentation and gaming – and so should be considered when any of these is especially important. Note however that they may have negative effects relevant to other dysfunctional phenomena as highlighted earlier:

8 nurturing long-term career perspectives among staff;
9 keeping the number of indicators small;
10 developing performance benchmarks independent of past activity.

The extent to which these and other potential solutions are relevant for the new national performance framework is a matter for further research and consideration.

In conclusion, we advocate a cautious approach to the implementation of the national performance framework. Current proposals represent an improvement over the previous methods of managing the NHS, but it would be a mistake to assume that only positive results will be produced. We have illustrated the potential for unintended and dysfunctional side-effects in the NHS and we have suggested some strategies which may be used to help reduce the extent to which they arise in the future.

However, until more is known about the behavioural impact of performance management systems, there will always be a danger that new systems will perpetuate the tendencies towards dysfunctional behaviour and even create additional ones. This suggests that the new national framework should be evaluated not only in terms of the degree to which it produces the expected improvements in the chosen measures, but also in terms of the unanticipated side-effects. A major research task is to identify the characteristics of schemes which influence successfully the behaviour of NHS staff. This would involve consideration of the impact of alternative dissemination methods (e.g. league tables, target setting, benchmarking, informal review) as well as the incentives and sanctions associated with the indicators (e.g. financial, peer pressure, reputation). This is the subject of our future research agenda.

NOTE

1 One of the aims of the study was to investigate the views of people at different levels in the organization on how their performance was judged and how they felt they were held to account. However, the results of this are not discussed further in this chapter but will be reported elsewhere. We also gathered views of a sample of general practitioner (GP) fund-holders, but again, these are not discussed in this chapter.

REFERENCES

Chassin, M.R., Hannan, E.L. and DeBuono, B.A. (1996). Benefits and hazards of reporting medical outcomes publicly. *New England Journal of Medicine*, 334(6), 394–8.

Conway, A.C., Keller, R.B. and Wennberg, D.E. (1995). Partnering with physicians to achieve quality improvement. *The Joint Commission Journal on Quality Improvement*, 21(11), 619–26.

Department of Health (1997). *The New NHS: Modern, Dependable.* London: The Stationery Office.

Finlan, J.K. and Zibrat, F.S. (1994). Struggles and successes: experiences of a beta test site. *The Joint Commission Journal on Quality Improvement*, 20(2), 49–56.

Ghali, W.A., Ash, A.S., Hall, R.E. and Moskowitz, M.A. (1997). Statewide quality improvement initiatives and mortality after cardiac surgery. *Journal of the American Medical Association*, 277(5), 379–82.

Goddard, M., Mannion, R. and Smith, P.C. (1999) Assessing the performance of NHS hospital trusts: the role of 'hard' and 'soft' information. *Health Policy*, 48, 119–34.

Goldman, R.L. and Thomas, T.L. (1994). Using mortality rates as a screening tool: the experience of the Department of Veterans Affairs. *The Joint Commission Journal on Quality Improvement*, 20(9), 511–21.

Greene, J. and Wintfield, N. (1996). Report cards on cardiac surgeons: assessing New York State's approach. *New England Journal of Medicine*, 332(18), 1229–32.

Jackson, P. (ed.) (1995). *Measures for Success in the Public Sector*. London: Public Finance Foundation.

Meekings, A. (1995). Unlocking the potential of performance measurement: a practical implementation guide. *Public Money and Management*, 15(4), 5–12.

Moller, J.H., Powell, C.B., Joransen, J.A. and Borbas, C. (1994). The paediatric cardiac care consortium – revisited. *The Joint Commission Journal on Quality Improvement*, 20(12), 661–8.

Nash, D.B. (1995). Quality of measurement or quality of medicine? *Journal of the American Medical Association*, 273(19), 1537–8.

Nelson, E.C., Batalden, P.B., Plume, S.K., Mihevc, N.T. and Swartz, W.G. (1995). Report cards or instrument panels: who needs what? *The Joint Commission Journal on Quality Improvement*, 21(4), 155–66.

NHS Executive (1998). *The New NHS – Modern, Dependable: A National Framework for Assessing Performance – Consultation Document* (EL(98)4). London: DoH.

Nutley, S. and Smith, P.C. (1998). League tables for performance improvement in health care. *Journal of Health Services Research and Policy*, 3(1), 50–7.

Rosenthal, G.E. and Harper, D.L. (1994). Cleveland health quality choice: a model of collaborative community-based outcomes assessment. *The Joint Commission Journal on Quality Improvement*, 20(8), 425–42.

Smith, P. (1993). Outcome-related performance indicators and organizational control in the public sector. *British Journal of Management*, 4(3), 135–51.

Smith, P. (1995). On the unintended consequences of publishing performance data in the public sector. *International Journal of Public Administration*, 18(2/3), 277–310.

Stewart, J.D. (1984). The role of information in public accountability. In A. Hopwood and C. Tomkins (eds), *Issues in Public Sector Accounting*. Oxford: Phillip Allan.

UK Government (1995). *The Citizen's Charter: Five Years On*. London: HMSO.

8

PERFORMANCE INDICATORS FOR MANAGING PRIMARY CARE: THE CONFOUNDING PROBLEM

Antonio Giuffrida,
Hugh Gravelle and
Martin Roland

INTRODUCTION

Increasing policy emphasis on quality in the National Health Service (NHS) has led to greater interest in performance indicators in all areas, including primary care. In setting out its future policy on the NHS in the White Paper *The New NHS: Modern, Dependable* (Department of Health 1997), the incoming Labour government stressed the need for a new performance framework to measure progress towards its objectives.

The recent consultation paper produced by the NHS Executive (1998) proposed additional performance indicators to compare the quality of primary health care in health authorities and the extent to which health authorities are effectively delivering appropriate health care. Health authorities will be responsible for monitoring the performance of the primary care groups (PCGs), established in April 1999 to commission and deliver health care. The PCGs will have responsibility for monitoring the quality of primary care delivered by their constituent general practices.

The greater emphasis on performance monitoring and accountability increases the importance of understanding the merits and drawbacks of the measures used. The aim of this chapter is to use one of the recently proposed primary care performance indicators to illustrate general issues raised in the selection and interpretation of performance indicators. The indicators examined relate to care for chronic conditions and are similar to those which have been widely used in the USA.

The usefulness of performance indicators depends on the extent to which they measure aspects of performance for which decision makers can properly be held to account, and whether they have unintended consequences for the behaviour of decision makers. Chapter 7 addresses the second of these issues. Our main concern here is with the first: in what sense are the indicators a measure of performance?

The first section discusses the suitability of hospital admission rates for three chronic conditions (asthma, diabetes and epilepsy) as performance indicators for primary care. The rationale is that such conditions are mainly managed in primary care, so that high rates of admission to hospital indicate that there is poor quality primary care. However, admission rates for the conditions may be influenced by socio-economic characteristics and the supply of secondary care, as well as by the quality of primary care provided. Chronic conditions indicators can be used to illustrate the implications of the general problem of 'confounding': performance indicators may reflect both the decisions of those whose performance is being monitored and factors which are outside their control. The next section is methodological and discusses different methods of allowing for such confounding. The following section is empirical and investigates the magnitude of the confounding problem using data on admission rates in English family health services authorities (FHSAs)[1] over a six-year period from 1989/90 to 1995/6. The final section summarizes the lessons to be drawn and makes suggestions for improvement in the set of primary care performance indicators.

CHRONIC CONDITION ADMISSION RATES AS PRIMARY CARE PERFORMANCE INDICATORS

The NHS Executive consultation document suggested a set of high level indicators to assess primary care performance in health authorities (NHS Executive 1998). The indicators were intended to measure whether health authorities have cost-effective delivery of appropriate health care. Some, such as the percentage of the female population aged 20 to 64 screened for cervical cancer and the percentage of children vaccinated, were previously included in the health service indicators produced by the NHS Executive over the years 1990/1 to 1994/5 (NHS Executive 1995). Additional indicators, relating to prescribing, hospital admission rates for certain acute conditions, and admission rates for three chronic conditions (asthma, diabetes and epilepsy) were proposed. In this chapter we focus on the chronic conditions indicator.

The chronic disease management indicator is an aggregation of age and sex standardized admission rates for asthma, diabetes and epilepsy. It is argued that the conditions are substantially managed in primary care so that 'high hospital admission rates for these conditions may indicate poor management of these conditions in primary care' (NHS Executive 1998: 32).

Admission rates for certain chronic conditions have been used in other countries, principally the USA, as measures of primary care performance (Arnold and Zuvekas 1989; Billings and Hasselblad 1989). Such conditions are often termed 'ambulatory care sensitive conditions' (ACSCs) and are defined as conditions where timely and effective ambulatory care could help reduce the risk of hospitalization either by preventing the onset of illness, controlling an acute episode of illness or better long-term management. The assumption underlying the use of hospitalization rates for ACSCs (Rutstein *et al.* 1976) is that informed patients receiving continuous and good primary care will require fewer hospitalizations. ACSC admission rates have been used extensively in the USA as measures of access to primary care (Arnold and Zuvekas 1989; Billings and Hasselblad 1989; Massachusetts Division of Health Care Finance and Policy 1995; Ricketts *et al.* 1998).

Previous research in the United Kingdom (UK) suggests that some characteristics of primary care which might reflect practice quality are related to ACSC admission rates. For example, lower admission rates for asthma have been found in practices whose prescribing patterns suggested better preventive care (Griffiths *et al.* 1996; Aveyard 1997), and lower admission rates for diabetes have been found in practices with better organized diabetic care (Farmer and Coulter 1990). Griffiths *et al.* (1997) found that higher admission rates for asthma in East London were negatively associated with numbers of partners in a practice and positively with high night-visiting rates. It was suggested that smaller partnerships found it more difficult to develop systems for identifying, reviewing and educating asthma patients. US studies also indicate that higher

ACSC admission rates are more likely among communities with poor access to primary care (Weissman *et al.* 1992; Begley *et al.* 1994; Bindman *et al.* 1995; Billings *et al.* 1996).

Confounding problems

The interpretation of admissions for the chronic conditions used in the proposed indicator is not straightforward because of the potentially confounding effects of hospital admission policies, the supply of secondary care and socio-economic factors which affect the prevalence of the conditions or propensity to seek care.

Although hospital admission for stabilization of diabetes used to be common, it is now rare, and secular trends in diabetes admission rates are likely to show a steady fall as a result of changing hospital practices. Most admissions for diabetic control are of insulin dependent diabetics who tend to be managed by specialists in secondary care. Non-insulin dependent diabetics are in the majority and are usually managed by primary care. They will normally only be admitted with the complications of diabetes which could indeed be related to poor primary care management. However, there may be a long time lag between poor quality primary care management of a case and resulting problems, such as blindness, which require admission.

Trends in asthma admission rates need to be interpreted against a background of encouragement to patients to seek admission when they are unwell, including allowing patients to admit themselves directly to respiratory wards. This policy is intended to reduce asthma deaths resulting from delayed admission or from failure to recognize the severity of an attack. Asthma admission rates may therefore be dependent on local secondary care policies and only partially dependent on the quality of primary care management. For example, Durojaiye *et al.* (1989) found that asthma admission rates in Nottingham increased markedly between 1975 and 1985, a period of time when there appeared to be improvements in primary care, possibly because of changing admission policies for asthma.

Watson *et al.* (1996) found that the asthma admission rate in the West Midlands was strongly associated with deprivation in the community as measured by the Townsend Index. Similarly, the finding by Griffiths *et al.* (1997) that practice-level asthma admission rates were associated with high night-visiting rates may be because high rates for night visiting might reflect higher patient demand from a less healthy population. US studies also find that socio-economic conditions affect admission rates (Weissman *et al*. 1992; Begley *et al*. 1994; Bindman *et al*. 1995; Billings *et al*. 1996).

In New Zealand, where hospital utilization is controlled via general practitioner (GP) gatekeeping, Brown and Barnett (1992) found that regional differences in diabetes admission rates were mainly explained by hospital bed supply, rather than the availability of GPs per population, even after controlling for socio-demographic characteristics of the population. However, a Spanish study (Casanova and Starfield 1995) of admission rates for children found that, unlike the US, they were not correlated with supply-side or socio-economic factors. The authors suggested that this was due to the provision of a universal free health service in Spain.

Although admission rates for similar conditions to those in the proposed chronic conditions indicator are widely used as markers of access to care in the USA, cultural, socio-economic and organizational differences between the USA and England, and the problems posed by confounding, may mean that the indicator is not a suitable measure of primary care quality in England. We address this issue in the next two sections. In the first we discuss four methods of allowing for confounding, and in the second we apply one of these methods (multiple regression) to English data. We examine the extent to which socio-economic factors and supply-side variables influence the admission rates used in the proposed performance indicator and thus cloud the relationship between it and the quality of primary care.

COMPARING LIKE WITH LIKE: ALLOWING FOR CONFOUNDING

Confounding arises when admission rates are influenced by other factors in addition to the quality of primary care. To assess performance it is necessary to remove the effects of factors which are outside the control of the decision makers whose performance is being measured. There are four methods of allowing for confounding so that the remaining variation in admission rates can be attributed to the quality of primary care.

Standardization

The characteristics of the population in an area could affect admission rates. Obvious examples are the age and sex composition of the population, but other possibilities include income, education level and car ownership, which may influence either health status or the propensity to seek care. The admission rate for an area may depend on the mix of such characteristics in the population.

Standardization is an attempt to correct for the impact of the population mix on admission rates. Because of the absence of data on other population characteristics, it is usual to standardize only for the age and sex composition of the population and to compare standardized admission ratios. The standardized admission ratio for an area is a weighted average of the ratios of the age and sex-specific admission rates in an area to the age and sex-specific admission rates for some reference population (typically the national population). In *direct standardization* the weights are the population shares in the reference population. A high standardized admission ratio is a signal that the area has relatively higher admission rates after allowing for the demographic mix in the area. Standardization has the advantages that it reduces the importance of random fluctuations in age and sex-specific admission rates and provides a single composite measure.

However, although standardization is relatively simple it has a serious drawback. In order for standardization to remove the effects of confounding by the population characteristics (in addition to age and sex) which affect admission rates it is necessary to calculate specific admission rates for the subsets of the population defined by these other characteristics. But routine data do not permit classification of the population by the other characteristics, such as employment status, which might affect admission probabilities, so that standardization cannot allow for the effects of potential confounders, apart from age and sex mix.

Cluster analysis

This method groups health authorities with similar socio-economic conditions together so that a health authority can be compared with the other health authorities in its socio-economic cluster. The Office of National Statistics has produced a general-purpose classification of health authorities which can be used for this purpose (Wallace 1996). Cluster analysis was used extensively in the NHS Executive consultation document on clinical indicators in secondary care in an attempt to allow for socio-economic factors which might confound comparisons of age and sex standardized rates – for example, for perioperative myocardial infarctions (NHS Executive 1997: 50). It was also used illustratively in the performance assessment consultation document (NHS Executive 1998: 10) to compare health authoritiy rates of emergency admission for those over 75 years old.

There are three problems with this approach:

- The provision of secondary hospital care is not one of the characteristics used to group health authorities, so that comparisons within clusters are still vulnerable to confounding.
- The same clusters of health authorities are used for all performance indicators. This would be justifiable only if the socioeconomic variables used to cluster health authorities affected the different admission rates in the same way.
- The method used to group health authorities with 'similar' socioeconomic characteristics into clusters rests on an essentially arbitrary concept of 'similarity' which takes no account of the way in which socio-economic characteristics may affect health or the use of health services.

Data envelopment analysis

Data envelopment analysis (DEA) is a means of comparing the admission rates for health authorities which are similar to each other in other respects so that potentially confounding factors are allowed for. DEA calculates the lowest possible admission rate which can be achieved with given levels of confounding variables measuring secondary care supply and socio-economic conditions. An area's performance is then measured as the difference between its actual admission rate and the best possible (lowest) admission rate that it could have achieved given its supply and socio-economic characteristics.

DEA is much more flexible than cluster analysis since the set of comparator health authorities for a health authority will vary with the performance indicator being considered. It has the conceptual advantage over cluster analysis that it is possible to give a sensible and policy relevant interpretation to the method by which DEA selects the set of comparator health authorities. However:

- Results can be heavily dependent on extreme observations.
- It is not possible statistically to test the underlying assumptions.

Multiple regression analysis

This method attempts to allow for confounding variables by using information on all the decision making units (health authorities) being compared (Aveyard 1997). The regression model predicts the admission rate that a health authority should have, given the values of the confounding variables. The difference between the actual value and the predicted value (the residual) is a measure of how well or badly the health authority is doing, given the values of the confounding variables. In effect, regression analysis standardizes for a range of possible determinants of the performance indicator.

Regression analysis has a number of advantages compared with the other methods of allowing for confounding:

- Flexibility: different confounding variables can by considered for different indicators.
- Statistical tests can be performed which indicate whether the assumptions used are good ones and whether observed relationships between potential confounders and admission rates are likely to be genuine or to have arisen by chance.
- Regression is relatively transparent compared with cluster analysis and with DEA.

AN ANALYSIS OF HOSPITALIZATION RATES

This section uses regression analysis to relate the variation in admission across areas to characteristics of primary care, secondary care and socio-economic characteristics of the areas. The aim is to assess the magnitude of potential confounding by these factors. To save space we concentrate on the results for asthma but all the substantive results hold for the other conditions.[2]

Data

The hospitalization data were obtained from the Hospital Episodes Statistics (HES) Unit at the Department of Health for each of the financial years 1989/90–1994/5. The data covered the 367 English local authorities, and were aggregated to FHSA level. (We use FHSAs, rather than health authorities because our other data are more readily available at FHSA level.) The measure of hospitalization for an area is the number of residents with ordinary admissions or day case episodes having asthma (ICD–10 codes J45-J46), diabetes mellitus (ICD–10 codes E10-E14) and epilepsy (ICD–10 codes G40-G41) as primary diagnosis. Hospitalization rates are measured per 10,000 residents. Summary statistics for hospitalization rates for asthma, diabetes and epilepsy are presented in Table 8.1. The table shows, for each of the six years 1989/90–1994/5, the unweighted mean FHSA admission rate, the minimum and maximum rates and the standard deviation (Std. dev.). Hospitalization rates for asthma were quite stable during the period, while both diabetes and epilepsy rates increased. For all three diseases there is a large variation in admission rates among the 90 FHSAs.

Impact of age-sex standardization

Even if there were no confounding factors apart from age and sex, direct standardization might not reveal the true primary care quality related differences in admission rates between areas. Unless improvements in primary care quality reduce all age and sex-specific admission rates by the same amount or reduce them all in the same proportion, direct standardization will not correct appropriately for differences in age and sex structure across areas (Freeman and Holford 1980). If quality does not act uniformly on age

Table 8.1   Unstandardized hospitalization rates per 10,000 population

Condition	Year	Mean	Std. dev.	Minimum	Maximum
Asthma	1989/90	19.908	6.036	9.778	35.997
	1990/1	19.619	5.972	6.397	35.404
	1991/2	21.574	5.825	9.443	35.827
	1992/3	20.948	5.780	9.938	36.468
	1993/4	22.173	5.687	12.579	40.922
	1994/5	20.273	5.873	3.241	34.728
Diabetes	1989/90	10.479	2.922	4.426	19.910
	1990/1	10.892	3.571	4.742	21.406
	1991/2	11.737	4.550	4.053	27.112
	1992/3	12.458	5.256	4.857	30.553
	1993/4	12.504	5.538	4.834	35.642
	1994/5	13.000	5.462	2.191	31.504
Epilepsy	1989/90	7.567	2.460	3.127	14.380
	1990/1	7.874	2.515	3.493	14.945
	1991/2	8.404	2.544	4.077	17.244
	1992/3	8.344	2.331	4.169	14.258
	1993/4	8.267	2.286	3.824	16.982
	1994/5	8.717	2.754	1.823	16.519

and sex-specific admission rates the analyst faces a dilemma. One can compare age and sex-specific admission rates across areas but such a mass of comparisons may be difficult to interpret. Or one can standardize and take a weighted average of the age and sex-specific rates knowing that such an aggregate may be misleading.

Faced with this dilemma one might be tempted just to use crude admission rates (total admissions for all age and sex groups divided by the total population) on the grounds that such aggregation is simple. The impact of using direct standardization compared with crude admission rates is shown in Tables 8.2 and 8.3. Table 8.2 shows the impact on the rankings of FHSAs in terms of their asthma admission rates and Table 8.3 the size of the changes in asthma admission rates.

Standardization has a marked impact, so that it clearly does matter whether one uses crude or standardized rates. It is conventional to assume that it is better to attempt to separate out differences across areas due to differences in demographic composition from those due to genuine area effects, even if the method adopted is accurate only under quite strong assumptions about the way quality differences affect admission rates. We agree and feel that standardization is better than using crude admission rates. In what follows we examine the impact of confounding by socio-economic and supply-side variables on the directly standardized admission rates, rather than on the crude admission rates.

Table 8.2   Impact of standization[a] versus crude rates on FHSA ranking by asthma hospitalization rates

Difference in ranking	1989/90	1990/1	1991/2	1992/3	1993/4	1994/5
<10	73	76	81	78	76	74
10–20	7	3	2	4	5	4
>20	10	11	7	8	9	12
Average[b]	8	8	7	7	7	9
Correlation[c]	0.797**	0.81**	0.833**	0.882**	0.861**	0.795**

Notes: [a]   Hospitalization rates are directly standardized for age and sex. The reference year is 1991/2
   [b]   Average absolute change in ranking
   [c]   Spearman's rank correlation
   **   Correlation is significant at the .01 level (2-tailed)

Table 8.3   Differences between crude and standardized asthma hospitalization rates[a]

Change in hospitalization rate[a]	1989/90	1990/1	1991/2	1992/3	1993/4	1994/5
< –5	6	5	4	3	4	5
–3 –5	1	1	0	1	0	0
–1 –3	6	4	5	4	5	3
–1 +1	65	68	67	67	68	71
+1 +3	6	5	9	9	8	2
+3 +5	0	2	0	1	0	2
> +5	6	5	5	5	5	7
Average[b]	2.101	1.868	1.815	1.657	1.487	1.746

Notes: [a] Per 10,000 per population
   [b] Average absolute change

Composite or separate indicators?

The NHS Executive consultation document suggests that the admission rates for asthma, diabetes and epilepsy be combined to yield a single composite indicator (NHS Executive 1998: 32). Combining the three rates is an attempt to reduce the influence of random factors which affect the rates for each condition and to make comparison easier by reducing the amount of information presented. But there is a potential disadvantage: the three admission rates may be measuring different aspects of the quality of primary care. If so, adding the rates will not necessarily yield a more accurate indicator of quality.

Table 8.4 reports the correlation between the hospitalization rates for the three conditions. The rates are positively and significantly correlated, as we would expect if they were all influenced in the same way by the same aspects of quality and the confounding factors, but the correlation is by no means perfect. Since it is clearly possible for GPs to devote different amounts of effort and resources to care of these three conditions, it may be more sensible not to aggregate them to provide a single indicator.

Stability of admission rates

If there are large random fluctuations in admission rates each year at area level their usefulness as indicators is undermined. Table 8.5

Table 8.4   Correlation[a] between hospitalization rates[b]

Asthma	1		
Diabetes	0.621**	1	
Epilepsy	0.674**	0.561**	1
	Asthma	Diabetes	Epilepsy

Notes: [a] Pearson correlation coefficient
    [b] Direct age and sex standardization
    ** Correlation significant at the .01 level (2-tailed)
    Number of observations: 540)

shows the distribution of changes in rankings between years and the correlations in the area rankings in consecutive years. There are quite large changes in rankings from one year to the next. Using the change in the rankings in terms of asthma admission rates between 1993/4–1994/5 as an example, we see that 23 areas moved between 10 and 20 places in the rankings and 13 moved more than 20 places. The correlation between area rankings in terms of asthma admission rates in these two years was 0.865.

Table 8.5 shows that adding up the three admission rates does not yield noticeably more stable rankings than any of the three rates used separately. Temporal stability is therefore not a strong argument for using a single composite measure. It would be better to use a moving average of several years' admission rates. This would reduce the importance of random fluctuations in any one year though it would take longer for genuine changes in admission rates to become apparent. A two- or three-year average would seem a suitable compromise.

Allowing for confounding with regression analysis

The literature suggests that admission rates may be influenced by both socio-economic factors and by the supply of secondary care. We used multiple regression to explore the confounding problem. We looked at the relationship between directly standardized admission rates and a large number of potential explanatory variables relating to both socio-economic conditions and the supply of care.[3]

The regression predicts the admission rate expected in an area after taking account of the potential confounding variables. The difference between the predicted admission rate and the actual admission rate (the residual) will arise from factors which have not

Table 8.5   Changes in FHSA ranking by hospitalization rates[a] between subsequent years

Change in ranking	1989/90–1990/1	1990/1–1991/2	1991/2–1992/3	1992/3–1993/4	1993/4–1994/5
All three conditions					
<10	49	53	67	65	62
10–20	24	25	19	23	18
>20	17	12	4	2	10
Average[b]	12	10	7	7	10
Correlation[c]	0.805**	0.85**	0.926**	0.946**	0.864**
Asthma					
<10	51	56	66	58	54
10–20	20	24	17	23	23
>20	19	10	7	9	13
Average[b]	13	10	8	9	10
Correlation[c]	0.776**	0.831**	0.911**	0.903**	0.865**

Notes: [a] Hospitalization rates are directly standardized for age and sex. The reference year is 1991/2
   [b] Average absolute change in ranking
   [c] Spearman's rank correlation
   ** Correlation significant at the .01 level (2-tailed)

been included as confounding variables. We used the residual as a measure of the effect of the unobserved quality of primary care on admission rates after allowing for confounding effects. The residual is the admission rate 'standardized' for the explanatory or confounding variables.

If there are factors which influence admission rates and which have been left out of the regression equation, the residual admission rates will still be confounded as measures of quality. For example, cigarette consumption, air pollution and pollen counts are likely to influence asthma admission rates. If such omitted confounders are correlated with the variables included in the regressions, then part of the variation in admission rates which is due to the omitted variables will be attributed to the included variables. The residual is then more reliable as a measure of the effect of primary care quality since more of the admission rate is explained by the included variables. How much faith is placed in the residual admission rate as a measure of quality depends on how important the omitted explanatory variables are and on the extent to which they are correlated with variables we have included. The failure to allow for all confounders means that the performance indicators should be used as a trigger for a more detailed investigation in individual health authorities, rather than as basis for immediate action.

The variables in use in the regression analysis are in three groups. Supply conditions in secondary care are measured by the number of hospital medical staff in general medicine per 10,000 population and by a variable which reflects the distance-weighted number of beds per head of population. The hypothesis is that admission rates will be positively associated with both variables.

The second group of variables measure socio-economic conditions in the FHSAs. The variables cover housing conditions, social class, unemployment and car ownership. We also included two variables, prescriptions and night visits, which reflect the propensity of the population to use primary care services. These variables reflect both the health needs of the population and their willingness to consult GPs. We would expect that greater use of primary care services is associated with higher admission rates for two reasons. First, greater utilization is associated with worse population health. Second, the greater the volume of work on GPs, the less time they have to provide high quality care for chronic conditions. We also included more direct measures of population health, such as the proportion of the working age population who were permanently sick and the standardized mortality ratio.

The third group of variables reflect supply conditions in primary care. The rationale for including such variables is that we expect the quality of primary care to be associated, positively or negatively, with some of the characteristics of primary care. Some of these variables, such as the number of GPs per head, the proportion of GPs over 65 and the average distance to practices are included in our data. Others, such as practice asthma clinics, the use of registers for proactive care, or special training for practice nurses, are not measured.

Although we cannot observe all the primary care determinants of quality we can use the information in the current data set on the observable variables and admission rates to make inferences about the unobserved factors associated with quality. After allowing for the primary care variables which we can measure, we assume that the unexplained variations in admission rates reflect the unobserved aspects of primary care which influence quality. Higher unexplained admission rates are a cause for concern and further investigation.

Regression results

The variables included in the regressions explained 41 per cent of the variance of standardized admission rates across FHSAs for asthma, 53 per cent for epilepsy and 31 per cent for diabetes. Some of the coefficients on the variables were broadly in line with expectations. Admission rates are greater in areas with more hospital beds and more hospital doctors and in areas with more prescriptions. Not all the variables were significant in the three equations. There are also some puzzling findings. For example, population density was negatively correlated with admission rates for diabetes but positively correlated with admission rates for asthma, perhaps because population density is correlated with air pollution.

Are hospitalization rates a proxy for quality?

The results concerning the primary care variables included in the regression analyses tend to support the suggestion that admission rates may be a proxy for some aspects of quality in primary care. Admission rates for all three conditions were significantly negatively related to the GP population ratio and the admission rate for asthma was significantly positively associated with the proportion of GPs over 65. Admission rates for diabetes and epilepsy were positively associated with distance to the nearest practice.

We do not report the regression results in further detail here (Giuffrida *et al.* 1998). We are concerned with the implications of confounding variables for the use of admission rates as quality indicators, rather than with testing the detailed implications of theories about the determinants of admission rates.

We investigate the importance of confounding in two steps. We first compare the rankings of FSHAs by age and sex-standardized asthma admission rates with their rankings after allowing for socio-economic variables. Then we compare the rankings after allowing for socio-economic variables with those after allowing for socio-economic variables *and* supply factors. We use the 'unexplained' variation in admission rates across FHSAs as a proxy for primary care quality. What is unexplained depends on what confounding variables we allow for. When FHSAs are ranked by age and sex-standardized rates all of the cross-area variation in the standardized rate is 'unexplained'. When we allow for the confounding variables via the regression analysis the 'unexplained' variations are the residuals from the regressions: the difference between the actual standardized admission rate and that predicted by the regression.

Allowing for socio-economic factors

Table 8.6 shows the change in rankings of FHSAs when they are ranked by their residual standardized admission rates after allowing for socio-economic factors, compared with their rankings by their standardized admission rates.[4] In 1994/5 the average change in rankings was 15 places and 33 FHSAs had ranking changes of more than 20.

Comparing Table 8.6 with Table 8.2 we see that allowing for socio-economic factors has at least as large or larger effect on rankings as allowing for demographic factors by age and sex standardization. The implication is that, if standardization is felt to be required to allow for confounding by demographic factors, then allowance should also be made for socio-economic confounding variables.

Allowing for supply factors

Next we examine the additional impact of secondary and primary care supply factors. We rank FHSAs by the difference between actual admission rates and those predicted from regressions

Table 8.6 Impact of socio-economic factors on FHSA ranking by asthma hospitalization rates[a]

Change in ranking	1989/90	1990/1	1991/2	1992/3	1993/4	1994/5
<10	36	30	27	28	26	32
10–20	31	27	24	28	26	25
>20	23	33	39	34	38	33
Average[b]	14	16	18	17	19	15
Correlation[c]	0.788**	0.703**	0.635**	0.677**	0.612**	0.734**

Notes: [a] Hospitalization rates are directly standardized for age and sex. The reference year is 1991/2
    [b] Average absolute change in ranking
    [c] Spearman's rank correlation
    ** Correlation significant at the .01 level (2-tailed)

containing both socio-economic and supply variables. Although we made a distinction between secondary and primary care supply factors in our regression analysis we found that their combined effect was small in comparison with the socio-economic factors. Hence in what follows, when we refer to supply, we mean both secondary and primary care supply factors.

Table 8.7 shows the change in rankings caused by allowing for supply variables in addition to the socio-economic variables. The average changes in rankings is around half that caused by the socio-economic factors and the correlations between the rankings allowing and not allowing for the supply variables is always greater than 0.95.

The supply variables are correlated with the socio-economic variables so that part of the effect of supply variables on admission rates is picked up in the regressions, which only included socio-economic variables. Hence we may be understating the effect of supply variables by comparing the regression with supply and socio-economic variables and with socio-economic variables only. To test for this we also estimated a regression containing only supply variables. We then compared the resulting ranking of FHSAs with the ranking from the regression containing supply and socio-economic variables. For all three conditions we found that the effects on FHSA rankings of adding socio-economic variables to the supply variables was greater than the effect of adding supply variables to socio-economic variables. Further, the explanatory power of the regression was greater when only socio-economic

Table 8.7   Impact of supply factors on FHSA ranking by asthma hospitalization rates[a] after allowing for socio-economic factors

Change in ranking	1989/90	1990/1	1991/2	1992/3	1993/4	1994/5
<10	84	83	71	76	73	72
10–20	6	6	19	14	17	17
>20	0	1	0	0	0	1
Average[b]	3	4	6	5	5	6
Correlation[c]	0.984**	0.978**	0.957**	0.964**	0.962**	0.953**

Notes: [a] Hospitalization rates are directly standardized for age and sex. The reference year is 1991/2

[b] Average absolute change in ranking

[c] Spearman's rank correlation

** Correlation significant at the .01 level (2-tailed)

variables were included than when only supply variables were included. For example, in the case of epilepsy, the R^2 was 0.339 with only supply variables, 0.491 with only socio-economic variables, and 0.528 with both sets of variables.

We conclude that supply variables are confounders but that it is more important to allow for socio-economic variables than supply variables.

Effects of confounding

Table 8.8 shows the ten FHSAs which had the highest ranks and the ten FHSAs which had the lowest ranks in the case of asthma admission rates when no allowance is made for demographic factors (Column 1), when admission rates are directly standardized (Column 2), when socio-demographic factors are also allowed for (Column 3) and when all the confounding variables are allowed for (Column 4). Notice that while seven of the directly standardized top ten FHSAs were also in the top ten by crude admission rate, only four of those in the top ten after allowing for socio-economic factors were in the directly standardized top ten.

Table 8.8 is further illustration that the ranking of FHSAs by admission rates is heavily affected by which confounding variables are allowed for and that socio-economic factors are at least as important as the age and sex composition of areas. The smaller impact of supply-side factors is shown by the fact eight of the top ten allowing for socio-economic factors are also in the top ten after allowing for supply effects as well.

Ranking or rates?

We have examined the importance of confounding by looking at its impact on the rankings of FHSAs, since performance indicators are frequently presented in the form of league tables. However, simple rankings, which depend only on whether an area has a higher or lower score than other areas, may not be the most appropriate summary of an area's performance. Rankings take no account of the magnitude of differences in scores between areas nor of the level of the score.

Policy makers may prefer to judge health authorities not by their rankings but by comparing their admission rate against a standard. For example, admission rates which are more than a certain proportion above the national average might be considered to be a

Table 8.8 Top ten and bottom ten FHSAs by asthma hospitalization rates, 1994/5

Rank	Crude rate	Directly standardized	Allowing for socio-economic factors	Allowing for supply and socio-economic factors
1	Manchester	Kingston & Richmond	Kingston & Richmond	Kingston & Richmond
2	Rochdale	Manchester	Buckinghamshire	Buckinghamshire
3	Liverpool	Liverpool	Enfield & Haringey	Berkshire
4	St Helens & Knowsley	Rochdale	Berkshire	Enfield & Haringey
5	Bury	St Helens & Knowsley	Rochdale	Coventry
6	Sheffield	Bury	Doncaster	Doncaster
7	Oldham	Doncaster	Rotherham	Rochdale
8	Doncaster	Kensington, Chelsea & Westminster	Cambridgeshire	Cambridgeshire
9	Coventry	Oldham	Norfolk	Rotherham
10	Sandwell	Coventry	Durham	Sefton
81	Cornwall and Isles of Scilly	Kirklees	Kirklees	Calderdale
82	Avon	Hampshire	Redbridge & Waltham Forest	Kirklees
83	Kirklees	Northumberland	Dudley	Salford
84	Essex	Somerset	Ealing, Hammersmith & Hounslow	Northamptonshire
85	Hampshire	North Yorkshire	Northamptonshire	Redbridge & Waltham Forest
86	Northumberland	Barnet	Salford	Ealing, Hammersmith & Hounslow
87	Somerset	Northamptonshire	Barnet	Barnet
88	North Yorkshire	Croydon	Derbyshire	Derbyshire
89	Derbyshire	Derbyshire	Croydon	Croydon
90	Bedfordshire	Bedfordshire	Bedfordshire	Bedfordshire

cause for concern. The fact that rankings based on admission rates change quite markedly does not mean that confounding variables have important implications for admission rates themselves. It is possible that confounding variables could have quite small, though statistically significant, effects on the level of admission rates and thus have little policy significance if health authority rates are being compared against a standard rate. Our regression results suggest that the confounding socio-economic and supply variables are important. They are statistically significantly associated with admission rates and jointly explain between 30 and 50 per cent of the variation in admission rates.

Table 8.9 is a further illustration of the importance of confounding for comparisons of admission rates against a standard rate. The z score for an area is the difference between its admission rate and the average admission rate, expressed as a proportion of the standard deviation of the admission rate. A z score greater than, say, 2 would suggest that the area has an unusually high admission rate. Table 8.9 reports the correlations for four z scores calculated from crude admission rates, age and sex-standardized admission rates, admission rates after allowing for socio-economic factors and admission rates after allowing for socio-economic *and* supply factors.

We see that the correlations are very similar to those between rankings of FHSAs using these four measures of admission rates. Even if the performance of a health authority is judged by the level of its admission rate, rather than by its ranking, socio-economic conditions and, to a lesser extent, supply factors should be taken into account.

CONCLUSIONS

Policy implications

We can draw some policy conclusions from the examination of the rationale for the new primary care performance indicators, the discussion of the alternative methods of allowing for confounding and the empirical analysis of six years of data on hospitalization rates discussed in the previous section:

- The fact that the hospitalization rates for the three chronic conditions are correlated with primary care variables which can be argued to reflect quality in primary care, provides some justification for their use as proxies for unobserved aspects of quality.

Table 8.9 Impact of confounding factors: correlations[a] of z scores[b] for 1994/5 asthma admission rates

	Crude	Standardized	Allowing for socio-economic factors	Allowing for supply and socio-economic factors
Crude	1			
Standardized	0.795**	1		
Allowing for socio-economic factors[c]	0.488**	0.780**	1	
Allowing for supply and socio-economic factors[c]	0.451**	0.755**	0.976**	1

Notes: [a] Pearson correlation

[b] z score for an area is the difference between its admission rate and the average admission rate as a proportion of the standard deviation of admission rates

[c] Residual rates from regression

** Correlation is significant at the .01 level (2-tailed)

- Hospitalization rates and rankings of FHSAs based on them are quite unstable between years. To reduce the impact of random variations unconnected with performance we suggest that the performance indicator should be based on a moving average of two or three years' data, rather than on a single year.
- The rates for the three conditions are imperfectly correlated and are likely to reflect different aspects of quality. The rates should not be added up to produce a single indicator.
- Standardization for age and sex has a major impact on the hospitalization rates and the rankings of FHSAs, compared with the use of crude admission rates. Hospitalization rates should be age- and sex-standardized.
- Regression analysis is the most appropriate means of comparing like with like and allowing for the confounding effects of socio-economic and supply-side influences on the chronic conditions admission rate indicator.
- Socio-economic differences across FHSAs have the same size-effect on the rankings of FHSAs by hospitalization rates as age and sex standardization. They should therefore be allowed for when comparing authorities.
- Supply-side factors also affect rankings but their effects are smaller than those of socio-economic factors. It is less important to allow for differences in supply conditions across authorities but we recommend it when data is readily available.

Practice level indicators?

We have empirically illustrated some of the issues concerning performance indicators by using health authority-level data. The application of similar indicators to individual practices or to PCGs raises the same types of problems, often in sharper form. In particular:

- Since fewer patients are admitted from individual practices than from health authorities, it will be more difficult to disentangle the effects on admission rates of random influences and practice decisions. Longer time horizons will be required.
- Socio-economic confounding will be no less important at practice level but the routine data available will only permit much cruder allowance for such confounding. Socio-economic data are on people in geographical areas, not on patients on practice lists. Attempts to use data on area populations to estimate the socio-economic characteristics of patients on practice lists can be misleading (Carr-Hill and Rice 1995).

A general lesson

Health care organizations use a mix of inputs to produce a large set of outputs. In evaluating performance on one dimension we must take account of performance on all the other dimensions. To properly compare like with like we must allow for the other outputs and their quality as well as the inputs. Such 'confounding' is a fundamental problem whenever we use a single indicator intended to reflect a single dimension of performance.

Primary care in a health authority may score badly on an indicator (such as the chronic conditions admission rate) because it is producing poor quality care or because:

- it is using its resources to produce higher quality in other respects (better health promotion, or child surveillance, or better quality consultations);
- it is producing a greater volume of services (more minor surgery, more night visits);
- it is using fewer resources;
- it is operating in a less favourable socio-economic environment than other health authorities;
- the indicator is adversely affected by variables controlled in other sectors

We have examined the last two sources of confounding and suggested a method of dealing with the confounding. The confounding problems arising from the multiple output, multiple input nature of health care must also be addressed and dealt with in a similar way (Giuffrida and Gravelle 1997). A single performance indicator is an inadequate guide to the overall performance of an organization since it covers only one dimension of performance.

Given the confounding problems and the imperfections in the data available, care is required in interpreting variations in the indicators as reflecting variations in performance by decision makers. Indicators are a useful management tool: when suitably adjusted they can signal the possibility of unusually good or poor performance and the need for further investigation of the specific circumstances in such unusual health authorities.

NOTES

1 The 90 FHSAs were responsible for the administration of primary health care services in England until April 1996 when they were replaced by 95

health authorities with roughly similar geographical coverage. The health authorities are responsible for both primary and secondary care.
2 Giuffrida *et al.* (1998) examine the other newly-proposed primary care performance indicators related to prescribing and admissions for certain acute conditions, and has a fuller set of empirical results.
3 Details of the data and the regression results are given in Giuffrida *et al.* (1998).
4 The residuals are from a regression of standardized rates on the socio-economic variables only. The regression results are obtainable from the authors on request.

REFERENCES

Arnold, J. and Zuvekas, A. (1989). *Using Health Outcomes to Evaluate the Primary Care System: A Manual.* Washington: US Department of Health and Human Services – Public Health Service, Health Resources and Service Administration.

Aveyard, P. (1997). Monitoring the performance of general practices. *Journal of Evaluation in Clinical Practice,* 3, 275–81.

Begley, C.E., Slater, C.E., Engel, M.J. and Reynolds, T.F. (1994). Avoidable hospitalizations and socio-economic status in Galveston County, Texas. *Journal of Community Health* 19, 377–87.

Billings, J. and Hasselblad, V. (1989). *Use of Small Area Analysis to Assess the Performance of the Outpatient Delivery System in New York City: A Preliminary Study.* New York: Health System Agency of New York.

Billings, J., Anderson, G.M. and Newman, L.S. (1996). Recent findings on preventable hospitalizations. *Health Affair Millwood,* 15, 239–49.

Bindman, A.B., Grumbach, K. and Osmond, D. (1995). Preventable hospitalizations and access to health care. *Journal of the American Medical Association,* 274, 305–11.

Brown, L.J. and Barnett, J.R. (1992). Influence of bed supply and health care organization on regional and local patterns of diabetes-related hospitalization. *Social Science and Medicine,* 35, 1157–70.

Carr-Hill, R. and Rice, N. (1995). Is ED-level an improvement on ward level analysis in studies of deprivation and health? *Journal of Epidemiology and Community Health,* 49, S.28–9.

Casanova, C. and Starfield, B. (1995). Hospitalizations of children and access to primary care: a cross-national comparison. *The International Journal of Health Services,* 25, 283–94.

Department of Health (1997). *The New NHS: Modern, Dependable.* London: HMSO.

Durojaiye, L.I.A., Hutchison, T. and Madeley, R.J. (1989). Improved primary care does not prevent the admission of children to hospital. *Public Health,* 103, 181–8.

Farmer, A. and Coulter, A. (1990). Organization of care for diabetic patients in general practice: influence on hospital admissions. *British Journal of General Practice*, 40: 56–8.

Freeman, D.H. and Holford, T.R. (1980). Summary rates. *Biometrics*, 36, 195–205.

Giuffrida, A. and Gravelle, H. (1997). *Measuring performance in primary care: econometric analysis and DEA*. Paper presented to Health Economists' Study Group Meeting, York, July.

Giuffrida A., Gravelle H. and Roland M. (1998). *Performance Indicators for Primary Care Management in the NHS*, CHE discussion paper series no. 160. York: University of York.

Griffiths, C., Naish, J., Sturdy, P. and Pereira, F. (1996). Prescribing and hospital admissions for asthma in East London. *British Medical Journal*, 312, 482–3.

Griffiths, C., Sturdy, P., Naish, J. *et al.* (1997). Hospital admissions for asthma in East London: associations with characteristics of local general practices, prescribing, and population. *British Medical Journal*, 314, 482–6.

Massachusetts Division of Health Care Finance and Policy (1995). *Improving Primary Care: Using Preventable Hospitalization as an Approach*. Boston, MA: Division of Health Care Finance and Policy.

NHS Executive (1995). *Health Service Indicators Handbook*. Leeds: NHS Executive.

NHS Executive (1997). *Clinical Indicators for the NHS (1994–95). A Consultation Document*. London: Department of Health.

NHS Executive (1998). *The New NHS: Modern, Dependable: A National Framework for Assessing Performance*. London: Department of Health.

Ricketts, T.C., Randolph, R., Howard, H.A., Pathman, D. and Carey, T. (1998). Do ambulatory sensitive condition admission rates identify access problems in rural and urban areas? Mimeograph. University of North Carolina at Chapel Hill.

Rutstein, D.D., Berenberg, W., Chalmers, T.C. *et al.* (1976). Measuring the quality of medical care: a clinical method. *New England Journal of Medicine*, 294, 582–8.

Wallace, M. (1996). *The ONS Classification of Local and Health Authorities of Great Britain*. London: ONS.

Watson, J.P., Cowen, P. and Lewis, R.A. (1996). The relationship between asthma admission rates, routes of admission, and socioeconomic deprivation. *European Respiratory Journal*, 9, 2087–93.

Weissman, J.S., Gatsonis, C. and Epstein, A.M. (1992). Rates of avoidable hospitalization by insurance status in Massachusetts and Maryland. *Journal of the American Medical Association*, 268, 2388–94.

9

REFERENCE COSTS AND THE PURSUIT OF EFFICIENCY

Diane Dawson and Andrew Street

INTRODUCTION

Both the White Paper, *The New NHS: Modern, Dependable* (Department of Health 1997), and the consultation paper on performance (NHS Executive 1998a) stress the importance of finding better measures of performance for the National Health Service (NHS) than the long-criticized purchaser efficiency index:

> The Purchaser Efficiency Index simply failed to reflect the breadth of what is important in the NHS and created perverse incentives which ran counter to the real priorities for the health service. The balance needs to be shifted so that due weight is given to the things that really matter to patients and the public – the cost and quality of care the NHS delivers and the benefit patients get from their treatment.
>
> (NHS Executive 1998a: 3)

A range of performance measures have been proposed, most of which will be used to assess health authorities (NHS Executive 1998a). Among these, reference costs are intended to summarize the efficiency of the hospital sector and, when aggregated over all the providers used by a health authority, to assess the efficiency of the health authority itself:

> 'reference costs' ... will itemise what individual treatments across the NHS cost. By requiring NHS Trusts to publish and

benchmark their own costs on the same basis, the new arrangements will give Health Authorities, Primary Care Groups and the NHS Executive a strong lever with which to tackle inefficiency.

(Department of Health 1997: 9)

Reference costs are based on costed health care resource groups (HRGs) and are available in three formats (NHS Executive 1998b):

1 A comprehensive list of the costs of every treatment offered by every NHS trust in England.
2 The *National Schedule of Reference Costs* (NSRC) provides summary statistics (mean, range, inter-quartile range) from all trusts for each HRG, by method of admission.
3 The *National Reference Cost Index* (NRCI) reports the weighted average of all HRG costs in a trust relative to the national average.

If efficiency measures based on costed HRGs are to be central to the new system, we need to be clear about what aspects of health care efficiency are better understood by availability of this costing information. As information itself does not lead directly to change, it is important to examine incentives to use information on HRG costs and whether attempts to use this information to regulate behaviour in the NHS are likely to lead to perverse, beneficial or neutral outcomes.

This chapter is organized as follows. In the first section we set out the principles behind the proposed technique for determining the cost of individual treatments described using HRGs. The next section considers the main strategies trusts might pursue to improve their league table position, while the following section assesses the intended uses of the schedule. The final section offers conclusions and suggestions as to how the system might be developed.

COST AND OUTPUT MEASUREMENT IN THE UK

To be a valid comparative index, a reference costing schedule must be standardized on three bases:

1 the means of describing units of activity;
2 the method for classifying patients into comparable groups; and
3 the approach to determining treatment costs for each group.

Hospital activity: finished consultant episodes

The NHS is unusual in its approach to measuring the activities of the hospital sector. Most countries express inpatient activity in terms of the number of patients admitted to or discharged (including deaths) from hospital, so that a unit of hospital activity is said to have been provided when the patient's stay in hospital is complete. In contrast, since 1988/9 the NHS has decomposed the hospital stay to reflect the number of consultants assuming responsibility for the patient. When the patient is discharged from the care of the consultant (or specialty), a completed unit of activity is said to have been provided. This may not correspond with the patient being discharged from hospital. The time between a consultant assuming responsibility for a patient and discharging the patient from hospital or transferring responsibility to a colleague is called a finished consultant episode (FCE). Because a patient may receive care from various consultants during any particular spell in hospital, if NHS activity is measured using FCEs, higher levels of activity will be apparent than if the number of discharges and deaths were used.

While this counting method makes international comparisons difficult, it also complicates comparison of hospital activity in the NHS both over time and across institutions. Comparisons over time are made difficult because of the possibility of 'episode inflation' whereby the number of recorded episodes increases at a faster rate than the number of discharges and deaths. This problem may have been further compounded by the introduction of the internal market and the use of FCEs as the currency for contracts between health authorities and hospitals. These changes have created incentives for providers to record as many episodes as possible, however short they may be. Further, the purchaser efficiency index, designed to encourage health authorities to secure non-funded increases in activity from the hospitals with which they contract, expresses desirable activity increases in terms of FCEs. Hospitals could claim activity improvements by simply coding internal transfers more completely.

Cross-sectional comparisons using FCEs are compromised by the amount of local discretion over what constitutes a completed episode. The implications of using FCEs as the basis for comparative cost assessment are recognized in the documentation material accompanying the software for Version 3 HRGs:

> one hospital may count the admission from A&E [accidents and emergency] as one FCE, the transfer to medical ward as

another, and the transfer to surgery for a gastroscopy and then back to the medical ward as two further FCEs; another hospital may class all these internal transfers as one FCE. Needless to say the resource use allocated to the one FCE in the second hospital will be much higher than any of the individual FCEs in the first hospital.

(National Casemix Office 1997: 21)

In the consultation document on reference costs this problem is recognized and it is proposed that by the second year of publication HRG costs will be based on aggregating FCEs into 'provider spells' (NHS Executive 1998b). This change is likely to be welcomed but it does create aggregation problems because of the current absence of a unique patient identifier with which to link FCEs forming part of the same spell, and in retaining casemix information.[1]

Casemix: healthcare resource groups

The second important condition for accurate cost comparison is that casemix complexity is adequately accounted for. It is difficult to force hospitals to accept they are relatively inefficient without first establishing that their patients are either no different from those treated elsewhere or that differences have been accounted for in determining relative performance. This implies that not only should hospital activity be described in terms of cases treated, but allowance should be made for differences in casemix complexity. If two hospitals are similar in all respects with the exception that one treats a higher proportion of patients with acute myocardial infarction and a lower proportion with varicose veins then the costs of the hospitals will differ. In order to take account of cost differences which are patient related rather than a reflection of the hospital's efficiency, some means is required of describing (groups of) patients according to their expected use of hospital resources.

The proposal to 'itemise the cost of individual treatments across the NHS' (Department of Health 1997: 19) will entail defining individual treatments in terms of HRGs. HRGs are groups of inpatient FCEs which are purported to have similar health care resource requirements, and efforts to encourage their use in the contracting process was first signalled in 1994 (NHS Executive 1994). HRGs are a locally modified version of diagnostic related groups (DRGs), first developed in the USA (Fetter *et al.* 1980). The National Casemix Office has been developing HRGs in the United Kingdom

(UK), and the third version was released in May 1997 (Benton *et al.* 1998b).

HRGs are formed from routine data about inpatients and day cases recorded in the hospital episodes statistics (HES) dataset. Clinical representatives from each relevant specialty are asked to indicate which types of information recorded in the dataset should be used in the refinement process, the aim being to improve the amount of within-group homogeneity in the length of stay of patients classified to the same HRG. This may lead to recommendations that the presence of secondary diagnoses, indicating complications and co-morbidities, should be accounted for, or that an age split should be made. These clinical judgements have been statistically tested using 1993/4 data for every patient admission for England.

Figure 9.1 depicts the process by which an FCE is assigned to an HRG. Each individual record in the HES dataset is grouped to a single HRG based on the data contained in the record, including procedures conducted, diagnoses, length of stay, age, discharge method and legal status. Where information in any field required for grouping is missing or invalid the FCE will be assigned to one of seven 'undefined' groups.

As well as restricting the type of information available for grouping, reliance on the HES dataset has meant that attempts to reduce within-group variance has focused on explaining length of stay as a proxy for cost, this being the only information vaguely related to resource use routinely available, although occasionally it has been supplemented by other types of information and clinical judgement (Sanderson *et al.* 1995; Benton *et al.* 1998b). Even the procedure hierarchy, designed to ensure that the most 'resource intensive' procedures are used for grouping, is based not on theatre time or equipment use but on the expected relationship between the procedure and post-operative length of stay.

Use of length of stay data to determine groupings is not peculiar to the UK (the original version of US DRGs also relied on it – Fetter *et al.* 1980) but strong assumptions must be made about the extent to which length of stay and cost are correlated. Where the correlation is weak, HRGs will poorly reflect casemix complexity. For example, a number of HRGs are formed by subdividing patients on the basis of age, because older patients (generally over 69 years) tend to be hospitalized for longer than their younger counterparts for the same condition. However, their longer hospitalization might be explained by greater difficulty in making

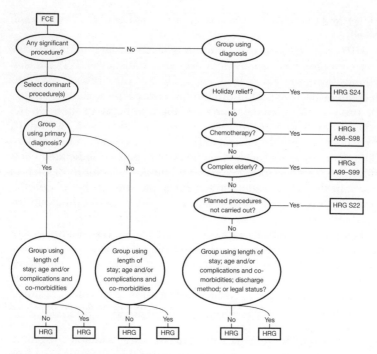

Figure 9.1   HRG grouping flow chart

discharge arrangements rather than their having greater care requirements. If so, the marginal resource implications of such delays may be minimal and it may not be appropriate to assume that a hospital treating a higher proportion of elderly patients in HRGs with an age split has a substantially more resource-intensive casemix.

Costs and cost allocation guidelines

The third requirement of a reference cost schedule is for 'costs' to reflect resource use. The NHS lags behind many other countries in terms of the routine cost data collected by health care providers. This reflects the historically loose relationship between hospital budgets and activity, and the absence of a significant private insurance sector requiring a detailed itemization of resource use for billing purposes. Even the introduction of the internal market failed to generate patient-related costing information.

In contrast to public sector hospitals in countries like Australia, where recording systems make it easy to determine the type and quantity of resources used by any patient during their hospitalization (Jackson *et al.* 1993, 1998), even basic data about the number of diagnostic tests, theatre time or nursing dependency are very difficult and extremely time-consuming to obtain in the NHS. Trusts rarely have automated information about the resources used by particular patients during their hospital stay. Because hospitals do not collect and record data on the use of resources by individual patients, almost all costing in the UK is undertaken on a 'top-down' basis.

This top-down process of allocating costs starts with collection of the annual financial returns of a hospital. These contain information on how much was spent on electricity, maintenance of buildings, catering, drugs, salaries, etc. This expenditure is then reallocated to 'patient treatment services': wards, operating theatre, pharmacy, etc. This reallocation may be direct – such as wages for the number of nurses normally staffing a particular ward; or indirect – for example, operating theatres may be allocated a proportion of the cost of hospital cleaning corresponding to their share of total hospital area.

These costs, once allocated to patient treatment services, are then reallocated to specialties: paediatrics, general medicine, general surgery, etc. Again, this reallocation may be direct – as where a ward only houses patients in one specialty; or indirect – for example, where the proportion of operating theatre time booked by a specialty is used to determine the share of operating theatre costs apportioned to that specialty.

Once each specialty has been assigned its share of total hospital expenditure, the specialty total is divided by the number of bed days occupied by patients coded to that specialty. This process is the basis for calculating what is essentially the accounting cost of an HRG.[2] In moving from the allocation of hospital costs by specialty to the subdivision of specialty costs by HRG, a 'care profile' may be constructed by a working group made up of clinicians, nurses and clinical managers. The care profile describes the resources expected for a typical patient and might include estimates of items such as theatre time, consultant time, radiology, significant drugs and consumables.

In general medicine, for example, a relatively simple approach to estimating resource use is recommended. The process of moving from the allocation of hospital costs to general medicine to the subdivision of these specialty costs by HRG can be illustrated using data taken from a National Casemix Office study (Dredge 1997). The total accounting cost of general medicine is divided by occupied bed days in the specialty in order to derive a cost per bed day:

$$\frac{\text{Total cost of general medicine}}{\text{Occupied bed days}} \quad = \quad £210 \quad = \quad \begin{array}{l}\text{Average cost per}\\ \text{bed day of a}\\ \text{patient in}\\ \text{general medicine.}\end{array}$$

The cost per bed day is then multiplied by the number of bed days attributable to the HRG of interest to derive total expenditure by HRG. This figure is then divided by the number of FCEs assigned to the HRG, to produce the HRG cost per FCE.

$$\text{Average HRG cost per FCE} \quad = \quad \frac{\text{HRG bed days} \times \text{cost per bed day}}{\text{HRG FCEs}}$$

As Table 9.1 illustrates, the cost per bed day is assumed not to vary across HRGs within a specialty.

This example reveals the main mechanisms by which a trust can improve its position in the reference cost league tables. The three most immediate measures are to reduce length of stay, increase throughput, or reassess cost allocation procedures. These strategies are discussed in more detail in the next section.

CLIMBING THE LEAGUE TABLE

Having consulted the published list of costed HRGs, a purchaser finds that one of its providers reports costs 25 per cent above the

Table 9.1   Cost allocation process

		HRG a16	HRG d25	HRG e38
	Bed days	456	850	662
*	Average cost per bed day	£210	£210	£210
÷	Number of FCEs	68	141	211
=	Average cost per FCE	£1408	£1265	£659

Source: adapted from Dredge (1997)

lowest cost reported in the NSRC for that HRG. The management of the health authority or primary care group (PCG) will be judged partly on the basis of the weighted average of costed HRGs of its providers. Unless the purchaser can get their providers to reduce costs, their own performance looks poor. What happens next?

Improving the quality of data used for assignment and costing

Coding to the appropriate HRG relies on the accuracy of information recorded in the HES dataset. This in turn depends on the ability of medical records staff to interpret clinical notes and the extent to which transcription of information is audited and checked. Increasing the accuracy with which support services and the cost of diagnostic procedures are assigned to patients using these services requires more information gathering and monitoring. Devoting additional resources to improving the accuracy with which patient treatment is recorded in hospital information systems and costs are allocated, will increase administrative and information technology costs.

In the past, hospitals and clinicians in the UK have had little incentive to improve the quality of their data collection, let alone report it. In countries like the USA or Australia, where reported costs can affect hospital income, there is a strong incentive to invest in administrative support for improving the quality of information: medical records personnel are better paid and departments better staffed than in the UK, and greater investments have been made in clinical costing systems.

Of course, there is a danger that hospitals will code patients in such a way that they are assigned to more resource-intensive HRGs in an effort to improve their league table position without addressing efficiency. There is evidence to suggest that hospitals in the USA adopted such behaviour following the introduction of DRG funding (Ginsberg and Carter 1986). However, if all hospitals act similarly and resource weights are revised periodically, the advantages to each hospital will not persist beyond the short term. In contrast, the health system will benefit from improved information because no hospital will be able to afford to record less completely than the rivals against which it is compared. Regulatory controls can also be introduced to limit coding inaccuracies. For example, the Victorian Department of Health and Community Services in Australia undertakes a random audit of 1 per cent of medical records to measure the accuracy of coding, provide advice on coding conventions and to reduce the extent to which casemix payments are subject to gaming (Duckett 1994; Health and Community Services 1994).

Increasing throughput

The 'cost' of an HRG can be reduced by:

* reducing length of stay and increasing throughput; and/or
* reducing fixed expenditure and thus the cost per occupied bed day.

If the efficiency of purchasers and of trusts is to be assessed by reference to an index of HRG costs, the short-run response is likely to be to encourage increased hospital throughput and reduced length of stay. Because HRGs currently do not apply to non-acute and non-hospital based activity it is not immediately obvious that these short-term incentives are very different from the actions encouraged by the purchaser efficiency index (Appleby 1996a).

Pressure to reduce length of stay has been associated with concern over two problems: cost shifting and reductions in quality of care. A hospital shifts costs on to general practitioners (GPs) or other carers if it discharges patients with a high level of dependency. There is evidence that this occurred after the introduction of prospective payment in the USA (Kosecoff *et al.* 1990). If the pressure to increase throughput leads to inappropriate early discharge, the result may be increased readmission rates (Henderson *et al.* 1989). The proposed publication of readmission rates may help limit such behaviour, but published clinical outcome data in the UK are likely to remain less comprehensive than those produced by other countries. Of those measures proposed (NHS Executive, 1998a), only a subset of about six hospital indicators are expected to be made available, at least in the short term.[3] This compares with 32 indicators currently produced for health districts and hospitals in Scotland (Clinical Resource and Audit Group 1994, 1996).

The second approach to reducing reported cost also involves changing clinical practice but, this time, indirectly. Most costs are labour, primarily nursing, along with diagnostic services, facilities management and estate costs. Given the age of hospital buildings and equipment, casemix and ward dependency there may be scope for management to reduce the 'cost' of treatments by reducing the use of and/or unit cost of these inputs. Fewer diagnostic services could be offered or the assumptions about dependency reviewed to allow reduced nursing costs. However, this approach may prove counter-productive.

Economists are ordinarily interested in costs only to the extent that they (fail to) reflect opportunity costs and thereby influence decisions that will affect overall economic efficiency. Unit costs, calculated in the form of a costed HRG, do not reflect opportunity costs. They do not show what additional resources will be required (or saved) if we increase the number of hip replacements by 5 per cent or if we shift the balance between surgical and medical admissions within a hospital, or if consultants in neurology reduce the number of scans performed. Because HRG costs do not reflect opportunity costs, care will need to be taken to ensure that use of the reference cost schedule does not create incentives for trusts to avoid what would be genuinely efficiency-enhancing moves. For example, suppose technical developments within one specialty permit an accelerated move from inpatient to outpatient treatment. If the trust implemented the new pattern of treatment, all the overheads currently assigned to patient bed days in this specialty would have to be reallocated to the other specialties in the trust. If the buildings and beds previously used to treat these patients cannot be disposed of rapidly, the costing methodology requires these infrastructure costs be reallocated to all other trust activity. The costs for HRGs (in, say, orthopaedics) rise because dermatology patients are no longer treated as inpatients but as outpatients. Managers and clinicians may have an incentive to slow down the movement from inpatient to outpatient treatment in order to avoid the opprobrium of being accused of having become less 'efficient' in the treatment areas where HRG costs have risen due to the reallocation of fixed costs.

The type of perverse incentive illustrated here will be present whenever proposals to improve patient care involve movement across institutional boundaries. The movement of patients from acute settings will raise the HRG costs of the patients whose treatment remains in the acute unit. These problems are inherent in any system of costing that is predominately one of allocating fixed and common costs rather than identifying marginal costs. It is like punching a beanbag: the volume is fixed and if you depress it at one point, it pops out at another.

USING REFERENCE COSTS

The consultation document sets out a formidable list of expected uses for reference costs in their various formats (NHS Executive 1998b: 3, 6). Purchasers and providers are to use them:

- as benchmarks for cost improvement;
- as indicators of technical efficiency;
- as a mechanism for identifying sources of inefficiency;
- as evidence to inform the negotiation of long-term agreements on improving performance;
- as a means of identifying good practice;
- in costing local health authority-wide Health Improvement Programmes (HImPs).

Ministers and the NHS Executive are to use them:

- in providing national information for funding transfers;
- in providing a better measure of efficiency;
- in ensuring public accountability for the use of NHS resources.

The public and patients are to use them:

- in assessing the efficiency of the NHS locally.

This array of anticipated use is discussed along lines that reflect relevant economic issues:

- Can we expect conclusions about relative efficiency to be statistically valid?
- Are the data appropriate for their intended use?
- What are the incentives to improve efficiency?

Making comparisons

Can the data used to construct the NSRC and NRCI ensure that conclusions about the relative efficiency of individual trusts are statistically valid? Even though the NHS has for the last five years provided guidelines for coding patients and allocating costs, large variations in the calculated cost per HRG remain. Table 9.2 provides examples. This shows the NSRC costs for the five most common HRGs, by each admission type. The highest cost varies from between five and nineteen times the lowest cost for these HRGs. Are we to infer that the efficiency of these trusts differs by as much as the difference in their published costs would suggest?

Table 9.2 Variations in NSRC HRG costs

HRG Description	Costs for all NHS Trusts			
	Trimmed FCEs	Mean (£)	Minimum (£)	Maximum (£)
Day cases				
L21 Bladder minor endoscopic procedure w/o cc	154,686	287	93	692
F06 Oesophagus – diagnostic procedures	140,242	258	49	815
M06 Upper genital tract intermediate procedures	121,382	397	116	1522
J37 Minor skin procedures – Category 1 w/o cc	116,562	343	125	1012
F35 Large intestine – endoscopic or intermediate procedures	111,852	313	50	846
Elective inpatients				
C24 Mouth or throat procedures – Category 3	90,367	674	262	2333
M07 Upper genital tract major procedures	63,345	1702	453	2822
M06 Upper genital tract intermediate procedures	36,440	547	210	1321
B02 Phakoemulsification cataract extraction with lens implant	31,547	847	165	1913
C22 Nose procedures – Category 3	30,907	714	317	1628
Non-elective inpatients				
F47 General abdominal disorders <70 w/o cc	67,032	546	114	2039
D20 Chronic obstructive pulmonary disease or bronchitis	63,543	1184	443	8403
E12 Acute myocardial infarction <70 w/o cc	49,060	1076	248	4226
E36 Chest pain <70 w/o cc	44,989	476	167	2602
S16 Poisoning, toxic effects or overdoses	44,846	321	94	1046

Source: National Casemix Office 1998

Clearly if the differences stem from variations in counting units of activity, deficiencies in casemix measurement, or local interpretation of the costing guidelines, such an inference might be misplaced.

Users of the schedule should also be aware that the costs reported by trusts might arise from chance rather than being statistically significant indicators of inefficiency. With there being 565 HRGs, there is a danger that individual trusts will see too few cases within a particular HRG to produce reliable cost figures.

The consultation document on reference costs recognizes this problem and offers several means of reducing its impact. First, it is proposed to exclude from the database 'those NHS Trusts which undertake a small volume of activity in a given HRG and those HRGs where, nationally, there is a small volume of activity' (NHS Executive 1998b: 7). Second, the interquartile range is to be included among the summary statistics as a measure of variation in reported costs. Reported costs are themselves averages and fail to take account of the variation in costs at HRG level within hospitals. It would be preferable to provide confidence intervals based on patient-level data rather than on information already aggregated at hospital level (Appleby 1996b; Goldstein and Spiegelhalter 1996). Third, 'outlier' cases (those with exceptionally high lengths of stay for their HRG) are to be trimmed from the returns made by trusts. This results in lower mean costs, as cases in the upper tail of the distribution are ignored.

Offsetting these adjustments, the problem of small numbers is exacerbated by the NHS Executive's requirement that trusts subdivide their HRG costs according to admission type and specialty (NHS Executive 1997). For example, for the treatment of varicose veins (Version 2 HRG e44), a trust in north-west region quotes one price in general surgery (£706), another in urology (£794), another in trauma and orthopaedics (£1,040), another in ENT (£422) and yet another in gynaecology (£543) (North West Regional Office 1997). Clearly, for ostensibly the same treatment, this variation is counter-intuitive (quite apart from it being odd to quote prices in some of these specialties!) and is probably nothing to do with differences in actual resource use across specialties. Rather, the explanation is either to do with differences in the cost allocation process by which specialty-based bed day costs are derived or to do with differences in length of stay, which may not be systematically related to clinical practice but are random observations from small numbers. It is estimated that 65 per cent of specialty HRGs at individual trust level contain between one and nine cases per year (Bates 1996). The cost estimates pertaining to such limited samples cannot be expected to be particularly robust.

Assuming we have dealt with problems arising from statistical significance and small numbers, there is the issue of whether remaining observed cost differences are likely to be due to factors other than the relative efficiency of managers and clinicians. Economic theory postulates that if economies or diseconomies of scale exist, efficient small hospitals will have different unit costs from efficient large hospitals. If economies of scope exist, the minimum cost of producing a particular treatment will depend on the set of other treatments provided, and hospitals producing different service mixes will have different minimum unit costs for each treatment. For example, a recent systematic review of the literature on economies and diseconomies of scale identified at least three distinct groups: hospitals with fewer than 100–200 beds, hospitals with more than 600 beds and the rest (Aletras *et al.* 1997).

The reference cost consultation paper (NHS Executive 1998b) recognized there may be sources of cost difference independent of efficiency and proposed that trusts be clustered, so that comparison was limited to other trusts within the cluster. Nineteen cluster groups (some of which were further subdivided) were suggested in the consultation document, these having been devised by the NHS Executive and the Audit Commission in previous examinations of performance.

Trusts are grouped on the basis of:

- size;
- teaching status;
- type of service (acute, children's, orthopaedic, community, learning disability, mental health, or some combination of these);
- whether in London or not.

The first published version of the NSRC and NRCI did not cluster trusts and, as reported in the press, implied all cost differences were due to managerial efficiency. The CD-ROM, containing the raw data, permits users to experiment with clusters. Clustering further undermines the problem of small numbers for comparison but, unless factors expected to affect costs but outside the control of management are accounted for, conclusions about the relative efficiency of hospitals will be spurious. Statistical and econometric techniques are available to identify the extent to which patient treatment costs in teaching hospitals are likely to exceed those in non-teaching hospitals, or the extent to which the presence of specialist units is likely to raise costs relative to hospitals offering more generalized treatment. If the government is to succeed in encouraging people to accept the NSRC or NRCI as valid indicators of relative efficiency, the techniques used to separate differences in costs attributable to efficiency from other sources of cost difference must be robust and transparent.

Appropriate for intended use?

Three different intended uses for data on reference costs appear in the government's list:

1 indicators of where problems may exist;
2 mechanisms for identifying the sources of inefficiency and good practice elsewhere;
3 financial information needed for funding changes in health care.

It is unlikely that a single accounting construct like the costed HRG will be appropriate for such a diverse set of functions.

The basic economic definition of technical efficiency is that inputs are minimized per unit of output of a given quality.[4] If we assume that trusts are clustered to reflect economies of scale and scope, that the main statistical problems have been dealt with, that coding is fairly uniform across trusts, that all interpret the costing guidelines similarly and that we are only interested in the existing institutional locus of services, then reference costs should be useful indicators of possible differences in the use of inputs. Whether this difference in use of inputs reflects a difference in technical efficiency requires the further assumption that there are negligible differences in the quality of care among trusts. Economists are understandably uncomfortable with policies that equate lower financial costs with higher efficiency. A treatment with higher financial costs per patient may be more cost-effective than an alternative with lower financial costs. The collection of outcome data lags far behind the collection of accounting data and, despite frequent references to the importance of quality and appropriateness, the NSRC will not and cannot relate to the cost-effectiveness with which resources are used.

The published form of reference costs will not be a useful 'mechanism' for identifying sources of inefficiency or best practice. In the absence of information on cost shifting and quality measures at HRG level, the 'lowest' reported cost cannot be treated as an indication that the trust producing it is the seat of 'best practice'. In order to trace the source of any inefficiency, the published costs will need to be decomposed. For example, a trust with a published NRCI = 1.3 is reported to be 30 per cent 'less efficient' than the national (or cluster) average, while a trust with NRCI = 0.94 is 6 per cent more efficient than the average. The first trust could have the most efficient paediatrics department in the country while the second might have the most inefficient orthopaedics.

If the NRCI figure is decomposed so that we can identify the orthopaedics problem in the 'efficient' trust and if that trust's orthopaedics HRG costs are themselves decomposed, we might find that the 'inefficiency' is due to the use of agency nurses. What we might expect is that in the process of assembling the data that must ultimately be reported for publication of the NSRC and NRCI, trusts will acquire internal information that may help them identify sources of their higher costs. In this sense, the mechanism for identifying possible sources of inefficiency will not be the publicly available data on NSRC and NRCI but the information collected locally.

The closest the economics literature comes to discussing efficiency in the way the NSRC and NRCI address the issue is in the analysis of 'x-inefficiency' (Leibenstein 1966). The assumption is usually that quality is constant but that a degree of monopoly power has permitted managerial slack to go unpenalized so that costs are higher than technically feasible levels. Quality and appropriateness are issues for the consumer and the problem of the management is 'merely' to seek out and implement cost-effective production processes. The problem for the NHS is more complicated because steps to reduce 'x-inefficiency' that have the consequence of increasing the use of inappropriate treatments or reducing quality will not necessarily be obvious to the consumer or regulator.

The one suggested use for reference cost data that is clearly inappropriate is that of financial planning and funding transfers. Costing a programme that involves a change in services requires information on marginal costs, not short-run average costs. Short-run average costs are backward-looking, representing investments in capacity that were made in the past. Government and the public may want to look backward at how managers and clinicians have used the resources at their disposal – much as auditing accounts take a backward look at stewardship and probity. However, financial planning, funding of revenue transfers and HImPs are all forward-looking and require that estimates of marginal cost be used in budgeting. The proposed reference costs, based on short-run average cost, will not be particularly suitable for these purposes.

For example, a HImP that includes shifting 30 per cent of maternity services from acute units into the community over the next three years could not be costed using HRG costs. The funding requirements of the programme would have to be estimated by asking how many resources would be released by the acute units each year and available for redeployment, and how many resources would be required in the community. The difference is the net cost of the programme and would bear very little correspondence to the present accounting cost of HRGs in obstetrics.

Similar issues arise if HRG costs are used by the NHS Executive for funding transfers. The government has announced its intention of replacing direct payment for what used to be called 'extra-- contractual referrals' by 'budget adjustments' for the main purchaser of trusts providing these services. If a trust located in one health authority permanently holds capacity for treating patients from another health authority, then transferring purchasing power from the second health authority to the first at a rate that reflects overheads (such as the costed HRG) would be appropriate. However if the activity is temporary, as with a waiting-list initiative, then the funding transfer should be at marginal cost.

Incentives to tackle inefficiency

In neither the White Paper nor the consultation document is there discussion of how publishing reference costs will 'create a strong lever with which to tackle inefficiency' (DoH 1997: 19). These documents give the impression that the mere availability of information will make 'high cost' trusts seek out and change the causes of their supposedly inferior performance. Comparative performance information has been available for some time from a variety of sources. What remains unclear is why some trusts act on this information and others do not, but it would not be difficult to imagine mechanisms for encouraging providers to pursue efficient behaviour.

One possibility would be to provide financial incentives and penalties for trusts, dependent on their position in the league table. Previous government policy was based on an expectation that purchasers would use comparative cost information to direct more of their resources to providers with lower costs but it is unlikely this approach would be favoured by the present government. The mechanism now dubbed 'name and shame' relies on embarrassment or loss of professional esteem as the incentive to ensure someone else appears at the bottom of any performance list that is published.

Another possibility would be a 'command and control' approach where a trust would be instructed to reduce the distance between some of its costed HRGs and the corresponding reference costs by a centrally determined figure (say 10 per cent per annum) during the next three financial years. Alternatively the NHS Executive could delegate responsibility to the health authority for setting the target cost reduction and this would be incorporated into the long-term agreements between PCGs and trusts.

It may be that the main incentive to comply with central directives is the usual one within command and control systems: a subordinate unit that fails to satisfy superiors will lose out in terms of future resources and the opportunity to undertake utility-enhancing activities. The NHS Executive now has more control over major investment by trusts, and health authorities have more control over the financial implications of the appointment of consultants and developments at specialty level. If a trust with relatively high reported costs in, say, cardiology HRGs, fails to meet cost reduction targets, the opportunity for clinicians in that specialty to develop and expand their activities could be curtailed. As with any firm trying to protect market share, hospitals or specialties within hospitals will have a strong incentive to avoid being labelled one of the weak performers and, therefore, one of the dispensable units.

A drawback of incentive structures related to 'industry' reconfiguration is that the most vulnerable are not necessarily the least efficient. Particularly in the public sector, hospitals with political influence and/or good news management can survive threats of being closed or having their activities significantly curtailed.

CONCLUSIONS

This chapter has attempted to examine how the information on reference costs is to be generated, how it is likely to be used and whether the way it is used is likely to contribute to the objective of a more efficient NHS. For years, individuals concerned with the efficiency and improvement of health care services in the NHS have complained of lack of data with which to evaluate the performance of this major part of our economy and public sector. While the policy of making more information available is to be applauded, it is important that this information is used appropriately and that users are aware of its limitations.

Use of reference costs to make comparisons is hampered because of variations in the ways that activity is measured and costs are apportioned across hospitals. At last, calls to abandon FCEs as the main counting method have been heeded (Clarke and McKee 1992; Radical Statistics Health Group 1995), and the introduction of a unique patient identifier will further enhance understanding of activity across health sectors. However, the absence of patient-level cost information continues to frustrate attempts to improve case-mix measures, and the application of cost allocation guidance is subject to a high degree of discretion.

Serious consideration of techniques for identifying the impact on cost of factors other than efficiency is required if the resulting efficiency index is to be credible. If efficiency league tables are to become a permanent part of government monitoring of NHS performance, there must be investment in producing better cost information and the information must be generated in a way that permits the average values appearing in the league tables to be accompanied by confidence intervals, so that users are better able to judge the significance of a trust's position in the table. This might increase the cooperation of trusts as the system would then appear to be fairer than the current form of publication. It would also help the NHS Executive by making it easier to identify the genuinely poor or very good performers.

Experience with the system can be expected to help identify solutions to some of these problems. It may be worth examining whether the objective of changing clinical practice through cost benchmarking might not be more effectively pursued by using an indicator of resource use other than the costed HRG. The absence of patient-related cost data and the desire to minimize resources devoted to collecting cost data in the NHS means variations in the cost of a particular HRG are virtually all due to variations in length of stay. Why is so much time and effort being invested in translating length of stay information into cost data? This question would not arise if, as in Victoria, we were collecting details of many different resources used by a patient. Translating this information into standardized monetary values is a convenient means of summarizing the different dimensions of resource use. But where resource use is proxied by a single dimension (length of stay), nothing is gained from reporting the measurement units on a different scale (money). Rather than providing greater clarity about variations in practice, it may obscure them for the very people we want to influence: clinicians. Peer group/professional pressure to alter practice may be more effectively mobilized if the league tables relate to characteristics of the service recognized to be professionally significant. If it is the managerial model of benchmarking that the government wishes to see adopted in the NHS then perhaps we should be benchmarking length of stay directly, rather than indirectly via reference costs.

It remains unclear what incentives exist for purchasers and providers to change their behaviour in response to published data on reference costs. Recent NHS experience suggests purchasers have tended to be weaker than providers and often had difficulty securing desired changes in activity. The creation of PCGs will further fragment purchasers and the encouragement of mergers will further strengthen trusts. In view of this it may be that the only incentive structure likely to be effective in securing the government's desired use of reference costs is one of command and control.

A problem with the command and control approach is that the data are not sufficiently robust to permit a target cost reduction of 10 per cent for one trust and 25 per cent for another with any confidence that the consequences will represent efficiency gains. The process of generating the data within a trust may well help managers and clinicians better understand the use of resources within their organizations, but the specific figure produced may not tell us much about the efficiency with which health care is produced in one trust when compared to another. In the absence of trust-specific HRG-level data on quality and appropriateness for each HRG costed, it is not possible to tell whether the trust reporting the lowest cost is producing a service of roughly the same quality as the trusts further 'up' the schedule of reference costs. Collection of information on reference costs may well lead to fruitful discussion at the local level (one of the government's aims) but it is unlikely to produce a useful basis for setting targets (also, it appears, a government aim).

The White Paper and various consultation documents promise that the 'new' NHS is to be distinguished from the 'old' NHS by widening the focus on efficiency to embrace quality. But, given costing methodologies, the primary way a trust can improve its NSRC or NRCI performance is by increasing hospital-based activity.

Unless care is taken in the way the centre uses the NSRC and NRCI, there is a danger that reference costs will reinstate the perverse incentives of the purchaser efficiency index.

NOTES

1 See Benton *et al.* (1998a) for a description of the approach being used by the National Casemix Office to aggregate FCEs into spells.
2 Various sources describe the process of cost allocation recommended by the NHS Steering Group on Costing. NHS Executive (1997) summarizes the principles that are set out in some detail in the *Costing for Contracting Manual* (NHS Executive 1993). Butler *et al.* (1998) provide a case study.
3 The indicators are: 30-day in hospital perioperative mortality by method of admission; 28-day emergency readmissions; discharge home within 56 days of admission with fractured neck of femur, by admission method; 30-day in hospital mortality for fractured neck of femur, by admission method; discharge home within 56 days following emergency admission for stroke; 30-day in hospital mortality from myocardial infarction.
4 Efficiency in *production* of a service requires more, in that the mix of inputs must, given factor prices, minimize cost per unit of output.

REFERENCES

Aletras, V., Jones, A. and Sheldon, T. (1997). Economies of scale and scope. In B. Ferguson, J. Posnett and T. Sheldon (eds), *Concentration and Choice in the Provision of Hospital Services*. London: *Financial Times* Healthcare.

Appleby, J. (1996a). Promoting efficiency in the NHS: problems with the labour productivity index. *British Medical Journal*, 313, 1319–21.

Appleby, J. (1996b). Relegating league tables. *Health Service Journal*, 14 November, 38–9.

Bates, T. (1996). Casemix grouping for standard GP fundholding. *Proceedings of the National Casemix Conference*, Birmingham, 22–3 October.

Benton, P.L., Azorin, D. and Sutch, S. (1998a). Linkage of patient episodes into spells. *Proceedings of the National Casemix Conference*, Brighton, 8–9 September.

Benton, P.L., Evans, H., Light, S.M. *et al.* (1998b). The development of healthcare resource groups, Version 3. *Journal of Public Health Medicine*, 20(3), 351–8.

Butler, A., Horgan, J. and Macfarlane, L. (1998). Case study: costing, contracting and resource management. In H. Sanderson, P. Anthony, and L. Mountney (eds), *Casemix for All*. Oxford: Radcliffe Medical Press.

Clarke, A. and McKee, M. (1992). The consultant episode: an unhelpful measure. *British Medical Journal*, 305, 1307–8.

Clinical Resource and Audit Group (1994). *Clinical Outcome Indicators, December 1994.* Edinburgh: The Scottish Office.

Clinical Resource and Audit Group (1996). *Clinical outcome indicators, July 1996.* Edinburgh: The Scottish Office.

Department of Health (1997). *The New NHS: Modern, Dependable.* London: HMSO.

Dredge, B. (1997). *The costing of medical specialties in Wolverhampton Hospital Trust.* National Casemix Office occasional paper 16, July.

Duckett, S.J. (1994). *The reform of public hospital funding in Victoria. Australian Studies in Health Service Administration number 77.* New South Wales: School of Health Service Management, University of New South Wales.

Fetter, R.B., Shin, Y., Freeman, J.L., Averill, R.F. and Thompson, J.D. (1980). Casemix definition by diagnosis related groups. *Medical Care*, 18(suppl.), 1–53.

Ginsberg, P.B. and Carter, G.M. (1986). Medicare casemix index increases. *Health Care Financing Review*, 7, 51–66.

Goldstein, H. and Spiegelhalter, D.J. (1996). League tables and their limitations: statistical issues in comparisons of institutional performance. *Journal of Royal Statistical Society*, 159A(3), 385–443.

Health and Community Services (1994). *Casemix Funding for Public Hospitals 1994–95.* Melbourne: Health and Community Services.

Henderson, J., Goldacre, M.J., Graveney, M.J. and Simmons, H.M. (1989). Use of medical record linkage to study readmission rates. *British Medical Journal*, 299, 709–13.

Jackson, T., Henderson, N., Tate, R. and Scambler, D. (1993). *Resource Weights for AN-DRGs Using Patient-level Clinical Costs*, (technical report 3). Melbourne: National Centre for Health Program Evaluation.

Jackson, T., Wilson, R., Watts, J., Lane, L. and Bayliss-McCulloch, J. (1998). *1997 Victorian Cost Weights Study.* Melbourne: Health Services Research Group, Centre for Health Program Evaluation.

Kosecoff, J., Kahn, K.L., Rogers, W.H. *et al.* (1990). Prospective payment system and impairment at discharge. *Journal of the American Medical Association*, 264(15), 1980–3.

Leibenstein, H. (1996). Allocative efficiency vs. 'x-efficiency'. *American Economic Review*, 55: 392–415.

National Casemix Office (1997). *Version 3 Documentation Set: Introduction.* London: NHS Executive.

National Casemix Office (1998). Reference costs 1998 [CD-Rom]. London: NHS Executive.

NHS Executive (1993) *Costing for Contracting Manual* (FDL(93)76). Leeds: NHSE.

NHS Executive (1994) *Comparative Cost Data: The Use of Costed HRGs to Inform the Contracting Process* (EL(94)51). Leeds: NHSE.

NHS Executive (1997) *Costing Requirements and the Use of Costed HRGs in 1998/99* (FDL(97)25). Leeds: NHSE.

NHS Executive (1998a). *The New NHS: Modern, Dependable: A National Framework for Assessing Performance – A Consultation Document.* London: The Stationery Office.

NHS Executive (1998b). *Reference Costs – A Consultation Document.* London: The Stationery Office.

North West Regional Office (1997). *Extra Contractual Referrals: Purchaser Arrangements and Provider Tariffs for 1996/97.*

Radical Statistics Health Group (1995). NHS 'indicators of success': what do they tell us? *British Medical Journal*, 310, 1045–50.

Sanderson, H.F., Anthony, P. and Mountney, L.M. (1995). Healthcare resource groups – version 2. *Journal of Public Health Medicine*, 17(3), 349–54.

10

A NICE START? ECONOMIC ANALYSIS WITHIN EVIDENCE-BASED CLINICAL PRACTICE GUIDELINES

James Mason, Martin Eccles, Nick Freemantle and Mike Drummond

INTRODUCTION

The recent consultative document *A First-Class Service: Quality in the New NHS* (National Health Service) outlines the establishment of a new National Institute for Clinical Excellence (NICE) (NHS Executive 1998). NICE is intended 'to give new coherence and prominence to information about clinical and cost-effectiveness' and to 'produce and disseminate clinical guidelines, based on relevant evidence of clinical and cost-effectiveness' (NHS Executive 1998).

Despite the proliferation of clinical guidelines, most do not address issues of cost-effectiveness, and indeed there may be unforeseen problems in introducing economic 'evidence' into guidelines. If recommendations produced by NICE are to lead to more cost-effective health care provision, it is important that any potential problems are addressed before NICE begins its work. This chapter provides a commentary on recent work to develop evidence-based guidelines to explicitly consider cost-effectiveness concepts.

A framework for formulating treatment recommendations is presented and the manner in which this differs from a common health-economic policy approach is discussed. The methodology of evidence-based guideline development is described briefly, showing the process required to include cost-effectiveness concepts. Examples of recent guideline work, addressing the use of angiotensin converting enzyme (ACE)-inhibitors and non-steroidal anti-inflammatory drugs (NSAIDs) in primary care, are provided and also a checklist for health economists becoming involved in guideline work. We will identify the strengths and weaknesses of our approach and move on to consider what questions now need to be answered, in the context of the present health service reforms in the United Kingdom (UK).

Why have economics in guidelines?

Within the UK, most guideline development has involved informal consensus processes, focusing on issues of clinical effectiveness. While a number of evidence-based guidelines have been published, these have, until recently, focussed on clinical effectiveness (Eccles *et al.* 1996; North of England Asthma Guideline Development Project 1996; North of England Stable Angina Guideline Development Group 1996). The introduction of cost considerations within guidelines has been argued for (Eddy 1992; Institute of Medicine 1992; Williams 1995), though it is unclear how the introduction of economic data would influence the recommendations produced by a guideline development group.

The reasons for considering costs are clearly stated by Eddy (1992: 90) 'health interventions are not free, people are not infinitely rich, and the budgets of [health care] programmes are limited ... While these payments can be laundered, disguised or hidden, they will not go away'.

The Committee on Clinical Practice Guidelines (Institute of Medicine 1992) recommends that every set of clinical practice guidelines includes information on the cost implications of alternative preventive, diagnostic and management strategies for the clinical situation in question. Their stated rationale is that this information can help potential users to better evaluate the potential consequences of different practices. Although they acknowledge 'the reality is that this recommendation poses major methodological and practical challenges' (Institute of Medicine 1992: 143) they suggest that, in the process of considering costs, five theoretical questions should be considered (see Box 10.1), going on to provide reasons why guideline developers will have difficulty finding the answers to these questions (see Box 10.2).

In addition to these questions and limitations, there is the further question of how to use cost data in a guidelines group. Should data be presented alongside recommendations based solely on clinical

---

Box 10.1   Questions to be considered in clinical guidelines

- What evidence suggests that the services are likely to affect outcomes for the condition or intervention being considered?
- What groups at risk are most likely to experience benefits or harms from the proposed course of care and its side-effects?
- What is known about the effects of different frequencies, duration, dosages, or other variations in the intensity of the intervention?
- What options in the ways services are organized and provided can affect the benefits, harms and costs of services?
- What benefits, harms and costs can be expected from alternative diagnostic or treatment paths, including watchful waiting or no intervention?

Source: Institute of Medicine (1992)

Box 10.2   Problems confronting guideline developers

- Scientific evidence about benefits and harms is incomplete.
- Basic, accurate cost data are scarce for the great majority of clinical conditions and services.
- While data on charges may be available, significant analytic steps and assumptions are required to treat charge data as cost data.
- Techniques for analysing and projecting costs and cost-effectiveness are complex and only just evolving.

Source: Institute of Medicine (1992)

effectiveness, or incorporated into the judgement process of deriving recommendations? Williams (1995) argues that guidelines based on effectiveness issues and then costed may differ substantially and be less efficient than guidelines based on cost-effectiveness issues. The complexity of this process, and the reactions it evokes, are reflected by the Committee on Clinical Practice Guidelines (Institute of Medicine 1992) report of 'much debate, and with some vigorous dissent'. There is no widely-accepted successful way to incorporate economic considerations into guidelines.

Furthermore, it is unclear how UK health care professionals will react to this process. Most health care professionals have a limited knowledge of health economics and economic modelling. Guidelines based on clinical effectiveness could be enhanced or undermined by the incorporation of economic considerations, depending on whether they are seen as attempts to achieve cost-effectiveness or cost-containment. It remains a research issue how the incorporation of economic considerations will affect the use of guidelines with individual patients, although the intention is to encourage a more explicit consideration of costs and consequences in each consultation where the guideline is used. UK health professionals are not accustomed to this process at anything other than an implicit level. With the prominence given to systematic reviewing and evidence-based guideline construction (Grimshaw and Russell 1993; Eccles *et al.* 1998f), it is unclear how 'evidence' from the methodology of health economics – with its reliance on limited cost data, modelling and assumptions – will sit alongside 'evidence' derived from the (perceived) rigour of systematic review. However, the absence of economic data from guidelines may severely limit their usefulness to medicine at both the policy and practice level.

Concepts underpinning economic evaluation

The development of economic evaluation has been driven by concepts of efficiency. A commonly-used objective in publicly-provided health care systems is to improve or maintain health, as far as possible, with available resources. To maximize health gains, cost-effective strategies in health care must be identified; these are ones that produce, in a therapeutic area, the maximum output for a given cost (or minimum cost for a given output). This criterion alone, though, is inadequate, since to maximize health in the population requires the various cost-effective strategies across all therapeutic areas to be implemented in proportions that achieve the socially optimal allocation of resources. The measurement of health has mushroomed as an academic and clinical pursuit in recent years, with one strand attempting to produce generic measures that reduce patient health status (and its changes over time) to a single index (e.g. the quality-adjusted life-year or QALY). Hence, theoretically, health gains could be compared across different diseases and patient groups.

One approach to economic evaluation, the 'decision-making' approach, recognizes that decision makers have a range of objectives besides efficiency (Williams 1972; Sugden and Williams 1978). Inputs to decisions may include the decision-makers' personal values and specific notions of equity. Current thought is to provide an index of output efficiency (the cost/QALY) to contribute to the decision-making process in the hope that decision makers will give such data a good weight. Literature considering the impact of cost-effectiveness studies shows little impact (Alban 1982; Davies *et al.* 1994; Ross 1995; Drummond *et al.* 1997) and it is possible that such studies may have been misdirected as to their audience. This may have been no bad thing, since the quality of the studies themselves has often been inadequate (Lee and Sanchez 1991; Adams *et al.* 1992; Udvarhelyi *et al.* 1992; Gerard 1993; Mason and Drummond 1995a, 1995b).

The decision-making approach also assumes the existence of an audience of social decision makers, interested in weighing the costs and benefits of policy changes to all affected parties, who may apply the results of cost-effectiveness studies. This assumption may be largely invalid in many health care systems. For example, in the UK, the foremost role of health authorities is (despite a history of reforms) to administer the flow of funds into primary and secondary care. Purchasers contracting for health services (often covering, in one service agreement, provision of a whole medical specialty) may have little use for an economic evaluation of an individual technology. In insurance-based systems, economic evaluations may be useful to health insurers where reimbursement follows (or can be refused) for a specified treatment, but in all health care systems it is the doctor who remains responsible for treatment decisions and ideally should own the conclusions of research findings. Thus, clinical practice guidelines offer the potential to resolve societal and individual patient-based decision making, since they address the pertinent audience.

The rationale underpinning economic evaluation has been the

belief that complex cost and benefit profiles associated with treatments can be aggregated, thus handing 'an answer' to aid decision making (at least with respect to efficiency). This has proved unproductive, in part because the methods and data have not been adequate to provide a simple answer, and in part because clinicians (the key audience) do not appear to think of appropriate health care in terms of economic outcomes, such as cost-effectiveness ratios.

The areas in which economic analyses have had some impact (formally or informally) are licensing and reimbursement decisions for new pharmaceuticals and in the introduction of some new 'big ticket' technologies such as heart transplantation (Buxton 1987). However, there is no evidence of impact upon already established health care technologies. This may generate a distortion in health care policy since new technologies are being evaluated with far greater stringency than existing care. The current evidence-based medicine culture potentially provides an environment for clinicians to review their existing practice. In recognition of the ubiquitous constraints on resources, it is important that economic analysis takes the opportunity to contribute appropriately to this process.

Guideline objectives

The guidelines development process recognizes the clinician as the decision maker, acting as the arbiter of appropriate treatment. In making decisions, clinicians balance their own preferences, those of patients and carers, patient-specific information, the benefits, side-effects and safety of treatment and, to varying extents (depending on the mode of reimbursement), cost. Consequently, the primary goal of guidelines development is not to derive a cost per QALY but rather to help the clinician perform the aggregation of attributes of treatment, and develop well-informed social preferences. Such a process still requires the assessment of costs and benefits of treatment to be methodologically sound. The novel aspect is the dynamic use of economic data (rather than as static published studies), alongside traditional clinical inputs in the development of clinician valuation of treatments and consequent recommendations. In the rest of this chapter, we describe and comment on our initial attempt to introduce economic analysis into the process of developing evidence-based clinical practice guidelines.

DEVELOPING COST-CONSCIOUS EVIDENCE-BASED GUIDELINES

The aim of a guideline is to provide recommendations, evidence-based where possible, to inform health care professionals about their use of health technologies. By constructing representative groups to work systematically through available, graded evidence and contextual issues, it may be possible to reach treatment recommendations that achieve the costs and benefits they predict while reflecting remaining uncertainties. A guideline does not replace but supports the responsibility of health care professionals to use general medical knowledge and clinical judgement in consultations. It is recognized that recommendations may not be appropriate for use in all circumstances, and decisions to adopt any particular recommendation must be made by the practitioner in the light of available resources and the circumstances presented by individual patients.

Each guideline involves a systematic appraisal of a medical intervention in terms of the areas shown in Box 10.3. This being the most current, pertinent and complete data available, each guideline sets out (or profiles) these attributes of treatment and, where appropriate, attempts a robust presentation showing the possible bounds of cost-effectiveness that might result. The range of values used to generate low and high cost-effectiveness estimates reflects available evidence and the concerns of the guideline development group. Simple and transparent presentation also permits reworking with different values from the ones used by the guideline group.

Consistent with prior belief, the guideline groups did not feel it helpful to consider a summary of previously published economic

---

Box 10.3   Areas for systematic appraisal in guidelines

- Effectiveness
- Quality-of-life
- Tolerability
- Safety
- Health service delivery issues
- Resource use
- Costs in the British health care setting

analyses which adopted a variety of differing perspectives, analytic techniques and baseline data. However, the economic literature was reviewed to position guideline findings against representative published economic analyses and interpret differences in findings when the group found it beneficial.

Guideline development

North of England guidelines development groups were convened during 1996–7 to develop evidence-based guidelines for primary care prescribing decisions in four clinical areas. These guidelines were developed for use within a trial evaluating the effectiveness and efficiency of evidence-based outreach visits. Guideline topics were chosen where there was perceived to be scope for appropriate change and where guideline messages were likely to vary in the scale of changes of costs and benefits involved. The four treatments addressed were: ACE-inhibitors in the primary care management of adults with symptomatic heart failure; aspirin for the secondary prophylaxis of vascular disease in primary care; the choice of antidepressants for depression in primary care; and NSAIDs versus basic analgesia in the treatment of osteoarthritis (Eccles *et al.* 1998b, 1998c, 1998d, in press).

Guideline development groups were composed of general practitioners (GPs), secondary care physicians, local authority medical and pharmaceutical advisers, pharmacists and a research team consisting of a guideline development methodologist (Martin Eccles, who acted as the group leader), a systematic reviewer (Nick Freemantle), and a health economist (James Mason). Clinical members brought to the group their knowledge of the disease, experiences in treating patients, and understanding of the practicalities of the health care system. The research team (Martin Eccles, Nick Freemantle and James Mason) were responsible for reviewing and summarizing the evidence relating to treatments and interactively feeding this information back to the group to allow the development of recommendations. Additionally, the research team were responsible for the drafting of the guidelines and the resourcing of the guideline development group. The working of the group can be characterized as a dynamic process where an understanding of the pros and cons of treatment emerges and is refined, questions are responded to with available evidence and uncertainties are assessed. A detailed report of the working of the guideline groups has been published (Eccles 1998e).

Levels of evidence and strength of recommendation

To critically assess clinical effectiveness for evidence-based guidelines, the reviewers followed a process of establishing the level of evidence provided by individual studies. Papers were categorized according to study design, reflecting susceptibility to bias, and questions were answered using the best evidence available. Evidence categories, shown in Table 10.1, were adapted from the US Agency for Health Care Policy and Research Classification (AHCPR 1992). When considering a question of the effect of an intervention, if the question could be answered by Category 1 evidence provided by a meta-analysis or randomized controlled trial, then studies of weaker design (e.g. controlled studies without randomization) were not reviewed.

Recommendations were graded A to D as shown in Table 10.2. However, categories of evidence do not always map easily onto one strength of recommendation. First, it is possible to have methodologically sound (Category 1) evidence about an area of practice that is clinically irrelevant or has such a small effect that it is of little practical importance and therefore attracts a lower strength of recommendation. Second, a statement of evidence may only cover one part of an area in which a recommendation has to be made, or evidence of similar quality may be contradictory. To produce comprehensive recommendations, a group has to extrapolate from the available evidence and this sometimes leads to lower strength recommendations based upon Category 1 evidence (Eccles *et al.* 1996). In addition to the strength of clinical evidence, recommendations reflect the applicability of the evidence to the population of interest; economic considerations; guideline developers' awareness of practical issues; and (inevitably) guideline developers' societal values (AHCPR 1992).

Table 10.1 Categories of evidence

1a	evidence from meta-analysis of randomized controlled trials
1b	evidence from at least one randomized controlled trial
2a	evidence from at least one controlled study without randomization
2b	evidence from at least one other type of quasi-experimental study
3	evidence from non-experimental descriptive studies, such as comparative studies, correlation studies and case-control studies
4	evidence from expert committee reports or opinions and/or clinical experience of respected authorities

Table 10.2   Strength of recommendations

A   directly based on Category 1 evidence
B   directly based on Category 2 evidence or extrapolated recommendation from Category 1 evidence
C   directly based on Category 3 evidence or extrapolated recommendation from Category 1 or 2 evidence
D   directly based on Category 4 evidence or extrapolated recommendation from Category 1, 2 or 3 evidence

To apply a strength of recommendation to cost information presents some difficulties. A large, well-conducted trial may estimate some overall resource savings for a new treatment, but unless these findings are generalizable to normal care they may not reflect the best evidence possible. Resource measurement from observational data (such as insurance claims databases), may be subject to unknowable influences, particularly selection biases, and similarly not provide a reliable view. Commonly, in health care, alternative treatment strategies feature small differences in outcome. Consequently, precise and internally valid trials were required not just to achieve a reliable measure of differences in health outcome, but also (correlated) differences in resource consequences.

The approach adopted was to apply the same categories of evidence used for effectiveness to resource use and additionally to establish the generalizability and relevance of findings by mapping their consequences onto current national patterns of resource use. For example, the studies of left ventricular dysfunction (SOLVD) trial, for the treatment of heart failure with an ACE-inhibitor (SOLVD Investigators 1991), reported rates of hospitalization for heart failure in the placebo group consistent with rates reported nationally for England. Hence, the reduction in hospitalization in the active treatment group was consistent with improved health outcomes reported in the trial and plausible in the English setting. The categories of evidence for both resource use and health outcome, as well as the generalizability of those data, therefore determined strengths of recommendations for cost-effectiveness. The overall quality and importance of evidence as interpreted by the group determined the grade assigned.

Handling costs

While a social perspective in economic evaluation is both desirable and formally correct, in practice, due to the (un)availability of data, analyses of cost were limited to those borne by the NHS. Unit cost data used in guidelines were those in the public domain; it was beyond the scope of the guidelines development process to conduct new costing studies.

The approach is incrementalist, thinking of the net costs and consequences of changes in practice. Costs were calculated by attaching published average national unit costs to resource items. Economists often argue that, for decision-making purposes, marginal costs are preferable to average costs (Mooney and Drummond 1982). While the problems associated with average costs are recognized, there is no generally valid or accepted method for presenting marginal costs on items or procedures: these will vary from locality to locality. The simple presentation of analyses permits decision makers to apply different unit costs where such information is locally available. Reflating of unit costs from different years of origin to a common year to adjust for health care cost changes over time was not conducted. In general, there was no more than a two-year gap between the oldest and newest values. Additionally, reflating is an ambiguous practice for certain items such as drug costs where, under UK reimbursement, the price tends to remain fixed over substantial periods of time.

Data on drugs

It is not the role of a guideline group to conduct original research, rather to synthesize obtainable information. However, in three of the four areas (i.e. excluding ACE-inhibitors), prescribing analysis and cost (PACT) data were obtained for English primary care from the Prescription Pricing Authority (PPA). These data provide the total number of prescriptions reimbursed and their cost for each drug. Because prescriptions may not adequately describe the volume of use of drugs (Bogle and Harris 1994), quantity data were adjusted using World Health Organization (WHO) tables of defined daily doses, to provide a measure of the patient years of prescribing reimbursed (World Health Collaborating Centre for Drug Statistics Methodology 1992). These are not necessarily the doses recommended in the British National Formulary (British National Formulary Number 32, 1996), but are intended to reflect the average maintenance dose in adults. Where WHO values were not available, the standard lower maintenance dose listed in the British National Formulary was used. Hence, it was possible to calculate the volume of use of each drug as well as comparative acquisition costs of drugs per patient for a set period of treatment (reflecting the mix of forms of each drug currently prescribed).

This data served two purposes: first to tell GPs the extent to which various drugs were being used and their acquisition cost, and second to act as a starting point for thinking about how net costs may differ from drug acquisition costs.

Examples of the guidelines

The full guidelines give a systematic presentation of the available evidence in each treatment area and the treatment recommendations derived from the guideline groups. Here we present shortened summaries of two of the guidelines alongside selected recommendations, to illustrate issues for the inclusion of cost-effectiveness information in guideline development.

Guideline 1: ACE-inhibitors for heart failure

Introduction

Heart failure is a common, chronic condition with a very poor prognosis: as many as half the patients with a diagnosis of heart failure may die within four years. However, only 20–30 per cent of patients assessed by British GPs as having heart failure are prescribed an ACE-inhibitor. Most patients who are investigated for heart failure receive chest X-ray and electrocardiography but only about a third undergo echocardiography. Diagnosis by clinical assessment has been estimated to be correct in about half of the cases when confirmed by echocardiogram. While it is possible that some patients are being inappropriately treated, it is likely that ACE-inhibitors are considerably under-utilized in patients who might benefit from them.

Effectiveness data

Trials of ACE-inhibitors use left ventricular ejection fraction, measured by an echocardiogram to detect heart failure. A meta-analysis of 39 studies found that the pooled relative risk of mortality using a fixed effects model was 0.83 (95 per cent CI: 0.76 to 0.90) when taking an ACE-inhibitor compared to placebo. The findings of the meta-analysis are consistent with the largest trial, SOLVD, which randomized 2569 patients with overt but stabilized heart failure and a left ventricular ejection fraction of 35 per cent or less to enalapril or placebo with average follow-up of about 41 months (SOLVD Investigators 1991). The average benefit from ACE-inhibitors estimated during the SOLVD trial was 2.4 months of extended life.

Quality of life data

Narang *et al.* (1996) reviewed aspects of quality of life reported in 35 double-blind studies, including 3411 symptomatic patients, comparing the effect of ACE-inhibitors and placebo. Exercise duration improved in 23 of 35 (66 per cent) studies while symptoms improved in 25 of 33 (76 per cent) studies. All nine studies with a sample size of more than 50, a follow-up of three to six months and using a treadmill exercise test showed improved exercise capacity as well as symptoms.

The single largest and most general assessment of patient quality of life comes from a subsidiary analysis of the SOLVD treatment and prevention trials (Rogers *et al.* 1994). This found interim improvements in self-assessed dyspnoea and social functioning in those patients treated with ACE-inhibitors that were statistically significant, although statistical significance did not persist for the full two years of follow-up. Another analysis of SOLVD symptomatic patient data using observed frequency of dyspnoea showed a statistically significant reduction achieved and maintained beyond two years (Pouleur 1993).

Resource and cost data

Trials consistently show a reduction in hospitalization for progressive heart disease when on ACE-inhibitor therapy. It is unclear whether these are lasting reductions or simply reflect a 'time-window' effect, with more patients on ACE-inhibitors completing the trial follow-up period without their heart disease progressing, but deteriorating in following years. The data do not suggest that greater hospitalization for other reasons offsets reduced heart failure hospitalization; ACE-inhibitors seem to have a positive effect on other-cause hospitalization in symptomatic patients. It is not generally safe to assume that hospitalization rates found in trials will be matched in clinical practice. As already noted, the hospitalization rate in the control arm of the SOLVD treatment trial matches the average rate reported nationally for England. Each GP could expect, on average, four inpatient cases with heart failure each year and SOLVD trial data suggest that ACE-inhibition might prevent (or delay) one of these hospitalizations.

The annual cost of purchasing ACE-inhibitors (at maintenance doses) ranges from £100–340 per year, considering doses reported in the British National Formulary. The incremental cost per patient using ACE-inhibitors in primary care may vary from a small cost saving through to a net cost of nearly £1600 over four years (see Table 10.3). In cost-effectiveness terms, it is likely that ACE-inhibitors for heart failure fall in the approximate range £0–10,000 per life year gained, given the range of assumptions listed and the remaining uncertainties. The important variables are the cost of the ACE-inhibitor itself and hospitalization savings. It is not possible in this simple model to explore the influence of compliance with therapy on the cost-effectiveness estimates presented. The trial data, analysed on an intention-to-treat basis, reflect the level of compliance achieved in the SOLVD trial; the degree to which this represents experience in general practice in the UK is uncertain. Where non-compliance involves withdrawal of prescription then both costs and benefits are foregone and the overall cost-effectiveness ratios are not significantly altered. Substantial crossover to ACE-inhibitor therapy in the placebo group in the SOLVD trial may mean the attributable benefits are underestimated.

Commentary

Within the effectiveness data, no extrapolation beyond the period of the trials has been attempted. The presentation of available evidence is relatively free of assumptions, and it is easy to explore values different from the ones used. The values presented reflected those felt appropriate by the group in discussion. It would, technically, have been better to make a fractional reduction in the drug costs over four years to reflect mortality. However, such an adjustment made no difference to the substantive findings and the group preferred the simplicity of the presentation shown. The purpose of the analysis was to confirm to the guidelines group that not only were the individual attributes of treatment favourable, but also the 'ballpark' cost-effectiveness. If treatment stopped at four years, there would be some additional benefit after cessation of therapy and the findings presented would be conservative, though it is

Table 10.3 Net cost and benefit per patient of ACE-inhibitors for heart failure

Assumptions (optimistic or conservative)[1]	Optimistic (£)	Conservative (£)
ACE-inhibitor £100/year or £340/year for four years	400	1400
Initiation of therapy by two GP visits or two outpatient visits[2]	20	138
Reduced hospitalization or no reduced hospitalization[3]	-626	0
GP visits related to heart failure unchanged or one extra visit/year for four years[4]	0	40
Net cost range	-206	1578
Increased life expectancy (based on placebo comparison)[5]	0.203 years	0.203 years
Incremental cost-effectiveness of implementing ACE-inhibitor therapy[6]	Small cost saving and health gain	£7770/life year gained

[1] Costs and benefits are shown which arise from the addition of ACE-inhibitors to current care. Diagnosis costs are excluded because of the variation in tests performed, the lack of adequate cost data and because these costs may occur in any case as part of normal care. For simplicity of presentation the consequences of treatment withdrawal are not modelled, hence drug costs are likely to be overestimated.

[2] Cost per:
 GP consultation: £10 (excluding prescribing cost) (Netten and Dennett 1997)
 Outpatient visit: £69 (CIPFA/HFM 1997)
 Costs of additional blood tests are excluded as no adequate cost data was found

[3] Calculation based on:
 Difference in SOLVD trial treatment and control hospitalization rates (21.9%–15.4%) × 4 years
 Inpatient stay of 14.5 days (McMurray *et al.* 1993)
 Cost of an inpatient day: £166 (CIPFA/HFM 1997)

[4] Since patients visit their GPs on average once a year in relation to heart failure it is not plausible to assume an optimistic reduction in GP visits although treatment does delay disease progression and associated morbidity.

[5] Based on the placebo-controlled findings of the SOLVD treatment trial, improved survival was highly statistically significant (p = 0.0036 by stratified log rank test). However, the survival gain calculation (using Irwin's Restricted Mean) does not provide a useful confidence interval. The point estimate is thus used in optimistic and conservative scenarios.

[6] Survival gains are truncated in the SOLVD trial, and it is reasonable to presume that if treatment stopped there would be some additional benefit after cessation of therapy. This is not modelled, since it is probable that therapy would continue and so both costs and benefits would occur after four years.

probable that therapy would continue, and that both costs and benefits would occur after four years. Future costs and benefits were not discounted because of the short, four-year time frame and because all important costs are distributed along with the benefit in time. Neither extrapolation nor discounting will substantially alter the cost-effectiveness ratios presented.

The strength of recommendation (see Box 10.4) for the cost-effectiveness of ACE-inhibitors for heart failure reflects the fact that worthwhile health benefits have been established in trials as well as the net impact upon resources (from the SOLVD trial) which appears generalizable to the British context.

Guideline 2: NSAIDs for osteoarthritis

Introduction

On average, approximately 3 per cent of patients on general practice lists will be recorded as suffering from osteoarthritis. However, osteoarthritis is one of a continuum of connective tissue disorders, and the extent to which these interrelate and share common treatment is uncertain. The prevalence of all such conditions (ICD 710–739) amounts to nearly 19 per cent of patients.

Currently, GPs in England spend approximately £150 million each year on NSAIDs for musculoskeletal and joint disorders. Annually, this corresponds to nearly 1.5 million person-years of treatment, with ibuprofen and diclofenac constituting respectively

---

Box 10.4   Selected recommendations from the heart failure guideline

- All patients with symptomatic heart failure and evidence of impaired left ventricular function should be treated with an ACE-inhibitor (A).
- Treatment of heart failure with ACE-inhibitors is cost-effective (A).
- As there is no good evidence of clinically important differences in the effectiveness of available ACE-inhibitors, patients should be treated with the cheapest drug that they can use effectively (B).

26 and 37 per cent of prescribed usage (prescribed use of ibupro-fen is underestimated due to its over-the-counter availability). Although used extensively, attempts to derive an evidence-based rationale to choose between NSAIDs have not proved fruitful. This is because of the poor quality of trials comparing different NSAIDs, which exhibit many biases (Gøtzsche 1989; Rochan *et al*. 1994). The guideline addressed a more fundamental question, raised by the group of GPs: when is it appropriate to use NSAIDs in preference to simple analgesia? Thus, the guideline addresses the decision to manage pharmacologically painful joints believed to be due to degenerative arthritis.

Effectiveness data

There are only three adequately designed trials (Parr *et al*. 1989; Bradley *et al*. 1992; Williams *et al*. 1993) which may, in combination, provide useful information about the appropriate place of NSAID use in primary care. These studies compare the short-term effec-tiveness (four to six weeks) of the NSAIDs ibuprofen and naproxen against paracetamol in osteoarthritis of the knee (Bradley *et al*. 1992; Williams *et al*. 1993) or the NSAID diclofenac versus co-proxamol in non-traumatic pain in hip, knee, ankle or wrist joints (Parr *et al*. 1989). In addition, the Bradley study uses two doses of ibuprofen: 'analgesic dose' or at 'anti-inflammatory dose'.

These studies indicate small benefits for NSAIDs over simple analgesia for pain at rest and pain in motion, using a visual analogue scale, but no significant change in time to walk 50 feet. One study (Parr *et al*. 1989) used the Nottingham Health Profile to describe different elements of the comparison between diclofenac and co-proxamol on broader health outcomes; the results suggest that there are no substantial differences in outcome for simple analgesia versus NSAIDs.

Compliance and safety data

Comparing NSAIDs and simple analgesia, treatment discontinua-tion was slightly less common for patients taking an NSAID, although the difference was not statistically significant. Overall, 3.3 per cent (95 per cent CI: −1.2 to 7.7 per cent) fewer patients dropped out of NSAID therapy over an average of four and a half months of treatment.

The absolute level of risk associated with individual NSAIDs and their safety relative to paracetamol is unknown. In a large US trial, the control group of patients took a variety of different NSAIDs for rheumatoid arthritis (Silverstein *et al.* 1995). In this cohort, the number needed to treat for a six-month period to expect one serious gastrointestinal event was 105 (95 per cent CI: 81 to 151), though it is unclear to what extent this risk is attributable to NSAIDs. Placebo controlled studies of aspirin in heart disease indicate that, while gastrointestinal disease is common in patients, the additional disease attributable to NSAIDs may be relatively small (Eccles *et al.* 1998b). Comparing the use of ibuprofen to no NSAID use, various case-control studies have estimated the rate of serious gastrointestinal damage to vary from no additional risk to a relative risk of two (Langman *et al.* 1994).

The relative risk of serious gastrointestinal complications with individual NSAIDs is reviewed systematically by Henry *et al.* (1996) who examine the relationship between drug use and admission to hospital. The review identifies 12 epidemiological controlled studies examining 14 NSAIDs for which comparison with ibuprofen can be made. Ibuprofen presents the lowest risk, and is used as a baseline to rank the relative safety of the other NSAIDs, although most differences are non-significant and the findings vulnerable to a range of biases. The review also suggests that the risk of gastrointestinal injury increases for higher doses of the same NSAID.

Resource and cost data

Paracetamol appears a cost-effective alternative to any NSAID because of lower acquisition cost and relative absence of gastrointestinal toxicity, while often providing adequate symptomatic relief and displaying similar levels of patient withdrawal from treatment. For the three NSAIDs for which randomized control trial data comparing with simple analgesia are available, the Henry *et al.* (1996) study suggests an ordering, on safety grounds, of ibuprofen, and then diclofenac or naproxen. While diclofenac and naproxen are similarly priced, ibuprofen is three to four times cheaper, given the forms in which these drugs are currently prescribed. Therefore, in the likely event that ibuprofen results in lower gastrointestinal injury and symptomatology, and without clear evidence of a general therapeutic advantage for naproxen or diclofenac, ibuprofen is the most cost-effective first-line NSAID.

There is wide variation in the purchase costs of different preparations of the same NSAID available on the NHS. There is no evidence to support the use of more expensive preparations over cheaper ones or the use of the modified release preparations.

In those patients requiring NSAID treatment it is important to consider what strategies may be available to minimize the risk of gastrointestinal injury. Such preventative strategies should not be confused with treatment of (common) dyspepsia where prescription or over-the-counter purchase of antacids may be considered when NSAID treatment cannot be modified.

Preventing NSAID induced gastrointestinal injury

Concerns about the high risk of NSAID-induced gastrointestinal injury have led to a number of trials of H_2-receptor antagonists (such as cimetidine and ranitidine) and misoprostol. A recent meta-analysis of trials focusing upon endoscopic assessment of lesions demonstrated a statistically significant reduction in the number of NSAID-induced gastric ulcers in patients randomized to take misoprostol, but not those taking H_2 blockers (Koch *et al.* 1996). Both H_2 blockers and misoprostol reduced the risk of duodenal ulcers in long term, but not short-term administration. However, it is recognized that endoscopically detected lesions may overestimate clinically important injury.

A recent large, double-blind trial randomized primary and secondary care patients, with rheumatoid arthritis and receiving NSAIDs, to receive misoprostol or placebo (Silverstein *et al.* 1995). The trial assessed the development of serious upper gastrointestinal complications detected by clinical symptoms or findings (rather than scheduled endoscopy) and found a small but borderline significant reduction in favour of the use of misoprostol. Twenty-five of 4404 patients receiving misoprostol, and 42 of 4439 patients receiving placebo suffered a serious upper gastrointestinal complication (odds ratio: 0.60; 95 per cent CI: 0.35 to 1.00) during six months of follow-up. The number needed to treat to prevent one serious gastrointestinal complication in this period is 264 (95 per cent CI 132 to 5703). In the first month of the study, 5 per cent more patients taking misoprostol withdrew, primarily because of diarrhoea and other side effects.

A rate of serious gastrointestinal events necessitating hospitalization for rheumatoid arthritis patients, associated with NSAID therapy, and preventable by misoprostol, can be estimated (see Table 10.4). Hence, for 1000 patient years of treatment, 10.6 events will be prevented (95 per cent CI: 0.4–15.1), at a purchase cost of

Table 10.4   Rates of serious gastrointestinal events with and without misoprostol in rheumatoid arthritis patients taking NSAIDs

Treatment	No. of patients	Follow-up	Person-years on drug	Events*	Event rate/year
Misoprostol⁺	4404	6 months	2202	25	0.0114
Placebo	4439	6 months	2220	42	0.0189

Notes: * Serious gastrointestinal events definitely attributable to NSAID use
       ⁺ Average daily dose: 680μg

Source: Silverstein *et al.* (1995)

Table 10.5   Net cost and serious gastrointestinal events prevented with misoprostol prophylaxis (for 1000 patients)

Scenario	Events avoided	Cost of misoprostol (£)	Savings in reduced hospitalization (£)*	Net cost (£)	Cost/event avoided (£)
High	0.4	230,000	1200	228,800	572,000
Best guess	7.6	230,000	22,800	207,200	27,300
Low	15.1	230,000	45,300	184,700	12,200

Notes: * The average cost of inpatient hospitalization across all specialities was £3000/episode for Scotland in 1995/6 (*Scottish Health Service Costs, Year ended 31st March 1996*, 1996).

misoprostol of £230,000 (using the average dose reported in the trial). The net cost/event prevented is calculated, and the confidence interval of events prevented is used to provide low and high estimates (see Table 10.5).

The rate of serious gastrointestinal complications in the control group in the Silverstein trial (Silverstein *et al.* 1995) was 1.9 per cent per person year of treatment. Extrapolation using the number of person years of treatment currently prescribed in England implies 30,000 hospitalizations for NSAID-associated gastrointestinal injury per year. Thus, half of the 60,000 annual gastrointestinal ulcer/bleed associated hospitalizations in England (Department of Health 1995) might be estimated to be NSAID-associated. Inclusion of over-the-counter NSAID use might suggest a bigger proportion. There were 4304 ulcer-associated deaths (ICD: 531–3) in England in 1991. Assuming that chance of fatality following hospitalization is independent of the underlying reason for gastrointestinal injury, then 2150 deaths per year can be attributed to NSAID-associated

Table 10.6 Modelled cost-effectiveness of misoprostol prophylaxis (for 1000 treated patients)

Scenario	Net cost (£)	Lives saved	Cost/life saved (£)
High	228,800	0.0276	8,290,000
Best guess	207,200	0.552	375,000
Low	184,700	0.883	209,000

injury, or 1.38 deaths per year in 1000 patients taking an NSAID for one year. This suggests that nearly one in ten serious gastrointestinal complications are fatal. The use of misoprostol led to a 40 per cent relative reduction in serious events (95 per cent CI: 65 to 2 per cent) and so might be argued to lead to a 40 per cent reduction in the average fatality rate. These figures are used to estimate the cost-effectiveness of a general policy of misoprostol prophylaxis in terms of the cost-per-life saved (see Table 10.6). High and low estimates are derived assuming lives saved are a constant fraction of serious events avoided.

The above estimates must be viewed as tentative, given the assumptions required to reach them. For example, hospitalization rates are generally higher in the USA than in the UK, and the relationship between hospitalization and mortality with ulcers of different underlying cause is unknown; notably there is currently no direct evidence of gastrointestinal injury-associated death being prevented by misoprostol prophylaxis. The purchase cost of misoprostol reflects additional separate prescription of misoprostol tablets. Combined NSAID and misoprostol tablets are available: subtracting the cost of non-proprietary forms of these NSAIDs, the combined drugs are generally a more expensive way of providing misoprostol, and if used will increase the net cost.

The mean ages of death in men and women due to ulcer, haemorrhage and perforation (ICD-9: 531–3) are 76 and 81 respectively. The average life-expectancy in the normal population for both genders at this age is about eight years (Department of Health 1996), so a crude calculation of cost per year-of-life gained is possible using the estimates shown in Table 10.6. The age distribution of ulcer fatalities presented in national statistics aggregates those ulcers caused by NSAIDs, those related to Helicobacter Pylori, and those due to other causes. These causes would need to be separated, and other modelling assumptions validated, before formal calculation of years-of-life saved is possible.

On the available evidence extrapolated from a trial of rheumatoid arthritis patients, it is not demonstrated that a strategy of routine and unselected misoprostol prophylaxis for patients taking NSAID therapy is cost-effective. Patient review and sequential therapy selection, beginning with simple analgesia, is likely to minimize adverse event rates in the general patient group.

It is possible, although not demonstrated, that misoprostol prophylaxis may be more cost-effective in a high-risk group for which current NSAID therapy has to be maintained. The Silverstein trial of rheumatoid arthritis patients (Silverstein *et al.* 1995) suggested greater relative risks of serious gastrointestinal injury for patients with age >75 (Odds ratio [OR] = 2.48), history of peptic ulcer (OR = 2.29), gastrointestinal bleeding (OR = 2.56) and heart disease (OR = 1.84). These risks factors have been presented in such a manner that it is not possible to calculate absolute reductions in the rates of serious events for each high-risk group, and the numbers of events in each instance are small. Without these, costs-per-life saved for high-risk groups cannot be estimated, but none of the risk factors individually appear very important, and the cost-effectiveness of misoprostol prophylaxis in high-risk NSAID-user groups remains undemonstrated.

Although it appears likely that omeprazole (a proton pump inhibitor) may be similar in effectiveness to misoprostol in NSAID-induced ulcer prophylaxis and healing (Hawkey *et al.* 1996), and better tolerated (although purchase costs are also higher), trials that rely on ulcers detected through endoscopy overestimate the effectiveness (and hence value) of protective agents in practice. No large, pragmatically designed trials with serious gastrointestinal events as primary outcome are available for omeprazole. Without such data it is not possible to recommend the routine use of omeprazole prophylaxis as an evidence-based strategy.

Commentary

The guideline group were not using the available evidence to rule out any drug given for osteoarthritis, since the evidence regarding any of the consequences of these treatments is not compelling. Instead, on the basis of broad arguments about superiority or (near) equivalence of attributes, they established a sequencing of treatment:

• Paracetamol is cheaper than ibuprofen, has most of the efficacy, is nearly as well tolerated, and is safer at therapeutic dose.

- Ibuprofen is cheaper than diclofenac or naproxen, is not known to be less efficacious, and is probably safer.
- Other NSAIDs are similarly more expensive and less safe than ibuprofen, and their relative efficacy to analgesia is not known.

The underlying quality of evidence is reflected in the strengths of recommendations in Box 10.5.

The group also wished to explore the appropriateness of prophylactic treatment in patients who were at risk of gastrointestinal injury and for whom symptomatic relief could only be obtained with an NSAID. Given the lack of direct evidence, the group requested a modelling exercise to explore the likely value of treatment and having been led through the model, with all its uncertainties, the group felt confident that the case for a general policy of prophylaxis had not been established.

Box 10.5   Selected recommendations from the osteoarthritis guideline

- In terms of cost-effectiveness, patients presenting with painful joints believed to be due to degenerative arthritis should initially be treated with paracetamol. If inadequate symptomatic relief is obtained, then ibuprofen is the most cost-effective alternative (C).
- Modified release preparations are relatively expensive, while no evidence demonstrates that they are more effective than standard therapy; therefore they should not be used (D).
- Prophylactic protective therapy (with misoprostol or proton pump inhibitors) should not be used routinely as it is not cost-effective for the reduction of serious gastric events (D).
- There are a group of patients who are at higher risk of upper gastrointestinal bleeding or perforation for whom prophylaxis may be cost-effective but further evidence is required (D).

Research issues

The four guidelines developed have some important similarities. Each addresses a highly focused question on the use of one, or several, classes of drug for the treatment of one condition in primary care. Each guideline assesses the available evidence using quantitative techniques appropriate to the task of informing the guidelines group. These factors may limit the value of the methodology presented in this chapter in other contexts.

Certain areas of medicine are not amenable to quantitative analysis and may only be summarized by *narrative review*. An example may be where individual trials for a medical condition use qualitatively different intermediate endpoints or outcomes. The need for narrative review will also increase as the focus shifts from treatment of one defined condition to the management of a whole disease. In these cases, the health economic component may be restricted to equivalence and dominance messages and not be able to offer clear advice where an alternative achieves (possibly conflicting signs of) a marginally greater effect at additional cost. Where the benefits of diagnostic procedures and treatments are patchy or unclear, it may prove difficult to set these against the costs of implementation.

The process of grading recommendations of costs alongside health consequences raised some interesting issues in the guidelines group, particularly in areas of uncertainty or broad equivalence of effect. An example came in the overall consideration of the relative value of selective serotonin reuptake inhibitor (SSRI) or tricyclic treatment in first-line treatment of depression. The effects of the treatments are broadly equi-poised with the evidence suggesting tricyclics are slightly more efficacious and SSRIs slightly better tolerated. A range of secondary claims concerning the advantages of SSRIs were explored (for example, they are safer in overdose than some but not all tricyclics) and were thought to be of minor worth, except where overdose was a genuine concern. In the light of inconclusive differences, it would be intuitive to suppose that any treatment recommendation favouring (if at all) either SSRIs or tricyclics would attract a low strength of recommendation. However, when the group had considered the net cost implications of using SSRIs instead of tricyclics they were certain that the additional costs were not worthwhile in the light of such uncertain benefits. Should the cost-effectiveness grading reflect the uncertainty of the treatment effect, the certainty of the cost consequence, or an amalgam? Ultimately, the strength of recommendation reflected not just the quality of evidence but the guidelines group's understanding of the importance of the message. An alternative would be to treat costs and effects separately and develop different grading systems for cost evidence statements and recommendations. Then, two grades would be attached to any cost-effectiveness recommendation. This would be at the expense of the simplicity of the method presented here, where a recommendation encodes the overall importance of a message.

The levels of evidence attached to the resource consequences of treatments mirrored those used for clinical effectiveness. The validity, susceptibility to bias and generalizability of different sources of resource data is, ultimately, an empirical question and different viewpoints are possible. Adoption of a different system would again suggest movement towards separate grading of costs and treatment effects.

Many clinical guidelines currently in the public domain do not address health economic concepts. It is possible to envisage retrospective inclusion of economic analyses in such guidelines and this raises the issue of whether the health economist needs to be present at all at the time of guideline development. A concern with retrospective 'bolting-on' of economic analyses is the (often) complex issues of managing patients and delivering health care alongside the technical nature of the treatments themselves. Health economists need to understand these issues and reflect them in their analyses; additionally, it would appear to be a retrograde step to pass off an important opportunity to work so closely with clinicians and other health care professionals.

DISCUSSION

Incorporating economic data into evidence-based guidelines introduces some methodological challenges: specifically in providing valid, generalizable cost estimates, in the grading of cost 'evidence', and in finding a presentation helpful to clinicians. The guideline development process reported here presents an attempt to address these issues.

In recognition of the disparate level and nature of information available for each of the treatment areas, a profile approach was adopted to set out the attributes of treatment. Evidence concerning the effectiveness, quality of life, compliance, safety, health service delivery and resource use associated with treatment options was presented and discussed in the guidelines group. A recurring theme in these discussions was GPs attempts to derive useful statements of how treatments would affect patients. In the case of ACE-inhibitors, the pooled relative risk of survival, reported in placebo-controlled trials, conveyed little and the average increase in life-expectancy was more helpful, though even this caused some debate, since the average increase masked a wide variation in benefit for individual patients.

Interestingly, the GPs in the group seemed comfortable moving from the very solid evidence presented on the value of ACE-inhibitors to the very speculative exploration of prophylaxis against NSAID-induced ulcer, when they themselves were participants in the steps and assumptions. A concern would be whether other clinicians outside the group could make such an investment to understand the issues.

Traditional summary presentations of cost-effectiveness were made, where available data permitted, but these provided only a partial view of the value of treatment. For example, the analysis of ACE-inhibitors in symptomatic heart failure suggests between £0 and £10,000 per life-year gained. These values do not inform on the quality of extended life or how the quality of existing life of patients might be improved when receiving an ACE-inhibitor, although this may be paramount in patient compliance. Clinicians asserted that the provision of simple presentations of the attributes of treatment and how these were aggregated was most useful: results could be 'unpicked', permitting other clinicians to apply their own values.

When reaching recommendations, the clinicians appeared to require treatments to leap two broad hurdles: first, did the treatment option really work (i.e. did changes in health and risks of consequent adverse events support the use of a treatment and could these benefits be delivered in practice?); and second, was the purchase worthwhile (for the benefits involved, what was the net requirement in health resource costs, and where did the costs and savings occur)? Additionally, they wanted an independent appraisal of the likely bounds of uncertainty for the various attributes of treatment (e.g. the likely range of the size of clinical effect and the likely range of the cost of achieving this effect).

The *raison d'être* of economic evaluation has (largely) been to achieve greater efficiency in health care delivery. In none of the areas examined was there adequate data to make an informative

estimation of a cost/QALY. Even if such calculation had been possible, it is unclear how much additional value would have been
attached to this information. Instead, the clinicians approached
decisions by thinking about treatment attributes and by using the
two-hurdle approach described above. This may reflect an appropriate response to the disparate effects of treatment – some good,
some bad – requiring a different cognitive model. Seldom can a
treatment's value be adequately captured by a simple, cost-
effectiveness construct and it is apparent that the GPs in the group
were not working with a predefined notion of 'worthwhile' in the
way that health economists often approach concepts of efficiency.
By contributing to the 'clinical group consciousness' of a guideline
development group, it may be possible to influence treatment
recommendations to appropriately consider concepts of cost-
effectiveness, consistent with clinical decision-making processes.
An overview is provided in Box 10.6, for health economists becoming involved in guidelines work, and for guideline developers considering the inclusion of a health economist.

The definition of a valid guideline is one that, when followed,
leads to the costs and benefits it predicts. This emphasizes the need
to use the best evidence available to produce the most valid guidelines and a variety of effective strategies to help clinicians to implement them. By these means, if economic issues are appropriately
incorporated, then they will maximize cost-effectiveness in the
limited way that current information permits.

A NICE START

Evidence-based cost-effectiveness guidelines are a fledgling science
with methodological development ongoing. However, it must be
this 'science' that the NICE is seen to communicate to the NHS,
without modification for political ends. Cost containment guidelines are likely to have no currency with the medical profession.
Credible guidelines stand the best chance of achieving an appropriate use of resources. For example, a recent guideline considering the use of donepezil hydrochloride for the treatment of
Alzheimer's disease concluded, on the basis of the available Phase
2 and 3 trials, that there was currently insufficient evidence to recommend its use, or to continue secondary care initiated prescribing
(Eccles *et al.* 1998a).

For products approaching the licensing stage, the NICE plans to

Box 10.6 An overview of guidelines development for health economists

- It is important to be clear about the process and objectives of guideline work, the conduct of group meetings and the role of each of the group members.
- Objective (if probabilistic) attributes of treatment decisions include effectiveness, side-effects, compliance, safety, quality of life, health service delivery issues and resource use. The outcomes of a guideline process are graded treatment recommendations, which may reflect some or all of these attributes.
- The health economist, together with other group facilitators, has a responsibility to provide a rigorous exploration of treatment attributes with the available evidence. A general understanding of other disciplines (statistics, epidemiology and health services research) is essential alongside training in economic evaluation methodology.
- Simple and transparent presentations, which permit exploration with different values, are most likely to be helpful to the guideline group and subsequent users of the guideline.
- Each attribute of treatment is assessed in turn on its own merits including bounds of uncertainty. Over-precision should be challenged and all uncertainties should be explored which are appropriate to the data or expressed in the group.
- Careful presentation and full discussion in the guidelines group is essential for an understanding of the attributes of treatment to evolve into a view of overall clinical importance. Data, although rigorously analysed are being used to put a treatment in a broad 'ballpark' with respect to its various attributes (e.g. safe, acceptable, effective, deliverable, cost-neutral).
- The importance attached to each attribute of treatment remains the responsibility of the guideline group as a whole and recommendations must be transparent and credible to the target audience. The process of aggregating up to an overall recommendation may be

facilitated by a summary table of attributes, presenting summary cost-effectiveness estimates when appropriate. Summary ratios need careful explanation and interpretation.

- A systematic review of previously conducted economic analyses relating to a treatment may provide useful background to the health economist but may have limited (or no) direct use in the guidelines process. If rigorously conducted, the guidelines process is likely to produce an understanding and evaluation of treatment inadequately reflected in any one published analysis.
- The scope for conducting traditional cost-effectiveness models may be limited or unhelpful in some therapeutic areas, especially where the various attributes of treatments contain conflicting messages. Where modelling is appropriate, clinicians appear more responsive to simple and transparent models than to complex 'black box' methods requiring greater assumptions and extrapolation.
- Grading of recommendations of cost-effectiveness is in its infancy. However, the grade of recommendation should reflect not only precision and susceptibility to bias of data but also generalizability.
- As with clinical effectiveness, it is acceptable to say 'we just don't know yet' in a recommendation about cost-effectiveness of treatment and that more precise data are required.

require access to trial data four months before product launch. Appraisal will follow a development and evaluation committee-style procedure using a cost per QALY framework rather than a guideline approach. The major problem with cost-utility studies has always been the quality and handling of limited data (Mason and Drummond 1995a). How will the NICE achieve a robust assessment of new technologies on the basis of trial data intended for licensing? In internal deliberations the most heroic assumptions will be required, and as regards the external audience of practising clinicians, a cost-utility framework does not contain the right information to advise treatment decisions.

A simplified, evidence-based guideline process may be possible when considering close analogue and 'me-too' products at the near-licensing stage. In four months, little more will be possible. To assess new pharmaceuticals and procedures in the context of the epidemiology of the disease, other available treatments and health service delivery issues may place insurmountable strain upon the appraisal process. An annual target of 30 to 50 appraisals and guidelines is evidently ambitious. The consequent danger is that the appraisal process will have to cut corners in the very circumstances where a full guideline is most needed. Tampering with the elements of the evidence-based clinical guideline process may threaten their validity and consequent authority in clinical decision making (Cluzeau *et al.* 1997). Where longer-term data are required, a continuing research period, either following or delaying the NHS reimbursement decision, is proposed – although how this will work is as yet unknown. A full guideline process would ensure the right questions are asked of any further research. The NICE should focus on evaluating medicines in robust and physical terms rather than calculating assumption-laden QALYs. If the science wins then the guidelines process may become a transparent and acceptable cost effectiveness hurdle for pharmaceuticals in the UK.

The ability of any guidelines to effect a substantial change in clinical practice remains a research issue. The decision-making environment will, in any case, change in England due to the introduction of clinical governance: a package of activities intended to ensure clinicians receive and act upon the best evidence concerning treatment, corporately monitor their performance and report to those with overall responsibility.

The impact of implementing guidelines

Substantial use is to be made of audit methodologies in informing the clinical governance process. To this end, the NICE 'will develop a range of audit methodologies that can be adapted for local use to support the guidance it produces' (NHS Executive 1998). Actual monitoring will come under the national framework for assessing performance initiative, led by the new Commission for Health Improvement (CHI). Although it sounds straightforward, there are a number of major informational challenges in implementing this model (Scally and Donaldson 1998). It will prove unrealistic to follow all clinical activities: instead tracer conditions will need to be identified, although these may vary from year to year. Information may be relatively easy to obtain for some activities: use of drugs in primary care, use of procedures in secondary care, and even some simple outcome data (e.g. 30-day operative mortality). However, appropriate use of these interventions (i.e. whether the right patient received the right intervention at the right time) may prove considerably more difficult and require linkage across different patient records.

Simply handing the NICE guidelines to clinicians would not be expected, on current evidence, to achieve substantial appropriate changes in health care. Clinical governance is intended to create a pincer against unacceptable variations in performance, and the government will consider introducing new powers for the NICE and CHI if problems persist. This reflects a belief that acceptable and unacceptable variations in practice are generally separable. The evidence for the appropriate use of many treatments provided by the NHS is inadequate and it is unclear how far such a strategy can be pursued. The government may need to consider in much greater detail the dual issues of measurability and enforceability implicit in its reforms. Clinical governance as described signals a shift away from clinical freedom and implicit rationing and towards protocol-driven health care and explicit rationing. Guideline methodology has been developed to improve the scientific basis of decision making; guidelines have never been intended for mechanistic use or to form the basis of legal argument about defensible health care.

REFERENCES

Adams, M.E., McCall, N.T., Gray, D.T., Orza, M.J. and Chalmers, T.C. (1992). Economic analysis in randomized controlled trials. *Medical Care*, 30, 231–43.

AHCPR (Agency for Health Care Policy and Research) (1992). *Acute Pain Management: Operative or Medical Procedures and Trauma*. Rockville, MD: Agency for Health Care Policy and Research Publications.

Alban, A. (1982). Economic appraisal: what is the use? Paper presented at the Third Nordic Health Economists' Study Group. (Available from the Danish Hospital Institute, Copenhagen.)

Bogle, S.M. and Harris, C.M. (1994). Measuring prescribing: the shortcomings of the item. *British Medical Journal*, 308, 637–40.

Bradley, J.D., Brandt, K.D., Katz, B.P., Kalasinski, L.A. and Ryan, S.I. (1992). Treatment of knee osteoarthritis: relationship of clinical features of joint inflammation to the response to a nonsteroidal anti-inflammatory drug or pure analgesic. *Journal of Rheumatology*, 19(12), 1950–4.

British National Formulary Number 32 (1996). London: British Medical Association and Royal Pharmaceutical Society of Great Britain.

Buxton, M.J. (1987). Problems in the economic appraisal of new health technology: the evaluation of heart transplants in the UK. In M.F. Drummond (ed.), *Economic Appraisal of Health Technology in the European Community*. Oxford: Oxford Medical Publications.

CIPFA/HFM (1997). *The Health Service Financial Database 1997* (CD-ROM). London: Chartered Institute of Public Finance and Accountancy.

Cluzeau, F., Littlejohns, P., Grimshaw, J.M. and Feder, G.S. (1997). National survey of UK clinical guidelines for the management of coronary heart disease, lung and breast cancer, asthma and depression. *Journal of Clinical Effectiveness*, 2, 120–3.

Davies, L.M., Coyle, D., Drummond, M.F. and the EC Network (1994). Current status of economic appraisal of health technology in the European Community: report of the Network. *Social Science and Medicine*, 38(12), 1601–8.

Department of Health (1995). *Hospital Episode Statistics 1994–5*. London: Department of Health.

Department of Health (1996). *Health and Personl Social Services Statistics for England 1996*. London: Department of Health.

Drummond, M., Cooke, J. and Walley, T. (1997). Economic evaluation under managed competition: evidence from the UK. *Social Science and Medicine*, 45, 583–95.

Eccles, M.P., Clapp, Z., Grimshaw, J.M. *et al.* (1996). North of England evidence-based guideline development project: methods of guideline development. *British Medical Journal*, 312, 760–1.

Eccles, M., Clarke, J., Livingstone, M., Freemantle, N. and Mason, J.M. (1998a). North of England evidence-based guideline development project: evidence-based clinical practice guideline – the primary care management of dementia. *British Medical Journal*, 317, 802–8.

Eccles, M., Freemantle, N. and Mason, J.M. (1998b). Evidence-based clinical practice guideline: aspirin for the secondary prophylaxis of vascular disease in primary care. *British Medical Journal*, 316, 1303–9.

Eccles, M., Freemantle, N. and Mason, J.M. (1998c). Evidence-based clinical practice guideline: ACE-inhibitors in the primary care management of adults with symptomatic heart failure. *British Medical Journal*, 316, 1369–75.

Eccles, M., Freemantle, N. and Mason, J.M. (1998d). Evidence-based guideline for the use of non-steroidal anti-inflammatory drugs (NSAIDs) versus basic analgesia in the treatment of pain believed to be due to degenerative arthritis. *British Medical Journal*, 317, 526–30.

Eccles, M., Freemantle, N. and Mason, J.M. (1998e). Methods of developing guidelines for efficient drug use in primary care: North of England evidence-based guidelines development project. *British Medical Journal*, 316, 1232–5.

Eccles, M., Freemantle, N., Mason, J.M. (in press). The choice of antidepressants for depression in primary care. *Family Practice*.

Eccles, M., Grimshaw, J. and Baker, R. *et al.* (1998f). Teaching the theory behind guidelines: the Royal College of General Practitioners Guidelines Skills Course. *Journal of Evaluation and Clinical Practice*, 4, 157–63.

Eddy, D.M. (1992). *A manual for assessing health practices and designing practice policies: the explicit approach*. Philadelphia, PA: American College of Physicians.

Field, M.J. and Lohr, K.N. (eds) (1992). *Institute of Medicine Guidelines for Clincial Practice: From Development to Use*. Washington: National Academy Press.

Gerard, K. (1993). Setting priorities in the new NHS: can purchasers use cost-utility information? *Health Policy*, 25, 109–25.

Gøtzsche, P.C. (1989). Methodology and overt and hidden bias in reports of 196 double-blind trials of nonsteroidal anti-inflammatory drugs in rheumatoid arthritis. *Controlled Clinical Trials*, 10, 31–56.

Grimshaw, J. and Russell, I. (1993). Achieving health gain through clinical guidelines, I: developing scientifically valid guidelines. *Quality in Health Care*, 2, 243–8.

Hawkey, C.J., Swannell, A.J., Eriksson, S. *et al.* (1996). Benefits of omeprazole over misoprostol in healing NSAID-associated ulcers. *Gut*, 38(Suppl. 1), T155.

Henry, D., Lim, L.L.-Y., Garcia Rodriguez, L.A. *et al.* (1996). Variability in risk of gastrointestinal complications with individual non-steroidal anti-inflammatory drugs: results of a collaborative meta-analysis. *British Medical Journal*, 312, 1563–6.

Koch, M., Dezi, A., Ferrario, F. and Capurso, L. (1996). Prevention of nonsteroidal anti-inflammatory drug-induced gastrointestinal mucosal injury: a meta-analysis of randomized controlled clinical trials. *Archives of Internal Medicine*, 156, 2321–32.

Langman, M.J.S., Weil, J., Wainwright, P. *et al.* (1994). Risks of bleeding peptic ulcer associated with individual non-steroidal anti-inflammatory drugs. *Lancet*, 343, 1075–8.

Lee, J.T. and Sanchez, L.A. (1991). Interpretation of 'cost-effective' (and soundness of) economic evaluations in the pharmacy literature. *American Journal of Hospital Pharmacy*, 48, 2622–7.

McMurray, J., Hart, W. and Rhodes, G. (1993). An evaluation of the cost of heart failure to the National Health Service in the UK. *British Journal of Medical Economics*, 6, 99–110.

Mason, J.M. and Drummond, M.F. (1995a). The DH register of cost-effectiveness studies: content and quality. *Health Trends*, 27, 50–6.

Mason, J.M. and Drummond, M.F. (1995b). Reporting guidelines for economic studies. *Health Economics*, 4, 85–94.

Mooney, G.H. and Drummond, M.F. (1982). Essentials of health economics – Part 1(continued): what is economics? *British Medical Journal*, 285, 1024–5.

Narang, R., Swedberg, K. and Cleland, J.G.F. (1996). What is the ideal study design for evaluation of treatment for heart failure? Insights from trials assessing the effect of ACE-inhibitors on exercise capacity. *European Heart Journal*, 17, 120–34.

Netten, A. and Dennett, J. (1997). *Units Costs of Health and Social Care.* Canterbury: Personal Social Services Research Unit (PSSRU), University of Canterbury.

NHS Executive (1998). *A First-class Service: Quality in the New NHS.* London: HMSO.

North of England Asthma Guideline Development Project (1996). Summary version of evidence-based guideline for the primary care management of asthma in adults. *British Medical Journal*, 312, 762–6.

North of England Stable Angina Guideline Development Group (1996). Summary version of evidence-based guideline for the primary care management of stable angina in adults. *British Medical Journal*, 312, 827–32.

Parr, G., Darekar, B., Fletcher, A. and Bulpitt, C.J. (1989). Joint pain and quality of life: results of a randomized trial. *British Journal of Clinical Pharmacology*, 27, 235–42.

Pouleur, H. (1993). ACE-inhibitors in the treatment of clinical heart failure. *Basic Research in Cardiology*, 88(Suppl. 1), 203–9.

Rochan, P.A., Gurwitz, J.H. and Simms, R.W. (1994). A study of manufacturer-supported trials of nonsteroidal anti-inflammatory drugs in the treatment of arthritis. *Archives of Internal Medicine*, 154, 157–63.

Rogers, W.J., Johnstone, D.E., Yusuf, S. (1994). Quality of life among 5.025 patients with left ventricular dysfunction randomized between placebo and enalapril: the studies of left ventricular dysfunction. *Journal of the American College of Cardiology*, 23, 393–400.

Ross, J. (1995). The use of economic evaluation in health care: Australian decision-makers' perceptions. *Health Policy*, 31, 103–10.

Scally, G. and Donaldson, L.J. (1998). Clinical governance and the drive for quality improvement in the new NHS in England. *British Medical Journal*, 317, 61–5.

Scottish Health Service Costs, Year ended 31st March 1996 (1996). Edinburgh: National Health Service in Scotland Information and Statistics Division.

Silverstein, F.E., Graham, D.Y. and Senior, J.R. (1995). Misoprostol reduces serious gastrointestinal complications in patients with rheumatoid arthritis receiving nonsteroidal anti-inflammatory drugs: a randomized, double-blind, placebo-controlled trial. *Annals of Internal Medicine*, 123, 241–9.

SOLVD Investigators (1991). Effect of enalapril on survival in patients with reduced left ventricular ejection fractions and congestive heart failure. *New England Journal of Medicine*, 325, 293–302.

Sugden, R. and Williams, A. (1978). *The Principles of Practical Cost-benefit Analysis.* Oxford: Oxford University Press.

Udvarhelyi, I.S., Colditz, G.A., Rai, A. and Epstein, A.M. (1992). Cost-effectiveness and cost-benefit analysis in the medical literature: are methods being used correctly? *Annals of Internal Medicine*, 116, 238–44.

Williams, A. (1972). Cost-benefit analysis: bastard science or insidious poison of the body politick? *Journal of Public Economics*, 1, 199–216.

Williams, A. (1995). How should information of cost-effectiveness influence practice? In T. Delamothe (ed.), *Outcomes in Clinical Practice*. London: BMJ.

Williams, H.J., Ward, J.R. and Egger, M.J. (1993). Comparison of naproxen and acetaminophen in a two-year study of treatment of osteoarthritis of the knee. *Arthritis & Rheumatism*, 36(9), 1196–206.

World Health Collaborating Centre for Drug Statistics Methodology (1992). *Anatomical Therapeutic Chemical Classification Index*. Oslo: World Health Organization.

11

CLINICAL GOVERNANCE: STRIKING A BALANCE BETWEEN CHECKING AND TRUSTING

Huw Davies and
Russell Mannion

INTRODUCTION

Clinical governance emerged as one of the big ideas central to the latest round of health reforms. It places with health care managers, for the first time, a statutory duty for quality of care on an equal footing with the pre-existing duty of financial responsibility (Warden 1998). Clinical governance tries to encourage an appropriate emphasis on the quality of clinical services by locating the responsibility for that quality along defined lines of accountability.

This chapter explores some of the implications of clinical governance using the economic perspective of principal–agent theory. It examines the ways in which principals seek to overcome the potential for agent opportunism either by reducing asymmetries of information (for example, by using performance data) or by aligning objective functions (for example, by the creation of a shared quality culture). As trust and mutuality (or their absence) underpin all principal–agent relationships these issues lie at the heart of the discussion.

The analysis emphasizes the need for a balance between techniques that seek to compel performance improvements (through externally applied measurement and management), and approaches that trust to intrinsic professional motivation to deliver high quality services. Of crucial importance in achieving this balance is the creation and maintenance of the right organizational culture.

Background

The United Kingdom (UK) health care reforms of the early 1990s were characterized by a clarification of budgetary responsibilities within the system, a linking of clinical practice to those financial responsibilities, and an attempt to use market mechanisms to force efficiencies. Almost a decade later, many of the structural changes introduced may have been retained (Department of Health 1997; Baker 1998) but the rhetoric has changed: competition is out, cooperation is in (Goddard and Mannion 1998). Further, both rhetorical emphasis and practical action are now firmly located around issues of health care quality (Thomson 1998).

The confluence of a great many factors have conspired to bring quality of care issues centre-stage (see Box 11.1). As a result, these and other trends have loosened a number of previously sacrosanct cornerstones of clinical autonomy and organizational hegemony (see Box 11.2). Thus there is an unprecedented opportunity for a radical overhaul of how health care is managed in the UK. Political will and public concern have ensured that the *status quo* is no longer an option. To their credit, many clinicians and their professional organizations do demonstrate a willingness to increase the scrutiny of professional practice. However, recent debates at the General Medical Council over revalidation and medical practice regulation suggest that such willingness is far from universal (Horton 1998b). What is more, experience from the USA has shown that failure on the part of the medical profession to maintain or improve quality while at the same time curbing costs may result in the widespread micromanagement of clinical practice, as epitomized by managed care (LeGrand 1998; Robinson and Steiner 1998). Such an outcome would undoubtedly be disturbing and distasteful for many, if not most, UK clinicians.

The nature of clinical governance

Concerns over corporate governance in the private sector welled up in the late 1980s, partly as a result of a number of high-profile corporate failures and scandals. The resulting 'Cadbury Code' on corporate governance (Cadbury Committee 1992) attempted to set

---

Box 11.1   Why the focus on quality of care?

- A burgeoning evidence base of what works in clinical practice (and what does not).
- The existence of widespread and unacceptable variations in clinical practice as well as clinical outcomes.
- A number of manifest and highly public failures of care.
- The emergence of sophisticated data systems and the expertise to mine these for performance-related information.
- A desire to curb costs (as poor quality may be seen in the overuse of treatments and/or iatrogenic harm).
- A political need on the part of the incoming government to find an issue around which to articulate public concern over the NHS which could serve as a focus for health care reform.

---

clear guidance in this area and brought a *'new public role to the internal control system'* (Power 1997: 56). These same principles have been extended to other public services including the National Health Service (NHS) (Scally and Donaldson 1998). Clinical governance emerged as a core theme in both the government White Paper (Department of Health 1997) and the ensuing policy document *A First-Class Service* (NHS Executive 1998a). The main components of clinical governance were spelled out as:

- *Clear lines of responsibility and accountability for the overall quality of care.* This includes giving the chief executive the ultimate responsibility for clinical quality, and placing an obligation on NHS trusts to arrange formal reporting structures that put quality issues on an even footing with financial matters.
- *A comprehensive programme of quality improvement activities.* Measures suggested are: a revitalizing of clinical audit, engagement with evidence-based practice; compliance with national service frameworks and other national standards; along with programmes for continuing professional development. High quality data systems and quality assurance programmes are seen as essential for meeting these requirements.

Box 11.2   Trends loosening clinical autonomy and organizational hegemony

- The development of general management within the NHS.
- The rise of clear financial accountability.
- The emergence of 'evidence-based medicine' as a powerful paradigm for clinical practice (together with the organization of a sizeable reliable evidence base).
- The explicit use of needs assessment to define desirable service provision.
- A gradual acceptance of the need for cost-effective health care.
- A calling into question of the appropriateness and effectiveness of professional self-regulation (Klein 1998; Smith 1998b).
- The centralization of standards of acceptable practice – for example, through national service frameworks (NHS Executive 1998b).
- Some tentative questioning of the appropriateness of the existing consultant contractual arrangements in a modern health service (Richards 1998).
- An apparent increase in the willingness to suspend clinicians in the face of allegations of poor performance (Bower 1998).

- *Clear policies aimed at managing risks.* Suggestions here emphasize both personal clinical responsibility and the need for effective systematic reduction of risk.
- *Effective procedures to identify and remedy poor performance.* Actionable points listed include the development of critical incident reporting and accessible patient complaint procedures as a way of identifying learning opportunities. Also highlighted is the need to support staff in their duty to report concerns about colleagues' performance to enable early remedial action to be taken.

Thus, government strategy on clinical performance has centred on a push for more and better information on clinical performance, as set out in the national performance framework (NHS Executive

1998b), pitched against clearly defined standards of expected practice to be developed by the National Institute for Clinical Excellence (NICE). A waiting policeman is also on hand to deal with
miscreants (the Commission for Health Improvement). The interface between provider organizations and these national enabling
initiatives, as well as the internal galvanizing of actions aimed at
quality improvement, are now gathered under the umbrella term
'clinical governance'.

Doctors have given this part of the White Paper a cautious welcome (Black 1998; News report 1998), some noting that clinical
governance largely clarifies and structures activities that have
always been regarded as the foundations of good professional practice (News report 1998). A recent review of general practitioners
(GPs) involved in total purchasing did reveal negative attitudes and
concerns about clinical governance, but also showed considerable
lack of understanding of its nature and implications (Malbon *et al.*
1998). Dissenting voices have focused on the lack of resources
available either to deliver high quality care or to put in place the
necessary infrastructure to support quality improvements (Frazer
1998; Richards 1998). As such, cynics suggest that clinical governance is just another tactic to distract clinicians from the bigger
issues of increased central control and tight fiscal settlements.
Nonetheless, leading articles have congratulated the government
for attempting to articulate a clear quality vision together with a
detailed and practical strategy aimed at supporting clinical excellence (Donaldson 1998; Scally and Donaldson 1998; Thomson
1998).

Framework for analysis

This chapter uses principal–agent theory to examine some of the
options for clinical governance. The first section explains the basis
of the theory (for non-economists) and outlines its prominent
implications. Two of the major approaches to dealing with these
implications are then described and evaluated. These are: checking
and modifying behaviour using hierarchical control (perhaps allied
to incentives); and developing intrinsic professional motivations
(through the creation and harnessing of trust). These represent
first an attempt to redress asymmetries of information, and second
an attempt to align principals' and agents' objectives. What links
these and provides a context for all approaches to governance is
organizational culture. Thus, culture and its implications for

organizational performance are also explored. Finally, the chapter rounds off with some normative remarks on the need for thoughtful deployment and careful balancing of the various approaches to governance.

PRINCIPAL–AGENT THEORY

Principal–agent theory analyses reciprocal (but nonetheless asymmetric) relationships within and between organizations (Laffont and Tirole 1993). Principals are those actors (individuals or organizations) who want things done. Agents are other actors who are engaged to accomplish these things at the principals' behest. The relationships between principals and agents can take many forms. They may be fixed, tightly controlled and contractual, or they may be loose, informal and shifting. Even when tightly controlled, softer information and informal relationships often underpin formal contracts (Goddard *et al.* 1998). However, a key feature in all these relationships (and the source of possible problems) is the presence of various asymmetries between the two parties.

Agency theory has much to say about the interaction between doctors and patients (Mooney and Ryan 1993). However it has also been used to elicit insights into the organization and operation of health services in a variety of other ways. For example, agency theory has been used to examine the financial flows in health services (Smith *et al.* 1997), to explain the emergence, stability and efficiency of different provider structures (Robinson 1997), and to explore the organizational behaviour implications of performance indicators (Davies *et al.* 1999). In an analysis of the previous NHS (market-style) reforms, Propper concluded that the reconfigured NHS could be viewed as a series of overlapping principal–agent relationships with varying incentives (Propper 1995).

In this analysis of clinical governance, *the principals* are service managers (non-clinical or clinical) with primary responsibility for health care quality within the health care organization (trust or primary care group). *The agents* are those health care professionals through whose effort quality of care may be achieved or lacking. The analysis exposes the difficulties and conflicts that may arise in these relationships and discusses some of the approaches which may be used to overcome these.

Of course, health care professionals (and physicians in particular) are not only the agents of service managers. They are also, most obviously, agents of their patients. This fiduciary relationship is one by which many physicians place great store as they seek to meet their obligations under the Hippocratic oath. Thus, clinical governance places physicians and other health care professionals in the position of holding multiple accountabilities which may interact and at times conflict (Shortell *et al.* 1998).

Problems arising from agency

Difficulties arise in agency relationships because of incongruities and asymmetries between agents and principals. Agents may differ from principals in two main and important ways:

1 *Objective functions:* ambiguity over the objectives of health care may lead to divergent implicit (or even explicit) aims between principals and agents. For example, health care managers may be seeking balanced budgets whereas clinicians may be seeking to maximize health benefits for individuals under their care. Further, principals and agents (even notional ones) are all *people* – with various beliefs, attitudes and values, some of which are stable, while others vary by time and context. Thus principals and agents may differ in other important ways – for example, in the values they attach to specific outcomes, or their attitudes to risk.

2 *Knowledge and information:* principals and agents have different (though often overlapping) technical knowledge and situation-specific information. They may therefore come to quite different understandings about situations and appropriate actions. For example, even when principals do share objectives, they may differ as to how those objectives are best reached.

These differences between principals and agents open up scope for divergence between what principals want and what agents are able or are prepared to deliver. Agents may for example make undesirable trade-offs between multiple competing objectives, or worse, they may exploit their powerful position to indulge in opportunistic behaviour to maximize their own gain at the expense of the principal. Such opportunism is by definition covert, what Williamson calls *'self-interest seeking with guile'* (Williamson 1993), and is therefore insidious. The accountable officer charged with ensuring health care quality within the organization thus needs to be cognizant of this potential for (from their perspective) dysfunctional behaviour.

Approaches to agent performance

Various possibilities appear for principals to tackle the potential for sub-optimal agent performance. First they can attempt to exert control through hierarchical organizational structures. For such control to be successful they must be able to measure and monitor those aspects of agent behaviour thought important, and they must have some means at their disposal of exerting influence over agent behaviour in response to observed deviations from desired practice. Such control may be conferred by legitimate power within the organization or it may be gained by judicious application of incentives (punishments and/or rewards).

A second approach is to seek a negotiated realignment of objectives, knowledge, beliefs, etc. – all the factors described above which might give rise to (perceived) agency waywardness. If, as far as possible, agents and principals share a broad and deep understanding about ends, means and the relationships between them, then the agency problems can be minimized without the need for (often costly) control mechanisms. Such a situation arises when principals and agents enjoy a relationship of *mutual trust*: principals trust agents to deliver desired performance; and in return agents trust principals to leave them unmolested in delivering that performance.

A number of linked questions of relevance to clinical governance emerge from this discussion:

- What aspects of agent behaviour and performance should be measured? And what are the strengths and limitations of using such measures to check on agent performance?
- How should performance information be used to prompt agent behaviour change – for example, what control structures are appropriate, and how might incentives be set?
- What is the role played by trust? What are the benefits and risks that might ensue when principals trust agents? And how does checking on agent performance impact on trusting relationships?
- How can principals and agents negotiate a convergence on the factors that contribute to unsatisfactory principal-agent relationships?

It is in seeking insights into these questions that we now address the relative roles of checking and trusting in prompting high performance in clinical practice.

CHECKING AND CONTROLLING

Checking performance and introducing measures to coerce behaviour change are instinctive responses by managers faced with securing performance improvement. In many cases such shocks to the system will indeed produce results. There is ample evidence that tightened control and the application of economic incentives and sanctions can have immediate and marked effects (Meekings 1995; Flemming and Mayer 1997). Such ready successes in various areas of application have legitimized the increased application of performance indicators to health care (Davies and Lampel 1998). The national performance framework document (released in support of the White Paper) outlined the multifarious ways in which performance measures are expected to be used to drive health care improvements in the 'new' NHS (NHS Executive 1998b).

Data *are* an essential tool for reducing one of the important asymmetries between principals and agents (that of information on agent behaviour and subsequent outcomes). Agents themselves also require good quality information if they are to identify deficiencies in practice and respond accordingly. Thus the provision of high quality information on the processes and outcomes of care has much to commend it. However, it is also clear that focusing on data to drive improvements has a number of limitations as well as the potential for deleterious effects. Some of these limitations are now outlined.

Interpretation difficulties

In using data to assess performance, we want to infer that poorly measured performance reflects poor actual performance. Unfortunately, many factors intervene to make such causal attribution weak at best and nonsensical at worst. Variations in apparent performance may arise because of data deficiencies, bias in the measures used, unadjusted casemix, differential ascertainment of severity data or even just chance variability (Davies and Crombie 1997, 1999). Further, data from different sources (for example, administrative data *versus* data derived from clinical records) may tell rather different stories about the quality of care (Hartz and Kuhn 1994). In consequence, poor quality of care may falsely be labelled adequate, or adequate care may unfortunately be judged poor. Thus, inferences about quality, especially from routine datasets, may lack both validity and reliability.

Dysfunctional consequences

Smith in particular (1995a, 1995b) has drawn attention to the various less than desirable ways in which organizations and individuals may respond to indicator data. There may, for example, be a tendency to focus on those aspects of care which are measured to the detriment of other important areas; or for emphasis to be placed on narrow or short-term objectives at the expense of long-term global or strategic ends. The fear of falling short on measured performance may also lead to a disinclination to innovate and may elevate a concern to be average over the desire to be outstanding. At the most extreme, powerful incentives may induce gaming behaviour, misrepresentation or even out-and-out fraudulent practice. While empirical research does find some support for these dysfunctional consequences (Luce *et al.* 1996; Goddard *et al.* 1998), more usually, unless closely tied to specific actions, indicators are largely ignored (Davies 1998; Goddard *et al.* 1998; Rainwater *et al.* 1998).

Backward-looking

A more fundamental concern with an over-reliance on performance measurement is that it is inescapably backward-looking. That is, using measures to make judgements reflects a concern with picking up past mistakes rather than on pre-emption of those mistakes in the first place. By the time they have been collected, collated, analysed, adjusted and disseminated, performance data may be years out of date. This clearly limits both the relevance and usefulness of these data in securing appropriate behaviour change. Although more recent work has emphasized the benefits of developing on-line measures, available in real time (Kaplan and Norton 1992), the fact remains that for many measures of health care performance – particularly health outcomes – delays are inevitable.

None of the above observations are to argue that data do not matter. On the contrary, data have an invaluable role to play in any quality improvement programme. Instead, the deficiencies outlined should counsel against demanding more from performance data than they can reasonably support. Many of the problems described arise in part because attempts are made to draw strong inferences from the data. Berwick (1996, 1998) has highlighted the importance of distinguishing between using data to inform quality improvement efforts, and using data to make judgements. Thus, the crucial consideration is not the data themselves but the underlying context and culture within which those data are used.

ORGANIZATIONAL CULTURE AND QUALITY PERFORMANCE

Recent re-examination of the assumptions underlying the economic perspective on organizational behaviour have led to a number of observations relevant to clinical governance (Granovetter 1992; Mannion and Small 1998). In contrast to the view of organizational actors as being 'utility-maximizing rational individuals', new economic sociology asserts that other powerful factors come into play, namely:

- that the pursuit of economic goals is also accompanied by the pursuit of non-economic goals such as status, power, reputation and peer approval;
- that actions are socially situated, embedded as they are in networks of social relations;
- that the institutions within which actions take place are not inevitable but are idiosyncratic and socially constructed.

This socialized view of behaviour enables a link to be made between the governance of individuals and the culture of the organization within which those individuals are situated. Various definitions of organizational culture have been proposed and, although they may differ, they contain a substantial common core: culture consists of that which is shared among organizational colleagues, including shared beliefs, attitudes, values and norms of behaviour. It is a commonly understood way of making sense of the organization that allows people to see situations and events in similar and distinctive ways (Morgan 1986; Langfield-Smith 1995; Williams *et al.* 1996).

The notion that organizations possess distinctive cultures that can be managed to improve performance has now entered mainstream management thinking. In the 1980s a number of popular management books also proved influential in establishing the notion that culture was the crucial variable separating 'excellent' organizations from the also-rans (Peters and Waterman 1982). The NHS has proved no exception to this trend and it is clear that the architects of the latest NHS reforms view the manipulation of culture as an important change driver to delivering higher quality services: 'There is a need to develop organisations to support a change in culture and deliver change . . . We want to create a culture in the NHS which supports and encourages success and innovation' (Department of Health 1997).

Here we examine the processes and factors associated with successful cultural change in the context of the proposed NHS reforms. First, it is now recognized that cultural change is no panacea for poorly performing organizations, and that to be effective such initiatives should be part of a wider set of mutually reinforcing improvement activities (Williams *et al.* 1996). In this respect, culture should be viewed as merely one of a range of critical variables that an organization such as the NHS should manage in order to improve performance. Other crucial variables that need to be actively managed include, for example, organizational structure, accounting systems and strategy formulation.

Second, changing an organizational culture is unlikely to be a 'quick fix' solution. Many corporate case studies show that transition is often a slow process and can take anything from five to eight years to achieve any real impact (Deal and Kennedy 1992). It seems therefore that the government strategy of evolution rather than revolution, and its commitment to a ten-year programme of modernization of the NHS, is a realistic assessment of the task ahead.

Third, the experience of many organizations throws into considerable doubt the traditional assumption that cultural change can be imposed top-down by macho-style leadership. It is becoming increasingly clear that changes which do not take into account the concerns and motivations of lower level staff do not generally produce significant and long-standing change (Beer *et al.* 1990). Successful cultural change initiatives appear to embody both clear leadership and attempts to facilitate lower level participation in the decision making process. All this must be fostered by developing a common sense of purpose through education, training and effective communications (Williams *et al.* 1996). This holistic approach is in contrast to the rapid improvements frequently sought by the application of measurement and control strategies – for example, recent evidence shows that there are few systematic attempts to communicate the importance and meaning of performance data to front-line staff (Goddard *et al.* 1998).

A final consideration is the *diversity* of cultures that may be contained within a single organization, each subculture with its own distinctive value system and affiliations to external social and professional groupings (Langfield-Smith 1995). The fact that multiple cultures can and do coexist within the same NHS trust (albeit with the dominant subgroup being the 'medical clan' – Bourn and Ezzamel 1986) makes any attempt to instil a unified culture somewhat problematic.

Clearly, changing the culture of the NHS will not be easy. A number of studies in the NHS have shown that, in the face of major restructuring, continuity is more apparent than change as the dominant culture attempts to neutralize the impact of any reform. For example, attempts to impose a general management culture on the medical subculture in the mid–1980s (through the development of resource management initiatives) met with strong resistance and largely failed to have substantial impact on clinician autonomy (Jones and Dewing 1997). Similarly, there is evidence to suggest that, at least initially, the internal market reforms had little impact on the culture of the medical clan (Broadbent *et al.* 1992). Thus, although cultural reform may be a *sine qua non*, all the evidence is that achieving deep and prolonged cultural shifts will be no easy task.

AN EXPLORATION OF TRUST

One key cultural variable receiving increasing recent attention in the social science literature is that of trust. All principal–agent relationships of necessity involve a certain amount of trust as a backdrop to the more explicit hierarchical control, contractual, or incentive-based arrangements. This happens because, in all except the most trivial of relationships, there will be aspects of the desired behaviour of the agent that will be beyond the scope of all reasonable checking. This is especially true of health care, which is so multifaceted, uncertain, often immeasurable and frequently hidden from view (consultations which occur in private, for example). Thus, even in well-specified and detailed contracts, or with comprehensive performance management systems, principals must nonetheless trust that their agents will attend with due diligence to those aspects of care which fall outside of these arrangements.

Even comprehensive control systems involving extensive measurement and audit do not obviate the need for trust. Instead, they demand trust of a different order: trust that the measurement or audit system is itself providing a good account (Power 1997). There is ample evidence that this second-order trust is often misplaced; that audit accounts can give false reassurance or provoke unnecessary alarm (Power 1997). Thus, trust of some sort is inescapable in almost any agency relationship: either direct trust without checking, or indirect trust in the reassurance provided by measures and systems.

The pervasiveness of trust means that it is a key component of many desirable organizational cultures. For example, empowerment as a means of releasing human potential relies on a mutual trust between the empowerers and the empowered. Over 20 years ago Golembiewski and McConkie (1975) asserted that *'perhaps there is no single variable which so thoroughly influences interpersonal and group behaviour as does trust'*. In the light of this, the next section examines the nature of trust and its implications for effective clinical governance.

The nature of trust

Trust by one person in another is the subjective assessment that that person will behave in an agreed manner regardless of monitoring, coercion or inducements (Gambetta 1988). Trust then is an *expectation* of competence, predictability and fairness on the part of agents (Zaheer *et al.* 1998). Trust arises when a number of conditions hold: when there is a relationship of interdependence and obligation between two parties; when there is uncertainty about the courses of action that may be taken; and when there is a deliberate decision to believe that obligations will be fulfilled.

A relationship where the principal has no choice but to place faith in the agent (i.e. when no alternative approaches are available) is not so much a trusting relationship but more one of dependency. The security of tenure of senior clinicians and the general lack of institutional leverage over their behaviour leads to some concern that the relationship between health care managers and clinicians may indeed be characterized by some dependency.

This description of trust highlights its interpersonal nature, but trust may also be said to exist between organizations (Lane and Bachmann 1998). For example, the reputation of high-status institutions highlights both the existence of trust lodged in an organization, and trust that is not dependent on personal experience. Trust may also be placed in specific groups: compare for example the high levels of trust usually commanded by doctors with the proverbial lack of trustworthiness ascribed to second-hand car salesmen. Note also that ascriptions of trust may or may not have a sound basis in reality.

Trust may be difficult and time-consuming to create – for example, it may result from repeated interactions over prolonged periods with slowly evolving confidence. In contrast, trust is easily dissipated through actual or perceived errant or aberrant behaviour. Thus, trust may be costly to develop, requiring an investment up front for uncertain pay-off, and it has the potential for lost investment if adequate trust is never gained or is subsequently lost.

Of necessity, trust also involves exposure to risks: trusted parties may fail to perform to expectations, and may exploit the lack of vigilance afforded by a trusting relationship. Even when opportunism is not a problem, high levels of trust may serve to lock-in parties to certain constrained modes of operation, thus reducing flexibility (Lane 1998). Attempting to renegotiate relationships may then result in a rapid shift from trust to mistrust. It is also worth noting that mistrust is not merely an absence of trust: mistrust brings with it an expectation of opportunistic behaviour (which may or may not be well founded) which demands defensive and costly reassurance arrangements (for example, detailed monitoring, or contracts and litigation).

Notwithstanding the costs and risks of trust, organizations that develop high levels of trust within both internal and external relationships can also expect significant advantages. An obvious benefit arising from trust is a reduction in transaction costs as the overheads associated with contracts and control mechanisms are reduced or eliminated. But this is not the only gain. Trust has been linked to a wide range of desirable organizational outcomes, including improved communication, better teamwork and increased worker participation (McCauley and Kuhnert 1992; Jones and George 1998; Sashittal *et al.* 1998). All of these in turn may foster empowerment, innovation and creative problem solving. Employee trust in senior managers has also been found to be a factor in job satisfaction (Driscoll 1978) and commitment to the organization (McCauley and Kuhnert 1992). Additionally, the existence of trust facilitates organizational learning (Koeck 1998).

Trust is starting to be examined as an explanatory variable in models of organizational performance. Even at a societal level, researchers have attempted to use different levels of societal trust to explain varying national economic performance (Fukuyama 1995). Within organizations, there is some evidence that practices which imply a lack of trust may have a deleterious impact on performance by displacing intrinsic motivations (Frey 1997). There are sound reasons why this might be so in health care (Davies and

Lampel 1998). However, these relationships are not simple. For example, some of the literature on performance-related pay suggests that the practice can damage trust and performance (Osterloh and Frey 1998), while others claim that in an existing high-trust environment performance-related pay can be advantageous (National Research Council 1991). Thus, the role of trust in improving organizational performance is certain to be highly contingent on the organizational context (including culture). What also remains unclear is whether high performance emerges as a result of high levels of trust within organizations, or whether high trust is a by-product of high-achieving organizations. That is, even if any relationship can be established between trust and performance, it is not immediately clear in which direction any causality may operate.

STRIKING A BALANCE BETWEEN CHECKING AND TRUSTING

Achieving accountability is all about principals calling agents to give an account of their activities and achievements. The main difficulties lie in deciding when an account is called for and what sort of account is appropriate. Following from this is the need to be aware of what it is that accounts (of whatever kind) miss out or de-emphasize, and the need to avoid the production of merely ritualistic accounts (accounts which placate but are neither truly informative nor instrumental – Power 1997).

Attempting to achieve the aims of clinical governance through measurement and monitoring represents a decision to focus on a certain type of account-giving. Such retrospective checking needs to be counterbalanced by developing an appropriate quality-focused and learning-oriented culture. Central to this is the need to develop high levels of trust in those delivering care so that real partnerships can be developed within the organization. Trusting in health care professionals may involve ceding some managerial control but it does not mean abdicating managerial responsibility. That responsibility encompasses articulation of the organization's mission, values and goals, the provision of leadership, and the development of organizational culture – what Rundall terms the 'bounding of empowerment' (Rundall *et al.* 1998). Thus, trust is not the abandonment of controls but is instead the re-emphasizing of the power of internal intrinsic motivations over external drivers; control based on shared goals and values, rather than incentives and fault-finding.

The appropriate balance between checking and trusting will depend crucially on the nature of the process at issue. When the nature of appropriate agent behaviour is unambiguous and easily measured, then checking may provide useful reassurance and control for principals. In health care, it is more often the case that the outputs from agents are ambiguous and difficult to measure, and the relationships between these outputs and agent behaviour is clouded. In such circumstances, what Ouchi (1980) calls 'clan control' may be more effective. That is, a reliance on shared values and beliefs, and an expectation of reciprocity or trust.

The theoretical benefits of trust receive some support empirically, but more work is required before we can claim to have a robust body of evidence. Nonetheless, the lack of research evidence to support much of the theoretical advantages of trust is more an absence of evidence of any kind rather than evidence that trust is of subsidiary importance. The concern is that insufficient attention will be paid to the sometimes nebulous concepts of trust and culture in a headlong rush for the more tangible appeals of measurement, monitoring and coercive control mechanisms.

CONCLUSION

Clinical governance provides an important new status for quality of care, giving it legitimate houseroom at all managerial levels. As such it may provide a stimulus to coordinating and integrating the multiplicity of activities and initiatives currently addressing quality issues. However, with the new responsibility may also come fears: fear of failure, fear of losing control, fear of the unknown. The natural response to such fears is increased measurement hand in hand with tighter control. Thus, the debate so far has often been dominated by discussion of how best to measure, monitor and correct aberrant behaviour. Recent high-profile instances of manifest failures in clinical practice and dilatory professional responses (for example, the Bristol case – Horton 1998a; Smith 1998a) have contributed to this atmosphere of regulation and restraint. Talk of 'policing' may be counterbalanced by soothing words on the need to engender the right 'culture' for quality and a renewed emphasis on the importance of leadership (Koeck 1998), but these two components remain uneasy bedfellows.

Measurement, monitoring and control are costly strategies. They are costly not only for the up-front expenses of putting in place information and accountability systems but also for the largely hidden opportunity costs associated with these systems' operation and use. Further, we are not yet clear what intangibles we lose when we abandon trust in professional motivation: '*a system that does not trust people begets people that cannot be trusted*' (Davies and Lampel 1998: 159). Thus, careless use of inappropriate control strategies may introduce new costs and actually impede progress towards quality objectives.

Measurement and explicit control is not the only approach open to those interested in wringing quality improvements from the NHS. As well as reducing information asymmetries, clinical governance also needs to pay sufficient attention to realigning objective functions. Thus, the complex nature of health care delivery requires a delicate balance between attempts at control and a fostering of high-trust relationships embedded in a quality culture.

REFERENCES

Baker, M. (1998). *Making Sense of the New NHS White Paper.* Abingdon: Radcliffe Medical Press.

Beer, M., Eisenstat, P. and Spector, B. (1990). Why changes programs don't produce change. *Harvard Business Review*, 68, 158–66.

Berwick, D.M. (1996). Primer on leading improvement of systems. *British Medical Journal*, 312, 619.

Berwick, D.M. (1998). The NHS: feeling well and thriving at 75. *British Medical Journal*, 317, 57–61.

Black, N. (1998). Clinical governance: fine words or action? *British Medical Journal*, 326, 97–8.

Bourn, M. and Ezzamel, M. (1986). Organisational culture in hospitals in the NHS. *Financial Accountability and Management*, 2, 203–25.

Bower, H. (1998). More doctors face suspension as managers flex their muscles. *British Medical Journal*, 317, 1101.

Broadbent, J., Laughlin, R. and Shearn, D. (1992). Recent financial and administrative changes in general practice: an unhealthy intrusion into medical autonomy. *Financial Accountability and Management*, 8, 129–48.

Cadbury Committee (1992). *The Financial Aspects of Corporate Governance.* London: Institute of Chartered Accountants in England and Wales.

Davies, H.T.O. (1998). Performance management using health outcomes: in search of instrumentality. *Journal of Evaluation in Clinical Practice*, 4, 150–3.

Davies, H.T.O. and Crombie, I.K. (1997). Interpreting health outcomes. *Journal of Evaluation in Clinical Practice*, 3, 187–200.

Davies, H.T.O. and Crombie, I.K. (1999). Outcomes from observational studies: understanding causal ambiguity. *Drug Information Journal*, 33, 153–8.

Davies, H.T.O. and Lampel, J. (1998). Trust in performance indicators. *Quality in Health Care*, 7, 159–62.

Davies, H.T.O., Crombie, I.K. and Mannion, R. (1999). Performance indicators in health care: guiding lights or wreckers' lanterns? In H.T.O. Davies, M. Malek, A. Neilson and M. Tavakoli (eds), *Managing Quality and Controlling Cost: Strategic Issues in Health Care Management*. Aldershot: Ashgate.

Deal, T. and Kennedy, A. (1992). *Corporate Cultures: the Rites and Rituals of Corporate Life*. Harmondsworth: Penguin.

Department of Health (1997). *The New NHS: Modern, Dependable*. London: The Stationery Office.

Donaldson, L.J. (1998). Clinical governance: a statutory duty for quality improvement. *Journal of Epidemiology and Community Health*, 52, 73–4.

Driscoll, J.W. (1978). Trust and participation in organizational decision making as predictor of satisfaction. *Academy of Management Journal*, 21, 44–56.

Flemming, J. and Mayer, C. (1997). The assessment: public-sector investment. *Oxford Review of Economic Policy*, 13, 1–11.

Frazer, M. (1998). The government's initiative may be stillborn. *British Medical Journal*, 317, 687.

Frey, B. (1997). *Not Just for the Money: An Economic Theory of Personal Motivation*. Cheltenham: Edward Elgar.

Fukuyama, F. (1995). *Trust: The Social Virtues and the Creation of Prosperity*. New York: The Free Press.

Gambetta, D. (1988). *Trust: Making and Breaking Co-operative Relations*. Oxford: Blackwell.

Goddard, M. and Mannion, R. (1998). From competition to co-operation: new economic relationships in the National Health Service. *Health Economics*, 7, 105–19.

Goddard, M., Mannion, R. and Smith, P.C. (1998). All quiet on the front line. *Health Service Journal*, 24–6.

Golembiewski, R.T. and McConkie, M.L. (1975). The centrality of interpersonal trust in group processes. In C.L. Cooper (ed.), *Theories of Group Processes*. New York: Wiley.

Granovetter, M. (1992). Economic institutions as social constructions: a framework for analysis. *Acta Sociologica*, 35, 3–11.

Hartz, A.J. and Kuhn, E.M. (1994). Comparing hospitals that perform coronary artery bypass surgery: the effect of outcome measures and data sources. *American Journal of Public Health*, 84, 1609–14.

Horton, R. (1998a). How should doctors respond to the GMC's judgements on Bristol? *Lancet*, 351, 1900–1.

Horton, R. (1998b). Yesterday's doctors. *Lancet*, 352, 1566–7.

Jones, C. and Dewing, I. (1997). The attitudes of NHS clinicians and medical managers towards changes in accounting controls. *Financial Accountability and Management*, 13, 261–80.

Jones, G.R. and George, J.M. (1998). The experience and evolution of trust: implications for cooperation and teamwork. *Academy of Management Review*, 23, 531–46.

Kaplan, R. and Norton, D. (1992). The balanced scorecard: measures that drive performance. *Harvard Business Review*, 70, 71–9.

Klein, R. (1998). Competence, professional self regulation, and the public interest. *British Medical Journal*, 316, 1740–2.

Koeck, C. (1998). Time for organisational development in healthcare organisations. *British Medical Journal*, 317, 1267–8.

Laffont, J. and Tirole, J. (1993). *A Theory of Incentives in Procurement and Regulation.* Cambridge, MA: MIT Press.

Lane, C. (1998). Introduction: theories and issues in the study of trust. In C. Lane and R. Bachmann (eds), *Trust Within and Between Organizations*. Oxford: Oxford University Press.

Lane, C. and Bachmann, R. (eds) (1998). *Trust Within and Between Organizations*. Oxford: Oxford University Press.

Langfield-Smith, K. (1995). Organisational culture and control. In A. Berry, J. Broadbent, and D. Otley (eds), *Management Control: Theories, Issues and Practices*. London: Macmillan.

LeGrand, J. (1998). US managed care: has the UK anything to learn? *British Medical Journal*, 317, 831–2.

Luce, J.M., Thiel, G.D., Holland, M.R. *et al.* (1996). Use of risk-adjusted outcome data for quality improvement in public hospitals. *Western Journal of Medicine*, 164, 410–14.

McCauley, D.P. and Kuhnert, K.W. (1992). A theoretical review and empirical investigation of employee trust. *Public Administration Quarterly*, Summer, 265–85.

Malbon, G., Gillan, S. and Mays, N. (1998). Clinical governance: onus points. *Health Service Journal*, 28–9.

Mannion, R. and Small, N. (1998). *Postmodern Health Economics*. Mimeograph, University of York.

Meekings, A. (1995). Unlocking the potential of performance measurement. *Public Money and Management*, 15(4), 5–12.

Mooney, G. and Ryan, M. (1993) Agency in health care: getting beyond first principles. *Journal of Health Economics*, 12, 125–35.

Morgan, G. (1986). *Images of Organization.* London: Sage.

National Research Council (1991). *Pay for Performance: Evaluating Performance Appraisal and Merit Pay*. Washington, DC: National Academy Press.

News report (1998). Clinical governance must be 'bottom-up'. *British Medical Journal*, 317, 214.

NHS Executive (1998a). *A First-class Service: Quality in the New NHS*. London: The Stationery Office.

NHS Executive (1998b). *The New NHS: Modern, Dependable: A National Framework for Assessing Performance*. Leeds: NHS Executive.

Osterloh, M. and Frey, B.S. (1998). Does pay for performance really motivate employees? In A.D. Neely and D.B. Waggoner (eds), *Performance Measurement: Theory and Practice*. Cambridge: Cambridge University Press.

Ouchi, W.G. (1980). Markets, bureaucracies, and clans. *Administrative Sciences Quarterly*, 25, 129–41.

Peters, T. and Waterman, R. (1982). *In Search of Excellence*. New York: Harper & Row.

Power, M. (1997). *The Audit Society: Rituals of Verification*. Oxford: Oxford University Press.

Propper, C. (1995). Agency and incentives in the NHS internal market. *Social Science and Medicine*, 40, 1683–90.

Rainwater, J.A., Romano, P.S. and Antonius, D.M. (1998). The California Hospital Outcomes Project: how useful is California's report card for quality improvement? *The Joint Commission Journal on Quality Improvement*, 24, 31–9.

Richards, P. (1998). Professional self-respect: rights and responsibilities in the new NHS. *British Medical Journal*, 317, 1146–8.

Robinson, J.C. (1997). Physician-hospital integration and the economic theory of the firm. *Medical Care Research and Review*, 54, 3–24.

Robinson, R. and Steiner, A. (1998). *Managed Health Care*. Buckingham: Open University Press.

Rundall, T.G., Starkweather, D.B. and Norrish, B.R. (1998). *After Restructuring: Empowerment Strategies at Work in America's Hospitals*. San Francisco: Jossey-Bass.

Sashittal, H.C., Berman, J. and Ilter, S. (1998). Impact of trust on performance evaluations. *Mid-Atlantic Journal of Business*, 34, 163–84.

Scally, G. and Donaldson, L.J. (1998). Clinical governance and the drive for quality improvement in the new NHS in England. *British Medical Journal*, 317, 61–5.

Shortell, S.M., Waters, T.M., Clarke, K.B.W. and Budetti, P.P. (1998). Physicians as double agents: maintaining trust in an era of multiple accountabilities. *Journal of the American Medical Association*, 280, 1102–8.

Smith, P. (1995a). On the unintended consequences of publishing performance data in the public sector. *International Journal of Public Administration*, 18, 277–310.

Smith, P. (1995b). Outcome-related performance indicators and organizational control in the public sector. In J. Holloway, J. Lewis and G. Mallory (eds), *Performance Measurement and Evaluation*. London: Sage.

Smith, P.C., Stepan, A., Valdmanis, V. and Verheyen, P. (1997). Principal–agent problems in health care systems: an international perspective. *Health Policy*, 41, 37–60.

Smith, R. (1998a). All changed, changed utterly. *British Medical Journal*, 316, 1917–18.

Smith, R. (1998b). Repositioning self-regulation. *British Medical Journal*, 317, 964.

Thomson, R. (1998). Quality to the fore in health policy – at last. *British Medical Journal*, 317, 95–6.

Warden, J. (1998). Duty of quality imposed on English hospitals. *British Medical Journal*, 316, 1261.

Williams, A., Dobson, P. and Walters, M. (1996). *Changing Culture: New Organisational Approaches*. London: Institute of Personnel and Development.

Williamson, O.E. (1993). Calculativeness, trust, and economic organization. *Journal of Law & Economics*, 36, 453–86.

Zaheer, A., McEvily, B. and Perrone, V. (1998). Does trust matter? Exploring the effects of interorganizational and interpersonal trust on performance. *Organization Science*, 9, 141–59.

12

THE NEW NHS:
A PRINCIPAL–AGENT
VIEWPOINT

Hugh Gravelle and Peter C. Smith

INTRODUCTION

Some of the most eminent economists have grappled with the problem of what shape an optimal system of health care might take
(Arrow 1963), and yet, as the opening chapter indicated, there
remain sharp divergences of opinion as to what advice to offer
policy makers. For many years the National Health Service (NHS)
– with relatively weak and rudimentary control mechanisms – was
generally considered to deliver one of the most cost-effective health
care systems in the developed world. Perhaps historically the most
remarkable achievement of the NHS in its first 25 years was the
ability to deliver broadly acceptable levels of health care while
remaining within public expenditure cash limits. This was despite
the fact that the major decision makers in the system – general practitioners (GPs) and consultants – were not responsible for the
resource consequences of their actions.

GPs, as the principal gatekeepers, had few incentives to restrain
demand for health care: they faced no budget or other constraints
on their referrals or prescribing, and their patients faced no money
prices, except to a minor extent for prescriptions. Demands for
emergency care were met and demands for elective or non-urgent
care were rationed by waiting (Martin and Smith 1999). Rationing
by waiting replaces money prices with time prices and – since time
is more equitably distributed than income – it is usually argued that
it is a fairer method of allocating scarce resources. However,
rationing by waiting gives much less clear incentives to providers to

respond to patient demands, as mediated through their GPs. The 'price' of care to patients (the time costs incurred), is not revenue for the providers, so they have no direct financial incentive to shift resources in response to changes in the relative length of waits for different treatments.

There were other serious problems with the unreformed NHS, though they were by no means unique to it. Budgets were allocated on a historical basis so that the geographical distribution of health care resources reflected that inherited in 1948. Broadly speaking, richer and healthier areas tended to have disproportionately large shares of resources. There were also doubts about the quality of care. Most health care interventions had not been subject to systematic and explicit evaluation, with the result that practitioners used techniques of unproven safety, efficacy and cost-effectiveness. This problem worsened with the increased pace of technological development and increased expectations of patients that developed over recent decades.

Further, there were considerable and unexplained variations in medical practice, with marked variations in referral and admission rates, lengths of stay for given conditions, and prescribing. Such variations suggest both inefficiency and inequity. If similar patients with the same condition in different areas have different chances of being referred and admitted for treatment there is clear horizontal inequity. Such differences in chances of treatment can also be argued to be inefficient. With different admission rates the marginal admitted patient in the high admission rate area gains less from treatment than the marginal patient in the low admission rate area. Hence health gain is not being maximized for a given level of resources (Phelps 1995).

From the mid-1970s a series of reforms were introduced which sought to address some, though not all, of these issues. Concerns about geographical equity led to the introduction of explicit formulae of increasing complexity and sophistication for the allocation of hospital and community health services within, though not between, the four parts of the United Kingdom (UK). The formulae led to a more equitable distribution of hospital and community health services (HCHS) expenditure, though as Carr-Hill, Rice and Smith (Chapter 3) point out, attempts to extend formula-funding to general medical services and prescribing are more recent and face a number of difficulties.

The 1991 internal market reforms were the first determined attempt at reform. However, the particular form chosen for the internal market resulted in a rather arbitrary type of control over the NHS. Supply-side competition was promulgated as the major discipline. Yet the extent of competition between providers was highly variable, and where effective competition did exist it sometimes led to clear inequities between patients. Purchasers also found it difficult to go beyond waiting times in specifying quality criteria. Thus the internal market, as implemented, emphasized financial restraint at the expense of clinical quality or equity. There must moreover be some doubt as to whether the uncoordinated and myopic character of the market would have allowed the NHS to implement strategic reforms to the configuration of local services when it became necessary.

As Chapter 1 indicated, the proposals for the 'new NHS' demonstrate a good understanding of the weaknesses of the internal market. What is more at question is whether the policy proposals that were inferred from that analysis will deliver the hoped-for improvements. The purpose of this chapter is to attempt to draw together the themes that have emerged in this book. A major policy change to health care, as embodied in the new NHS proposals, can be considered as an attempt to change the model of control over health services. The central economic model of control to have emerged in recent decades adopts what has become known as the principal–agent framework. This chapter therefore views the reforms and the foregoing commentaries from a principal–agent perspective. The next section introduces the salient features of the economic theory of principals and agents, the following section comments on the new reforms in the light of this theory, and the final section offers some conclusions.

THE HEALTH CARE CONTROL PROBLEM

In a social system of even moderate complexity it becomes necessary for an individual or organization (the principal) to delegate some activities to an agent, who is expected to carry out the wishes of the principal in return for some sort of reward. As Propper (1995) notes, the health care system – of whatever design – is replete with interlocking agency relationships: that is, with relationships between principals and their agents. Examples in the UK include the relationship between the central NHS Executive and health authorities; between health authorities and providers; between NHS trusts and hospital physicians; between GPs and hospital physicians; and between patients and physicians. Recent legislation has introduced more principal–agency relationships. For example, under the National Health Service (Primary Care) Act 1997, health authorities may seek to vary the standard contract with general practitioners to induce them to alter the range of services they provide or to attract them into underserved areas. The changes in the 'new NHS' will create further examples: health authorities will have primary care groups (PCGs) as their agents and PCGs in turn will have their constituent practices as their own agents.

Delegated decision making is only unproblematic either if the principal has full information or if the objectives of principal and agent coincide. The outcomes from the agents' decisions depend both on their own actions and also on factors outside the control of the agent. For example, in providing influenza vaccinations to their elderly patients, GPs must decide on the amount of effort to put into persuading patients to be vaccinated and the choice of patients to be offered vaccination. The outcome is the health gain in the eligible population which depends on the numbers of patients vaccinated, their personal characteristics, the type of influenza prevalent in the period, and a purely random element.

If the principal (say a PCG) knew how the actions of the GP and the uncontrolled factors affected the health gain, and it could observe both the GP's actions and the uncontrolled factors, it could design an optimal vaccination policy and ensure that it was carried out by a suitable contract with the GP. It could make payment contingent on the agent carrying out the action that was optimal given the uncontrolled factors. Alternatively, if the principal knew the outcome (health gain) and the factors other than the GPs actions affecting health gain, it could also achieve its optimal vaccination policy by making payment to the GP contingent on achieving the health gain which was optimal given the other factors.

In either case, it would also be possible to achieve an optimal sharing of risk between the principal and the agent. For example, if the GP was averse to bearing risk and the PCG was concerned only about the expected payment, the payment would be the same regardless of the uncontrolled factors and would depend only on the agent taking the appropriate actions or the outcome being at the optimal level given the uncontrolled factors. Thus, it would be possible to achieve both the optimal policy and an efficient bearing of risks.

Unfortunately, the principal will not usually have sufficient information to implement such a policy. It will not be able to observe all the GP's actions: the PCG can monitor the number of vaccinations but it will not be able to observe the GP's efforts directly: there will be a problem of *hidden action*. The PCG is also likely to face a problem of *hidden information*: it will not know enough about patients to determine whether a higher vaccination rate reflects greater effort by the GP, or a patient population who are easily contacted and persuaded to be vaccinated, or simply chance events. And the PCG will not be able to measure the (outcome) health gain since this requires detailed information on individual patients, such as their initial health state, their valuations of alternative health states and so on.

Hidden information and hidden action are pervasive but would not matter if the objectives of principal and agent coincided. This requires not only that principal and agent care about the same aspects of health care but that they place the same relative valuations on them so that they would make the same decisions when confronted with a given set of alternatives. This state of affairs seems highly unlikely. Doctors may care about the health of their patients, and possibly patients care about the effort of their doctors, but it seems plausible to suggest that the patient's valuation of health (relative to the effort of the doctor) is greater than the doctor's.

Thus, a principal–agent problem exists where there is asymmetric information and non-identical objectives, and many agency relationships in health care seem to satisfy both requirements. The difference between the principal's welfare when there is full information or coincidence of objectives and when there is not, is known as the *agency cost*. The principal will seek to devise managerial, information, budgetary and payment systems to mitigate the cost of agency, taking account of the direct costs of such systems, which we can call *transaction costs*. The principal will aim to choose a system which minimizes the sum of agency and transaction costs. Economists have examined two ways of mitigating agency costs: implementation of incentives and enhancement of information.

The first type of solution is for the principal to put in place a set of *incentives* which encourage the agent to carry out actions in accordance with the principal's requirements. These incentives are typically embodied in a contract which rewards or punishes the agent for certain actions or outcomes. Frequently, within a competitive market environment, part of the contract is an implicit threat that an alternative agent might be chosen if performance is deemed to be unsatisfactory. The cost of any rewards must be borne by the principal, who has to balance the costs paid out in the form of rewards to the agent against the improvement they might secure in the performance of the agent.

Principal–agent contracts typically attempt to motivate the agent by making their income depend positively on the outcomes valued by the principal. However, such contracts will, in a world in which outcomes depend on both the actions of the agent and on uncontrolled factors, impose some risk on the agent. Since it is usually the case that the agent is more risk averse than the principal, the optimal contract will embody a trade-off between insuring the agent against risk and providing them with incentives to pursue outcomes favourable to the principal (Shavell 1979).

A second feature of optimal principal agent contracts is that, when there is an observable signal either of the agent's effort or of the other factors affecting the outcome, the agent's reward should depend on the signal as well as the observed outcome (Holmstrom 1979). In the example of influenza vaccination sketched above, this suggests that the PCG should make the payments to the GP depend on the characteristics of the elderly population served by the GP. However, when the signals available to the principal about the actions of the agent or the environment in which the agent operates are weak or 'noisy', principal–agent theory suggests that the agent's reward should not depend very strongly on the signal (otherwise, unnecessary risk is imposed on the agent) and the principal will not benefit greatly from the environmental information.

There is an additional, and in the case of the NHS, important problem concerning the signals or information available to the principal. Agents in the NHS allocate their effort across many tasks. For example, doctors allocate their time among different types of patient and among different activities while seeing patients. There will be good signals about some of these activities and weak or no signals about others. Linking rewards to the signals can lead to distortion of effort in favour of activities where the signals are strongly correlated with effort and away from activities where the signals are weak. When the relative strength of signals differs greatly between activities, principal–agent theory suggests that, even when there are good signals available on some activities, the optimal contract will not link rewards to them (Holmstrom and Milgrom 1991).

The second type of solution to the principal–agent problem is for the principal to invest in an *enhanced information* base, which facilitates improved monitoring of the agent's actions and output, thereby reducing the associated asymmetry of information. Here the instruments might include extending the scope of existing information systems, or enhancing the audit function to improve the reliability of information sources. Again, of course, the costs of securing enhanced information will in general be borne by the principal. Principal–agent models of agents with many tasks indicate that the greatest benefit would be in improving the information available about activities where information is poorest. Thus, although NHS costing and accounting systems are poor compared with those in most private sector firms, routine information on outcomes and quality of care is appalling or non-existent, so that this is where the main information priority in the NHS should be.

There exists a third type of solution to the principal–agent problem which has received little attention from economists: *realignment of objectives*. The principal can seek to affect the perceptions and preferences of the agent so that the agent's objectives become more closely aligned to the objectives of the principal. Again, if such action is successful, it will effectively diminish the agency problem. This course of action presumes a certain malleability in the preferences of agents, a possibility that economic analysis has in general been reluctant to entertain (Goddard and Mannion 1998). Yet many commentators note that the success or failure of many innovations in health care management depend not so much on the management systems as on the involvement and enthusiasm of key actors. Securing such commitment may be a delicate and mysterious process.

In seeking to gain control of a complex health care system, a government or other principal must seek to analyse, and where necessary amend, the nature of a plethora of principal–agent relationships. In the early years of the NHS, little policy attention was paid to such relationships. Broadly speaking, there was a prevailing attitude that doctors and other health care professionals worked in the interests of both government and patients, and that the NHS control problem in the hospital and community sector was principally one of seeking adherence to annual cash limits. Indeed in general practice there was no explicit attempt to control, other than in the very loose form of some public health screening and vaccination targets.

The Griffiths proposals for general management in the NHS represented a first attempt to gain control of the NHS (Griffiths 1983). The objectives of this initiative were modest, in effect merely seeking to identify which parties were to be held responsible for which parts of the NHS, without explicit design of incentives. It is never-theless noteworthy that the first set of performance indicators in the NHS coincided with the rise of general management, and were explicitly designed to 'help [managers] assess the efficiency of the services for which they are responsible' (DHSS 1983). Some attempt was therefore being made to address the information element of the principal–agent problem. However, in practice little use was made of NHS performance indicators (Smith 1987), perhaps because there was no change in the basic set of incentives in the system.

In contrast, the NHS internal market reforms reflected an em-phasis on the incentive element of the principal–agent relationship, manifested in the form of contracts, particularly between purchaser and provider organizations. The hope was that competition within the internal market would encourage providers to deliver services at minimum cost, and that the contracts would ensure that the right mix of services was provided at the required level of quality. In the event, as Le Grand *et al.* (1998) document, there is some evidence that some of the anticipated benefits have indeed materialized. The purchaser-provider split and the introduction of fundholding moved decisions on service provision closer to the ultimate princi-pals (the patients) and their agents (the GPs). The system therefore became somewhat more responsive to demand and long waiting times had a greater role in allocating resources. However, the broad conclusion must be that the impact of the market reforms has been quite small, not least because the market has never been allowed to operate in anything like an unfettered form. The market that de-veloped was heavily regulated, restricted in scope and there was no effective change in the ownership of assets. Such a market should not be expected to replicate all the features (good or bad) that characterize markets in the private sector.

GAINING CONTROL IN THE NEW NHS

The proposals for a 'new NHS' reflect a more comprehensive understanding of the various principal–agent problems that exist within the NHS than that which informed the preceding market reforms. Some of the important incentive elements of the internal market remain in place, and are strengthened by the increased emphasis to be placed on quality. However, the incentives are to be augmented by a much extended informational framework. Further-more, and perhaps even more ambitiously, the talk of cooperation and partnership signals an acknowledgement of the desire to secure a closer alignment between the objectives of principals and agents.

Thus the latest reforms demonstrate a keen awareness of the nature of the control problem within the NHS. However, this is no guarantee that the search for improved control will necessarily secure the desired improvement in performance of the NHS. After all, the Soviet planning system was designed in the light of an apparently good understanding of the problem confronting the planner, yet failed abjectly in its objectives (Milgrom and Roberts 1992). More specifically, it is possible that the search for increased control may in some circumstances prove counter-productive. Titmus (1970) argued that the introduction of explicit financial incentives for blood donors would reduce the supply of blood and worsen its quality, because it undermined altruistic behaviour by donors.

Likewise, it could be suggested that explicit incentives and controls will undermine professional ethics and lead to a worse alignment of objectives between principals and their medical agents. Critics of this argument would perhaps suggest that reliance on a system of professional ethics and self-regulation has produced somewhat mixed results in terms of quality of care. Thus the key question is not whether the proposed reforms will lead to improved control; rather, it is whether they will be translated into improved performance. Only experience can answer this question definitively (and evaluation of the internal market reforms has demonstrated that even with the benefit of hindsight it may be possible to draw only cautious conclusions).

The preceding chapters have sought not so much to predict the outcome of the new arrangements, but rather to highlight some of the many issues that may be relevant in determining the success or otherwise of the reforms. Much will depend on implementation details and the extent to which the NHS can secure that elusive commitment of managers and health care professionals alluded to above. This book has nevertheless noted some key considerations that, at least in principle, might imperil the success of the latest reforms, and compromise the ability to secure the desired organizational control. We summarize some of the main observations under six headings: the regulatory framework; internal commissioner control; commissioner-provider relations; internal provider control; information; and cooperation.

The regulatory framework

The new arrangements introduce some important strategic inno-vations into the NHS organizational control structure. These include a new information base (the performance framework), the National Institute for Clinical Excellence (NICE) to promulgate best practice, and a potentially powerful enforcer in the form of the Commission for Health Improvement. Taken together these developments suggest a heightened desire to secure control and considerable accretion of power towards the centre.

The proposed reforms cannot be implemented without major investment in new managerial expertise. To some extent this may be secured by redeployment of management capacity released from (say) GP fundholding. However, new managerial skills will be required in consulting the public, developing health improvement programmes, implementing clinical governance, and in devising and implementing budgetary incentives and control systems in PCGs. In a principal–agent framework, transaction or management costs are incurred to reduce the agency costs arising from non-aligned objectives and information asymmetry. Given the changes in the budgetary arrangements and the increased emphasis on monitoring and control it is difficult to see how reduction in management costs anticipated by the government can be secured without a deleterious effect on agency costs. The question should not be whether management or transaction costs have been reduced, but whether the sum of transaction and agency costs has been reduced.

Internal commissioner control

At a local level, the health authority will in time become principally a planner, overseeing local services and producing a Health Im-provement Programme (HImP). Commissioning decisions will, to a greater or lesser extent, be devolved to the new PCGs. Important control issues arise in these new arrangements. How will health authorities hold PCGs to account? Will they be able to achieve the 'difficult balancing act in ensuring administrative, clinical and political accountability' (Chapter 5)?

And how will PCGs hold their constituent general practices to account? It is all very well introducing national clinical guidelines and devolving most of the NHS budget to the local level, but if PCGs or general practices choose to ignore advice or overspend, what sanctions exist to encourage compliance? The discussion has indicated that there will always be a need for considerable clinical freedom in choice of treatment (Chapter 11) and a large tolerance in spending requirements (Chapter 3). The hitherto untested PCG will need rapidly to develop sensitive managerial skills in balancing the desire for control against legitimate aspects of clinical freedom.

On top of the structural reforms, a key additional development will be the introduction of 'unified' budgets for health care. These abolish previous distinctions between expenditure on general hospital and community services, fundholding procedures, prescribing and practice infrastructure. Their introduction may lead to major new efficiencies, giving GPs the ability to use the most cost-effective treatments, unfettered by budgetary and service definitions. In this respect, the potential to form primary care trusts (PCTs) may offer primary care an enormous opportunity to change the pattern of NHS health care. On the other hand, the unified budget removes some important freedoms from the NHS – most specifically, effectively imposing a cash limit for the first time on prescribing expenditure, albeit within an overall health care budget. Will it prove feasible to impose such a limit, or will GPs merely ignore the implied constraint?

Further, there are dangers that self-interest may lead to misallocation of expenditure within the unified budget. Expenditure on practice infrastructure will benefit GPs through their ownership of premises as well as patients, and in the future PCTs will be able to commission services from their constituent practices. Will the principals (the NHS Executive, the health authorities or the PCTs) be able to devise systems which align the agent practices' incentives with their own and reduce the extent of misallocation?

Commissioner–provider relations

Although contracts between commissioners and providers will remain in place (albeit in the guise of 'agreements'), important changes will take effect. The proposals imply a switch of emphasis from financial issues to clinical quality, and an associated change in incentive structure. The abandonment of cost-per-case contracts implies less of a direct imperative among providers to attract additional patients. The abolition of fundholding will reduce the number of contract negotiations and the associated financial uncertainty. The reformed financial regime may therefore be more stable for providers than hitherto.

Most principal–agent relationships of any complexity are long term. Under these circumstances, any contract will be incomplete as it becomes impossible to embody all possible contingencies into the contract. The desire of the agent to maintain a reputation for reliability and quality may nonetheless be an important factor contributing to good performance. Economic actors have an incentive to build reputations for trustworthy behaviour and to invest in long-term relationships to the extent that they know they will gain in the future from their current behaviour in failing to exploit temporary advantages over trading partners. If the future gains accrue to their organization after the current actors have departed, then the incentives to build up reputation are reduced. In the private sector this problem is partially mitigated by markets where owners of firms can sell their firms as going concerns and expect a payment for the 'goodwill' resulting from the firm's reputation for trustworthy behaviour (Kreps 1991). In the public sector this direct incentive is by definition absent and other means must be sought to induce trustworthy behaviour with long-term pay-offs. The encouragement to build long-term relationships between principals and agents is therefore to be welcomed, even if the stated emphasis on long-term contracts may be an irrelevance (Chapter 4).

With the emphasis on stability and the elimination of GP fundholders, the reforms signal a distinct shift of power from purchasers/commissioners to providers in the reformed internal market. Furthermore, the lead taken by GPs (rather than managers) in the commissioning arrangements will probably mean that clinical quality plays a more important part in the commissioning process than hitherto, at the expense of price considerations. The combined effect of these developments may result in a lower profile given to provider costs, perhaps resulting in looser cost control than previously. If budgets are binding, the effect of increased unit costs will be reduced throughput, which – coupled with increased demand generated by higher quality – may, other things being equal, lead to longer waiting times.

Internal provider control

Hitherto little research attention has been paid to how NHS trusts secure control of their own resources. Despite some experiments with clinical budgeting and resource management, progress with developing usable managerial tools has been slow. However, the new arrangements concerning clinical governance may result in major changes in the way that hospitals and hospital physicians operate. How will hospital physicians react to the publication of guidelines and increased scrutiny of their activity? This is uncharted territory, and much will depend on how trusts choose to implement the new arrangements. Will they choose the right balance between coercion and persuasion, between checking and trusting?

Information

An over-reliance on information as the sole means of control may lead to a range of dysfunctional consequences that will be familiar to the student of Soviet planning (Nove 1980). While the new performance framework will – if used with discretion – undoubtedly lead to improvements in decision making and control, its limitations are manifest, and a failure to recognize and accommodate such limitations carries immense dangers (Chapter 7). The high profile given to *Patient's Charter* waiting-time data has led to a number of 'unintended consequences', such as some neglect of non-surgical specialities and strategic manipulation of waiting lists (Smith 1995). How will the system react if similar attention is applied to clinical outcome data?

The emphasis on cost data in the new arrangements is particularly troubling (Chapter 9). While cost data are readily produced at a fine level of detail, there must be some doubt as to whether much of the variation in observed speciality costs signifies anything more than accounting choices. If the interest is in variations in resource use (such as length of stay), then why not measure such phenomena directly? Certainly it seems clear that quite careful analysis will be needed to secure meaningful messages from the proposed cost data.

More generally, crude league tables of performance rarely offer a helpful story in health care. At the very least, there is usually a need for some sort of adjustment to accommodate casemix or population characteristics, often leading to quite large changes in ranking of performance (Chapter 8). Furthermore, there is considerable scope for debate about the precise methods to be used for such 'risk adjustment', leading to the potential for unresolved debates about the messages contained in many data (Iezzoni *et al.* 1996).

Cooperation

The White Paper on the new NHS makes much of the need to replace the culture of competition with a spirit of cooperation. As noted above, valuable efficiency gains might in theory be secured if such cooperation can be secured, and the agency problem reduced. In this respect, potential gains might be particularly important in the relationship between PCG and NHS trust, between individual GP and hospital physician, and between NHS trust and hospital physician. However, an over-reliance on the trust associated with cooperation increases the potential for opportunism (Chapter 11). Much will depend on the mechanisms chosen to nurture a culture of cooperation, a topic on which the White Paper is largely silent. In particular, as Goddard and Mannion (1998: 105) suggest in relation to NHS providers, principals will need to 'tread a fine line between competition and co-operation in order to reap the benefits of both'.

CONCLUSIONS

The proposals for a new NHS represent a major leap in the dark. It may be the case that, as Baker (1998) claims, they represent the most far-reaching reform yet of the NHS. However, until the nature of implementation is seen it will be impossible to say whether the apparently major changes contained in the proposals represent a real change to the system of UK health care. We have nevertheless suggested that the mechanisms are being put in place to secure much increased control of the NHS at all levels. There will be important changes in the associated incentive structure. Whether and how these changes affect the actions of individual health care professionals remains to be seen, and whether any changes lead to improved performance will be the touchstone of success.

This chapter has raised many questions about the likely impact of the new arrangements. Some will be relatively easy to answer. It will, for example, be fairly easy to observe the regulatory style adopted by the Commission for Health Improvement. However, the majority of the central questions raised here and throughout the rest of the book require more subtle investigation. In this respect, there is a large research agenda suggested by the reforms. As well as indicating whether or not the anticipated benefits are materializing, the research community should also be in a position to help to identify elements of best practice, and to offer guidance on the optimal ways of delivering the new NHS – in short, to identify 'what works' at both a policy level and a practice level.

In this respect, it is worth recalling the Conservative government's scornful rejection of the value of research at the time of the internal market reforms (Robinson and Le Grand 1994). This attitude led to a fragmented, underfunded and in some respects ineffectual research effort which yielded useful results in some areas (for example, fundholding) and almost no evidence elsewhere (for example, provider delivery methods). Since then, a more enlightened attitude towards the value of research has emerged, and it is to be hoped that an extensive, well coordinated programme is put in place to evaluate the latest reforms. It will then be up to the research community to rise to the challenge and to offer useful evidence on the important issues raised by the change to the 'new' NHS.

REFERENCES

Arrow, K. (1963). Uncertainty and the welfare economics of medical care. *American Economic Review*, 53, 941–73.

Baker, M. (1998). *Making Sense of the NHS White Paper.* Oxford: Radcliffe Medical Press.

DHSS (Department of Health and Social Security) (1983). *Performance Indicators: National Summary.* London: DHSS.

Goddard, M. and Mannion, R. (1998). From competition to co-operation: new economic relationships in the NHS. *Health Economics*, 7(2), 105–19.

Griffiths, E.R. (1983). *NHS Management Inquiry.* London: DHSS.

Holmstrom, B. (1979). Moral hazard and observability. *Bell Journal of Economics*, 10, 74–91.

Holmstrom, B. and Milgrom, P. (1991). Multitask principal-agent analysis: incentive contracts, asset ownership and job design. *Journal of Law, Economics and Organization*, 7, (special issue), 24–52.

Iezzoni, L.I., Shwartz, M., Ash, A.S. *et al.* (1996). Severity measurement methods and judging hospital death rates for pneumonia. *Medical Care*, 34(1), 11–28.

Kreps, D.M. (1991). Corporate culture and economic theory. In: J.E. Alt, and K.A. Shepsle (eds), *Perspectives on Positive Political Economy.* Cambridge: Cambridge University Press.

Le Grand, J., Mays, N. and Mulligan, J. (eds) (1998). *Learning from the NHS Internal Market.* London: King's Fund Institute.

Martin, S. and Smith, P. (1999). Rationing by waiting lists: an empirical investigation. *Journal of Public Economics*, 71, 141–64.

Milgrom, P. and Roberts, J. (1992). *Economics, Organization and Management.* Englewood Cliffs, NJ: Prentice Hall.

Nove, A. (1980). *The Soviet Economic System.* London: Allen & Unwin.

Phelps, C. (1995). Welfare loss from variations: further considerations. *Journal of Health Economics*, 14, 253–60.

Propper, C. (1995). Agency and incentives in the NHS internal market. *Social Science and Medicine*, 40, 1683–90.

Robinson, R. and Le Grand, J. (eds) (1994). *Evaluating the NHS Reforms.* London: King's Fund Institute.

Shavell, S. (1979). Risk sharing and incentives in the principal and agent relationship. *Bell Journal of Economics*, 10, 55–73.

Smith, P. (1987). Performance indicators: are they worth it? In A. Harrison and J. Gretton (eds), *Health Care UK 1987.* Hermitage: Policy Journals.

Smith, P. (1995). On the unintended consequences of publishing performance data in the public sector, *International Journal of Public Administration*, 18(2/3), 277–310.

Titmus, R. (1970). *The Gift Relationship: From Human Blood to Social Policy.* London: Allen & Unwin.

INDEX

CONTEMPORARY PRIMARY CARE
THE CHALLENGES OF CHANGE

Philip Tovey (ed.)

Primary care is currently going through a period of substantial change. The high profile alteration of structures is occurring at a time when many issues of practice are presenting new or renewed challenges. These are issues grounded in the complexities and dissatisfactions of contemporary society as well as in the changing policy context.

This book has been produced in order to bring together critical and thought-provoking pieces on these wide-ranging challenges, by authors from an equally wide range of disciplines, including anthropology, clinical psychology, disability studies, public health, sociology, as well as general practice.

Beginning with a think piece on the nature of primary care and what an emerging vision for it might look like, the book continues with contributions on the changing form, organization and delivery of primary health care, before going on to examine specific areas of provision and some significant research issues. The book will be of interest to all those involved in the study or development of primary health care services.

Contents
Introduction – Part 1: Challenges of context and organization – Vision and change in primary care: past, present and future – The changing character of service provision – The changing nature of primary health care teams and interprofessional relationships – Part 2: Challenges of practice – Commissioning services for older people: make haste slowly? – Disability: from medical needs to social rights – The new genetics and general practice: revolution or continuity? – Socio-economic inequality: beyond the inverse care law – Part 3: Challenges of research – Locality planning and research evidence: using primary care data – Counselling: researching an evidence base for practice – Complementary medicine and primary care: towards a grassroots focus – Postscript – Index.

c. 192pp   0 335 20009 5 (Pbk)   0 335 20452 X (Hbk)

**CHANGE-PROMOTING RESEARCH FOR HEALTH
SERVICES**
A GUIDE FOR RESOURCE MANAGERS, RESEARCH AND
DEVELOPMENT COMMISSIONERS AND RESEARCHERS

Selwyn St Leger and Jo Walsworth-Bell

Health services globally are changing, strategically, structurally and
clinically. Research and Development (R&D) plays a key role,
because only good research can elucidate and challenge the status
quo or future possibilities for effective healthcare.

Researchers and managers have a duty to collaborate with clinicians, to understand and make the most of each others' skills. This
necessitates a new paradigm of health service research which is part
of a change management culture and change promotion. A clear
philosophical and practical distinction is required between R&D
and fundamental biomedical science.

This book has been written for people who make decisions and
bring about change, at all sorts of levels, and in a wide range of disciplines. They include clinicians in many specialities, as well as administrative staff, and general managers of healthcare organizations. It
is also for people doing, or wanting to do, research and development
in this fascinating area.

Contents
*Part 1: Background and rationale – Research and development in a
changing health service – The new paradigm – Part II: Commissioning research – Commissioning: an overview – Putting commissioning
into practice – Part III: Doing and using research – Doing research –
Using research – Notes – Index.*

256pp   0 335 20220 9 (Pbk)   0 335 20221 7 (Hbk)

CRITICAL CHALLENGES FOR HEALTH CARE REFORM IN EUROPE

Richard B. Saltman, Josep Figueras and Constantino Sakellarides

This volume explores the central issues driving the present process of health care reform in Europe. More than 30 scholars and policy makers from all parts of Europe draw together the available evidence from epidemiology and public health, economics, public policy, organizational behaviour and management theory as well as real world policy making experience, to lay out the options that health sector decision-makers confront. Through its cross-disciplinary, cross-national approach, the book highlights the underlying trends that now influence health policy formulation across Europe. An authoritative introduction provides a broad synthesis of present trends and strategies in European health policy.

Contents

Introduction – Part 1: The context for health reform – Part II: Demand-side strategies – Part III: Supply side strategies – Part IV: On state, citizen and society – Part V: Implementing health reform – Assessing the evidence – Index.

448pp   0 335 19970 4 (Pbk)   0 335 19971 2 (Hbk)